When Charity Destroys Dignity

Overcoming Unhealthy Dependency in
the Christian Movement

A Compendium

Glenn J. Schwartz

World Mission Associates
Lancaster, Pennsylvania

ISBN: 978-0-9669735-4-9

World Mission Associates
600-C Eden Road
Lancaster, PA 17601
www.wmausa.org

For information on bulk pricing for this book up to 80% discount,
contact World Mission Associates at wmabookinfo@wmausa.org.
In the subject line, include the words WMA BOOK INFO.

DEDICATION

This book is dedicated to those African church leaders and missionaries who, through no fault of their own, live with the consequences of unhealthy dependency on outside resources.

CONTENTS

ACKNOWLEDGEMENTS

As many others have said, it is risky to mention some and leave out others when acknowledging contributions to a work such as this. Knowing that risk, I will mention some, with apologies to those who are left out.

First of all, I am indebted to the Lord who saved me, called me, and through His grace, made my Christian ministry possible. To have His companionship on this journey is a privilege beyond description.

I am indebted to scores of African church leaders, missionaries and mission executives who shared personal experiences with me in the course of collecting this information. Many of them are not identified in the text, but it does not diminish my appreciation to them for the illustrations they provided.

I am indebted to the professors of the School of World Mission (now the School of Intercultural Studies) at Fuller Theological Seminary in the 1970s who affirmed the potential they saw in me. In particular, I owe much to the late Professors Alan R. Tippett and Donald A. McGavran. Dr. Arthur F. Glasser still impacts my life and, as of this writing, is ninety-two years of age. The influence of these and others could be identified on page after page of this book. I am also grateful to Dr. Ralph Winter who first suggested in 1996 that I put this material into video format which eventually became the basis of this book.

There is no way I could have done this without the support and encouragement of the Board of Directors and my colleagues at World Mission Associates. They helped me in many more ways than I could begin to recall.

How does one acknowledge the support of my life-long best friend and wife, Verna, who has been by my side for more than forty-two years of ministry? She was long-suffering as we traveled together over a period of years, many times staying up all night on airplanes and sleeping in different beds night after night. In addition, she gave countless hours in the typing and editing of this material. Her knowledge of good English is an important part of making this text readable. Where it is not, I take responsibility.

I wish to express appreciation to Steve Saint for writing the Foreword for this book. As you will see in my biographical statement, the death of his father and four other missionaries in Ecuador in 1956 was influential in my call to ministry.

Finally, I am indebted to the wise counsel of Joe McCullough at Author House who guided me through the publication process. He was not only professional and competent, but a pleasure to work with. I also wish to thank Robby Butler for helping me make some important changes as I was preparing to send the manuscript to the publisher.

Thanks to many others not mentioned here for helping me attain this goal. Again, I accept responsibility for the final text, knowing that there are many other ways it could have been improved.

FOREWORD

There are many difficult things in life that are only words to us – until we experience them for ourselves: a terminal illness, family break-up, financial failure. Until these words take shape in experience, touching us or someone dear to us, they are just unfortunate things that happen — usually to other people and often far away.

A **cerebral hemorrhage** used to be just a medical term to me. Not any more. A few years ago, during a welcome home party for our only daughter Stephanie, she complained of a headache and wanted me to pray that it would go away. Shockingly, as I prayed, she lost consciousness and died in my arms. Her headache turned out to be a massive cerebral hemorrhage! Because of our family's experience, a *cerebral hemorrhage* will always be more than just a condition in a medical textbook.

Dependency was just such a word to me until I faced it head-on among the people I had come to love – the Waodani of Ecuador. As a young boy, I experienced the loss of my father and four other missionaries at the hands of these people, whom the world then called Aucas. God later called my Aunt Rachel Saint and Elizabeth Elliott, and a Waodani Christian woman called Dayuma, to live among these people. Over the years, many of them discovered the truth of "God's carving" (the Bible) and gave themselves to Jesus, thus ending countless years of bloodshed among them and their neighbors. While I lived for some years among the Waodani as a lad, eventually I returned to North America, married and began a successful business.

During the 1990s, I responded to a call from the Waodani to return to live among them with my family. It was then my turn to experience unhealthy dependency in bold relief. Proud, capable men that I had known as a boy were now living without dignity under the influence and protection of outsiders beholden to them in many ways. What had happened to these people? It was during this period of soul-searching, anger and disappointment that someone handed me a copy of *Mission Frontiers* that contained several articles on dependency written by Glenn Schwartz and others.

Suddenly I realized that what I had been experiencing was something real – the awful effects of full-blown dependency. I was relieved to learn that it was a sickness with a name – and a cure – as I found out later on. For the first time, I began to see the Great Commission from the **receiving** end, rather than the **giving** end. It was both mind numbing and gut wrenching to see what dependency had done to my friends, the Waodani. I found myself angry with those who had allowed these once proud people to be less than I knew they could be.

I also realized that if I did not take care, I, too, could spread this debilitating sickness. We had come to Ecuador at the invitation of the Waodani. What they were asking me to do was to **teach** them skills to help take care of the physical and spiritual needs of their own people. They were not looking for handouts. I needed to exercise great care in how I would proceed.

You probably hear someone like Glenn Schwartz or me mention dependency, and it is hard not to lose interest, especially if you don't know anyone who has been devastated by it. But, you do care about hurting people coming to know Christ, don't you? Well, you can't really care about Christ's Great Commission and not care about unhealthy dependency, because it is one of the greatest obstacles keeping us from fulfilling the Great Commission today. Dr. Ralph Winter has said that it is one of the most significant issues in missions in the twenty-first century.

One day I found myself called upon to attend to a pregnant woman in the midst of a difficult delivery. Making a long story short, God guided me through an experience for which I had little training. Thankfully, the lives of both mother and baby were saved. What a wonderful feeling for me! But I realized that without Christ, these people were doomed spiritually. And without others trained to do what I had just done, more would die physically. How could I provide training and materials so that the Waodani could assist their own people who have similar health problems, and then use such knowledge as a witnessing tool wherever they go?

The last several years of my life have been dedicated to doing this in the best way I know how. There are now Waodani people trained in basic health care and dental work. Tementa, one of their church elders, has learned to fly an aircraft specially designed for the jungle, paid for by the Waodani, and built on location. God helping me, I have purposed not to prolong dependency but to help the Waodani, whom I love, to break free from it and have something to offer the rest of the world.

Ignoring the problem of dependency won't make it go away. We have to do something about it. Christ never intended that the ministry of taking the Gospel to an unreached world should be a spectator sport where masses of His followers sit in the stands and watch a few "Westerners" build churches, paint school buildings or distribute handouts at Christmas – while local people sit back and watch it happen or let it happen. He intended the Great Commission to be more like a military engagement—gathering active recruits along the way.

Can you understand what it is like to feel left out—to have your dignity destroyed? Do you know what it feels like to have to get out of the way of so-called "experts"? And how can anyone help overcome the negative effects of dependency around the world, if they don't understand how complex the issues are?

That is the purpose of this book – to describe the dependency syndrome and to help us all search for solutions. Glenn Schwartz – and others on the World Mission Associates team – are dedicated to helping us *understand* and *overcome* dependency where it exists and to help *prevent* it from developing elsewhere. Like me, Glenn acknowledges that he was once part of the problem. But he dedicated himself to wrestling with this monumental problem and now he encourages others to do the same.

It has taken me a long time to begin to understand this sickness called dependency. Glenn has been studying it and writing about it for decades. He shares with you what he has learned through experience and observation, so that you, too, can help to avoid or overcome the problem.

Glenn, I had to feel the pain to understand the problem. Thank you for helping me understand the remedy.

Steve Saint
Ocala, Florida

PREFACE

This book is a compendium of the author's writings over the past decade or more. It is not a concise, concentrated treatment of dependency in the Christian movement. Nor does it seek to address one audience only. Sections of it are addressed to church leaders, others to missionaries, mission executives and short-termers. Some sections are addressed to donors, such as chapter 4 regarding what westerners should do with their money. Someone should do more targeted writing about dependency and self-reliance for each of these audiences, but were I to attempt to do that now, it would further delay publication of this which has been too long in process already.

The key to understanding what I present in this book can be found in the biographical statement which I have called *The Biography Behind the Issues: The Personal Journey of the Author.* At the beginning of that prologue, I explain the part that biography has in a subject such as this.

If you are convinced that American or other outside funding is the key to planting churches cross-culturally, you will be disappointed with what this book contains. I am using my experience in Africa to show that the Western Christian movement is much in need of finding a new way of utilizing personnel and other resources for its expansion.

There are some who will benefit from what I have written here. Indeed, many have already told me how much my research and writing has meant to them. There are others who will be disappointed, disconcerted or even hostile to what I have written. I apologize in advance to anyone who concludes that this is not appropriate as we seek to meet the needs of a hurting world. I can only pray that, together, we will view each other's contribution with Christian charity and understanding.

For those who feel strongly one way or the other about these issues, I welcome interaction. Perhaps we can both find common ground and new ways to be helpful to each other.

I recognize that at the beginning of the twenty-first century some of the winds in missionary circles tend to be blowing in the opposite direction from what I am saying here. This will be true in several areas.

First, there is a significant move away from self-supporting indigenous churches toward what are called "international partnerships." I usually refrain from the using the term "partnership" because of the current usage. I feel that it is often used when the term sponsorship would be better, something that I have been saying for a long time.

A **second** way the wind is blowing has to do with simply sending money rather than people in order to fulfill the Great Commission. Some feel this is the new way to do missions economically and efficiently. I see this as not new, but something old that needs to be challenged as we seek to overcome unhealthy dependency in the Christian movement. Those committed to just sending money are not likely to be pleased with what I have written in this book.

A **third** wind that is blowing has to do with the rise of short-term missions (STMs). Estimates are that more than a million young and older people are going out from North America each year for terms as short as ten days or two weeks. For some, short-term mission trips have become their only way of missionary ministry. A friend recently said that he was invited to speak at a missionary conference and was given the topic "A Lifetime Commitment to Missions: Short-Term or Long-Term." If a "lifetime" commitment to missions is to short-term missions, that is quite different from what I am dealing with in this book. I emphasize language and culture learning as well as building relationships, something that is virtually impossible in ten days or two weeks, even if repeated from time to time.

I firmly believe there is a place for long-term missionaries who are willing to do the following: 1) dig deep into cultural issues, 2) demonstrate loving concern through language learning, and 3) grapple with biblical issues cross-culturally. Unfortunately, those things are often considered to be too difficult or time consuming for many westerners who feel they are either a waste of time or something we can simply pay others to do.

One more word is in order at the outset. Some will accuse me of not being sympathetic toward the needs of the poor. I believe those who are truly in need should be helped. Jesus commanded it and reserved harsh criticism for those who offended the poor. My purpose here is to advocate helping those in need in a way that does not create long-term dependency. That means making a concerted effort to find resources which are close at hand whenever possible, rather than those that are in the global community far away.

My prayer is that we in the Christian movement, will learn what some governments have learned – that long-term subsidy for those who are in need can and should be replaced by helping people learn how to stand on their own two feet. And, as can be shown, there is Biblical evidence for everyone learning to carry his or her own part of the load.[1]

Glenn Schwartz
January 2007

Postscript to the Preface

Since this text was submitted to the publisher several weeks ago, a new book on missions giving has come on the market. That book says essentially the opposite of what I am calling for here. My readers should know that I am well aware of its emphasis and seriously concerned about it, but I will not be commenting on it anywhere else in this book for reasons I give below.

That book advocates a "Marshall Plan" of mission giving to mobilize large amounts of money in western churches in support of cross-cultural church planting. It represents a massive donor-driven missiology which is characterized more by compassion for the donor's need to give, than for preserving the dignity of those who are to be helped. In that respect, it represents the tragedy of well-meaning compassion. If such an emphasis is carried out, it will increase rather than decrease the number of those affected by unhealthy dependency. And that means that overcoming such dependency will be an even greater challenge than it already is.

---

[1] Those who wish to interact with the author can do so by e-mail at GlennSchwartz@wmausa.org.

Since that book[2] appeared after this text was submitted to the publisher, there will be no other mention of it in these pages. Doing so would have increased the cost and further delayed production. Suffice it to say, readers will need to decide for themselves whether unhealthy dependency in the Christian movement is harmless - or whether it is a syndrome that needs to be dealt with seriously. In this text, I seek to deal with it seriously.

GJS

---

[2] *To Give or Not To Give* by Dr. John Rowell is published by Authentic Publishing in Tyrone, Georgia, 2007.

Prologue

THE BIOGRAPHY BEHIND THE ISSUES
The Personal Journey of the Author

Introduction

This biographical statement is presented to show the basis on which this treatment of dependency and self-reliance is based. Professor Alan Tippett told us as missionaries and church leaders studying in the School of World Mission at Fuller Seminary that **one cannot understand missiology apart from biography**. The reader will better understand why I deal with issues of dependency and self-reliance after learning something of my personal missionary journey.

I came to know the Lord in rural Pennsylvania through concerned neighbors who took my family to Sunday School and worship services in a Brethren in Christ Church. At age 13 I accepted the Lord and at age seventeen I was called to Christian service through reading the story of five martyred missionaries in an Ecuadorian jungle. It was on a Sunday afternoon that I read that story in the Reader's Digest, of all places. (I acknowledge that it is a bit unusual to get a call to Christian service through reading the Reader's Digest.)[1] In any case, the Lord spoke to me as clearly as if there were someone in that room. It was a simple message as I sat on the bed with the magazine on my lap. The voice simply said, "There is a time and place for you in Christian service." It was no more or less dramatic than that. But, from that time on, I took one step at a time, walking through the doors the Lord opened for me over the next five decades.

My First Experience in Africa

In January 1961, I left for Africa by ocean-going freighter, sailing from New York City to Capetown. The journey lasted eighteen long days, and I am not a good sailor. Sometimes I have said I was seasick only one time, but it lasted for eighteen days! I was uncomfortable and somewhat bored on the long journey. After all,

---

[1] I have since learned that thousands of people have dedicated their lives to Christ or been called to service after learning about this story.

there were only six passengers on this "freighter." Thankfully, I was one of the last to be sent out by ship, and I shed no tear at the passing of sea travel to the mission field. One struggle I remember was the battle to spend time with the Lord even amidst a schedule that only included three meals a day and having to play checkers with the Captain. More on that later.

The sight of Capetown with Table Bay and Table Mountain was most welcome. However, my most exhilarating moment after arriving in Africa came several days later as we drove across South Africa to what was then Southern Rhodesia (now Zimbabwe). I remember the excitement as the first African villages (with round houses and traditional grass roofs) appeared on the horizon. I knew then that I was in Africa.[2] Homes like those would have increasing meaning for me as the years unfolded.

My two years as a volunteer in Southern and Northern Rhodesia were in some respects not very eventful. The spiritual battle with quiet times continued, but on the positive side I found great reward in learning to speak the language of the people. I bought primary school textbooks (grades one through six) with pictures and simple words. At the end of the day I sat down with an African friend and he helped me to unravel the mysteries of this fascinating language, complete with "clicks" unique to several Bantu languages.

I was never very good at Sindebele, but my determination to try was noticed by many African friends. Even my meager success drew a few snide remarks from older missionaries who had rationalized around acquiring the language. By the time I left Central Africa at the end of two years, I could pray publicly and give a simple sermon in Sindebele when asked. But it was elementary at best.

Re-entry to the USA

During this short period in Africa I saw sin in a new way. I saw alcoholism, witchcraft, adultery and a host of other things almost daily – things from which I was sheltered in my conservative upbringing in Pennsylvania. Among those things I encountered was political violence about which I knew nothing. In the early

---

[2] The city of Capetown was very modern and different from the pictures of rural Africa often shown in missionary presentations.

1960s, frustrated people in Southern Rhodesia were derailing trains and burning the thatched roofs off school buildings in rural villages. At one point, the police phoned our mission station every fifteen minutes to see if we were safe. That says something of the times in which we lived.[3] Having witnessed all that, I returned to Pennsylvania in January 1963 to the ethnic church[4] in which I grew up.

Coming back to my home church was my first real encounter with culture shock. Soon after returning to the USA I attended an evangelistic service at my home congregation where the evangelist was preaching against the sin of wearing a necktie. I sat somewhat in disbelief as I reflected on what I had seen in Central Africa. My first response was (and still is today), "This man doesn't know what sin is." The cultural dissimilarity I mentioned above stood out in bold relief.

I have come to believe since then that the theology of such preaching is a serious confusion of Christianity and culture and the result of a seriously inadequate Biblical hermeneutic. What happened to me at this point was only a partial awakening to the tension between Christianity and culture. Later, after studying missiology, I would come to understand much more about this conflict – a conflict not unrelated to issues of dependency.

What happened to me at that evangelistic meeting is worth some reflection. When I joined the Brethren in Christ Church, I was converted culturally as well as spiritually. In other words, there was a fair amount of social dislocation involved. Though I had never worn plain clothes (as was typical of the Mennonites or Amish), I did stop wearing a necktie and wore only conservative colored clothing. I then joined the brotherhood (including today, bishops) in making the transition to wearing first a black necktie, then one that was dark green and eventually those of various colors. Some who read this will not understand the significance of these practices designed to show separation from the world.

---

[3] That violence was mild compared to what happened in Zimbabwe during the war for independence in the 1970s.

[4] My use of the term "ethnic church" differs from popular usage. To understand how I use it, see the introductory statement at the beginning of chapter 15.

As I reflect on what I encountered, it strikes me that there were few in my generation who accepted such radical social dislocation in order to enter the Kingdom of God. I wonder how many might have responded differently if they had not been asked to make so great a cultural transition in order to enter the Kingdom of God? We have no way of knowing. But, as I mentioned above, that social dislocation has an important part to play in the development of the dependency syndrome. More on this will be included in Chapter 15 on issues of ethnicity.

Preparing for the Return to Africa

Following the completion of a four-year college degree in 1965 it was decision time again. By this time I was married to Verna (Oberholtzer), and we were asked by our denominational mission director to consider going out to Africa because "secondary school teachers were very much needed." I was not attracted to the idea because I felt there was a preoccupation in African missionary work with programs that made me uncomfortable. In our denomination there were large mission-run farms, some ranging from 3,000 to 7,000 acres each. There were hundreds of schools, several large hospitals and various other activities that I considered to be part of the cultural mandate. I felt God had called me to be involved in the evangelistic mandate. I didn't know those terms then, but learned the important distinction after eventually getting cross-cultural missionary training. I felt that many of those programs in Africa were like large-scale businesses run by missionaries while the adult population remained largely unevangelized or only marginally evangelized.

When approached by the mission board to return to Africa, I expressed my reservations and asked not to be sent there. I requested that my wife and I be sent to Japan where I understood that church planting and evangelism were the priority of our mission. My request was declined. "The situation in Japan is not as rosy as it appears," was the reply, "and furthermore, teachers are needed in Africa." Eventually I came to learn that large mission-established institutions are like living organisms with a huge appetite. To keep them alive requires large sums of money and, in those days, many "foreign" missionaries. They also require time, time, time. In spite of my request, Verna and I accepted the call of the church to fill teaching posts, first in a secondary school and later in a teacher training college, both in Zambia.

Beginning Missionary Service as a (Married) Team

Because I did not have cross-cultural training, I was not only ill prepared for missionary work in general, but I felt particularly unsuited for the secondary school classroom. My heart was not in teaching the English language, social studies or a course on "commerce", something that in a place like Zambia is culturally conditioned. The students had to tell me that local property taxes are called rates, and I was to be their teacher! At the same time, I had a strong desire to learn the local African language and the way things were done in the local social setting, the African village.

When we accepted the call to return to Africa we were assigned to Zambia, not Southern Rhodesia or Rhodesia where I had been before. This meant learning a new language, Tonga, instead of Sindebele. I poured my heart into learning Tonga and passed the second year examination after only about four months of study. Having learned some Sindebele previously was an advantage.

Mercifully, I was soon moved out of the classroom that I loathed. But it was as superintendent of a large mission station that I got caught in another dilemma of cross-cultural missions. I was assigned to a task bigger than I was ever prepared to undertake. I was assigned to oversee a three thousand acre farm. I would become a farmer, businessperson, manager of several boarding schools, and pastor of a church with seven hundred in attendance each Sunday when schools were in session. Fewer than a hundred attended when schools were not in session.

More than that, at the age of 28, I had more responsibility and influence in that rural district of Zambia than most African village headmen and perhaps, in some ways, more than the chief himself. As I look back now, it is very embarrassing. But it reflects something of missions in colonial Central Africa. To question the situation often elicited the response, "This is the way all missions are in Central Africa." Unfortunately, that was true of many churches and missions in that part of the world. I learned years later, however, that not all missions around the world function on that paradigm. I once met a missionary to Thailand who, upon hearing about mission work in Central Africa, made the statement, "I have heard about mission situations like that but never met anyone who was from one of them."

During the next five and a half years in Zambia, I carried an enormous load of activities, sometimes seeking to solve problems that were far above my ability or competence. For example, managing the budget of the mission was clearly beyond my ability. Among other things, the only homes that had electricity on the mission were within "the mission fence." Of course those were primarily missionary homes. When I began electrifying homes of African staff who lived outside the fence, the costs were high. As a result, the mission ran a deficit, but at least the disparity between those who had electricity and those who didn't was beginning to be corrected. This was only one example of the difficulties I had.

Taking Hold of my Schedule

Then one day it struck me: I must delegate this work to others. And so, I gave most of what I was doing to capable assistants — unfortunately, much went to missionary volunteers from North America — but I did take control of my schedule. Each Monday I pursued serious language study. I was soon giving all Sunday sermons in the Tonga language. Wednesday afternoon was given to a Bible study with local pastors and evangelists. Friday was reserved for village evangelism. I began to lead daily devotional times in the Tonga language with all mission workers and with a team of African men who were making bricks nearby. Simultaneously, Verna had a growing ministry among village women. It appeared that we had turned an important corner. We felt tremendously rewarded as our effectiveness became evident. That year the mission budget regained half its previous deficit, and it looked as if we were being rewarded for getting our priorities right. But we still had some way to go.

Into that rewarding ministry of personal evangelism, however, came a change as radical as a meteor from outer space. The ruling field committee — made up mostly of missionaries — decided that a position needed to be filled in a teacher training college about two hundred miles away. Once again I was to become a classroom teacher, in fact, a teacher of teachers. That is hardly the thing for someone who did not feel at home in the classroom in the first place. I begged to remain where I was. Leaving ministry in the local language to teach English was an enormous letdown, and I knew I was unsuited for it.

None of my attempts to persuade differently worked, so I had to leave the rural ministry I had come to love. My new assignment included weekend pastoral duties in a local congregation. But it was during this time that I experienced my most severe disillusionment with the missionary paradigm of Central Africa.

I learned, for example, that 84% of those being taken into church membership in our denomination each year were leaving by attrition through a well-greased back door. In other words, between 1959 and 1969, our mission and church baptized about 5,000 people and the membership increased only between four and five hundred. In addition, I became aware of the power of missionaries (outsiders) in the decision-making of the church and mission. Largely because the money and the decision-makers came from North America, it was obvious that the church in Central Africa was being kept dependent. During the time I was there, the constitution and bylaws for the church were hammered out by a group of 50-60 North Americans with only a small handful of Africans present. I clearly remember listening, as the legal terminology was debated — in English, of course.

I was also impressed with how little our missionary message had to say about demon possession, witchcraft, polygamy and other issues of cultural importance. In addition, many of my missionary colleagues could not preach a sermon in the local language. Some who could do so used the language in a denigrating manner. In the words of one African brother, "Some missionaries speak our language well, but they use it to despise our people." Sadly, that is the kind of missionary situation I encountered in Central Africa in the 1960s.

Needless to say, my growing restlessness left me disillusioned. The more I learned, the more I questioned the paradigm on which we as missionaries were functioning. The more vocal I became, the more alienated I became from the missionary administration.

Sadly, through the years an adversary relationship developed between the missionary establishment and some members of the African church, many of whom were leaders. There were several evidences of this. One example was a remark an older missionary made to me only a few days after I arrived in Africa years before. She said, "Glenn, one thing that will strike you is the harsh manner in which some missionaries speak to local people." That word was prophetic.

Another evidence of this adversary relationship was seen in remarks such as the following made by more than one African colleague through the years: "A missionary is either well-liked by us Africans or he is well-liked by the mission administration. The ones we appreciate the most have a lot of problems with the mission administration."

Something else was happening that I did not understand very well. Because of the stand I took, I found myself crossing over into the frame of reference of African brothers and sisters who were watching my changing relationship with the mission establishment with great interest. To them, it became increasingly clear that when the chips were down, I would stand with them. Space does not permit examples of how things like this occurred.

Needless to say, when my missionary term of five and a half years ended in 1971, it was decided by the missionary administration that unless I changed there was no possibility of my returning to that mission field. It was understood, though it was not said in exactly those words until later on as you will soon see.

The Search for Help

As my disillusionment grew, so did my search for answers. I learned about the emerging Church Growth school of thought in Pasadena, California. As I read one thing after another which they produced, I was convinced that I was not alone. It was reassuring to learn that others were verbalizing what I was feeling. During this time I engaged in deep inner searching to see what made me react so strongly to the way I and many of my African brothers and sisters were being treated. There came a time that I began to wonder if I were off base spiritually or maybe even mentally. That was a scary thought. But then I learned that there were others — from the outside — who saw things similar to the way I was seeing them. For me that was like regaining some of my psychic equilibrium. What a tremendous relief!

One missionary from another society in a different part of Southern Africa visited our area and gave me a few reassuring words: "Glenn, when you leave here and go to California to study, you will find that you are not so radical after all. You will only be middle of the road. They will confirm many of your suspicions." That word of encouragement proved to be prophetic.

The Return to the USA

In 1971 my family and I left Zambia. I had been greatly enriched, yet somewhat disillusioned concerning the nature of missionary work in general and Central Africa in particular.

I recall one incident vividly. We boarded a plane in Livingstone, Zambia for Lusaka and the long journey back to the USA. As the plane raced down the runway the door to the cockpit was left open, something that could not happen these days. As I watched, the pilot pushed forward the levers on the powerful jet engines, and to my surprise, the co-pilot gently laid his hand behind the hand of the pilot. He held it there as we lifted into the sky. I hadn't known about that practice in which the co-pilot shows support for the pilot during take-off.

As I watched, I cried. My thoughts turned to my experience of the past few years. I realized that I could not put my hand behind the hands of those in charge of the mission society of which I was a part. There was too much with which I disagreed. My sense of justice told me that something was very wrong indeed. Something clearly needed to change. As you will see later, it needed to change in me and in that situation.

Missionary Training for the First Time

I felt compelled to follow God's leading to study and enrolled in the School of World Mission at Fuller Theological Seminary.[5] Prior to that, however, I worked for six months (May to December of 1971) overseeing the building of the covered bridge that now stands on the campus of Messiah College.

When some of my missionary colleagues from Africa heard that I was building a bridge they chided me. I had spoken so much about

---

[5] This school is now called the School of Intercultual Studies (SIS)

the brick and mortar approach to mission work in Central Africa that they wondered how I could ever become involved in building a bridge. They taunted me by saying that it must be one of Dr. McGavran's *Bridges of God* — the title of his book that launched the Church Growth Movement.

The bridge was completed in December 1971, and in January 1972 our family (including our two children born in Africa) moved to California where we lived at the Christian and Missionary Alliance complex in Glendale while I studied at the seminary in Pasadena.

What I learned in that program was not only reassuring, but also somewhat more radicalizing. I was carried further down the road I had begun in Zambia. I became more and more convinced that there was something wrong with the colonial approach that the missionary enterprise followed in Central Africa. As I mentioned earlier, it characterized not only our mission society but many others in Central Africa as well.

I received a great deal of affirmation through what I was learning, but there was another major benefit from enrolling in this program. I met and learned to know scores (later hundreds) of other missionaries and church leaders from many parts of the world. One thing struck me: while colonialism exists in many places, I met some missionaries who knew nothing of the kind of experience I had encountered. Of course, there were many who could understand where I was coming from. Some of them became close friends with whom I could work through the implications of what I had experienced.

As I progressed through that graduate level program in missiology, I began to analyze the church and mission in Zambia. For my masters thesis I wrote about the church and mission with which I had been affiliated. I first gave it the title "Crucial Issues of the Brethren in Christ in Zambia." One administrator from our mission looked at the title and laughed, as if to indicate that it was presumptuous to indicate that our church faced any "crucial issues." I later dropped the words from the title, though the word 'crucial' was hardly inappropriate.

By the time I finished the two-year course at Fuller, it became increasingly clear that I could not return to Zambia. I clearly needed to seek another ministry at least for the foreseeable future.

I should add that as decision time drew near (1973), I was approached by our mission director and asked to consider returning to Zambia. I was told, however, that I would need to accept what the mission was doing without vocalizing my concern. I declined the offer and responded to another invitation to stay in California to work.

Service at Fuller Seminary

I was given an invitation to work in the School of World Mission at Fuller Theological Seminary as Administrative Assistant to the dean, Dr. Arthur F. Glasser. Before coming to Fuller he had been a missionary in China with the China Inland Mission (CIM) and, for many years served as North American Director of the Overseas Missionary Fellowship (OMF).

From 1973-1979 I served as Assistant to Dean Glasser, as well as faculty secretary and International Student Advisor for the seminary. The experience was unparalleled in terms of the scope of activity and personal reward. On a daily basis I was a servant of Drs. Donald McGavran, Alan Tippett, Ralph Winter, Pete Wagner, Charles Kraft, J. Edwin Orr and others. In addition, I learned to know hundreds of missionaries and international church leaders from all over the world.

My African Experience Catches Up with me

Early in my time in Pasadena I began to feel the full impact of my Africa experience. While in Africa I vocalized my feelings. In some ways that vocalizing upset others, but it kept me from getting an ulcer.

In California, however, I was not speaking out as before, and the resentment resulting from my earlier experience was now being internalized. As a result, I became ill with stomach and chest pains. On several occasions I was taken to the hospital in the middle of the night thinking that I was having a heart attack. I had all the symptoms, including pain or numbness in the arms. Such experiences were disquieting.

Over a period of a year and a half, I had one medical examination after another with hundreds of dollars of expense. Today it would be tens of thousands of dollars! No one could find a physical cause of my problem, yet I was often in great distress. On two different occasions medical doctors said to me, each using similar words, "There are five things that cause your kind of problem: fear, resentment, bitterness, anxiety and unmet goals." One said, "Before you get well, you may need to face up to what happened to you in the past." Again, these were prophetic words given to me by God's grace at the right time!

About that time, the Lord brought into my path a missionary by the name of Joe Arthur who had served with the Christian and Missionary Alliance (C&MA) in the Philippines. He was one of the many mid-career missionaries that I learned to know at the School of World Mission. He sensed my struggle and one day said, "Glenn, if you want help, I'll try to help you." He proved to be a genuine provision from the Lord. I accepted his offer, and for twenty-two days we met in his home for one hour each afternoon as I learned about my problem. He made me say nothing, but rather he spoke in great detail about the effects of unresolved inner conflicts. I listened and took copious notes.

At the end of those twenty-two one-hour visits with my missionary friend, a true peer therapist, I was convinced of one thing: I had unresolved inner conflicts; and if I were to get well physically, these conflicts would need to be resolved. A heavy personal assignment lay ahead of me. With Verna's patient help, I wrote letters to all those with whom I felt my past relationship was either strained or broken. Some were African church leaders, others were missionaries, and several were mission executives.

On the advice of my missionary friend, Joe, I wrote sixteen letters in which I assumed full responsibility for all that had happened. I blamed no one. The responses I got back were varied. Some wrote to say that they, too, were sorry that our relationship had been broken and they were glad to have it repaired. A few came to see me personally. One missionary wrote something to the effect that, "That's the way you are. I tried to tell you differently, but you wouldn't listen. Furthermore", he said, "when one is five years old his attitudes are set for life, so for you there is little possibility of change." As for me, I had taken my place and I was free because I had done all that I knew to do. Such freedom is priceless.

One Zambian brother had an interesting response to my letter. He was about fifty years of age at the time. When he received my letter, he took it to a missionary near to where he lived and asked, "What's the meaning of this?" The missionary responded by saying, "Glenn has written you a letter of apology." He replied, "But what am I to do with it?" "Forgive him," the missionary said, "that's all he is asking for." This African church leader who had worked with missionaries for several decades said, "No missionary has ever apologized to me for anything." This remark was symptomatic of the relationship that existed between the missionary establishment and many of our African brothers and sisters. I am happy to report that this Zambian brother subsequently sent me a wonderful letter, one that I treasure highly to this day.

Once I wrote those sixteen letters, the burden began to lift, and gradually the stomach and chest pains left. There were no more visits to the hospital in the middle of the night. I praise the Lord for the insight and intuition of my missionary brother, Joe. At the time of this writing, more than thirty-five years later, thankfully those symptoms have not returned. I give praise to the Lord.

Through all of this I learned one important lesson – and it is significant. I learned that resentment and bitterness are not worth the burden they represent. I heartily encourage anyone in similar circumstances to consider the cost of unresolved inner conflicts, and make the decision that they are not worth carrying through life. The cross of Christ is the place to deposit them. Had I not done that, I have no doubt they could have taken my life.

Another Call to Return to Africa

When it became clear that my time at Fuller Seminary was coming to a close in the late 1970s, I was faced with another period of decision-making. Thoughts turned again toward Africa and the mission. The mission society approached the African church about their need for missionary assistance.

By now there was a major change in the church and mission administration in Zambia where I had served. The missionary administration had been replaced in the mid-1970s with an African bishop and an African assistant. In addition, the ruling field committee to which I referred earlier was by now made up mostly of Africans—many of whom knew me well.

Another significant change had taken place. The overseas secretary from North America was replaced. On a survey trip to Zambia, the new secretary asked the ruling field committee the following question: "Who served with you before as a missionary that you would be willing to have come back?" The committee, now mostly Zambians, suggested my name. The invitation I was given by the church was to serve as principal of a Bible institute in Zambia. When the request was relayed to me, I declined on the basis that, after more than 70 years of mission activity in Zambia, obviously there was a qualified Zambian to fill that post. I agreed that I might teach there some day, but I could not head the program.

When my sentiments were sent back to the Zambian Church, they accepted my decision and appointed a senior African church leader to be the principal. Had I taken the position, I would have kept yet another African church leader out of leadership.

Reflections On Spirituality

I mentioned several times my struggle with quiet times. This is a struggle many in active Christian service have experienced. As time went by, I observed that some of my missionary colleagues appeared to be quite "spiritual." Sometimes I was tempted to envy them because they seemed to live above the human struggle that was evident in my life.

But in retrospect, I view the situation somewhat differently. Some of those who appeared to be the most "spiritual" I found were the most impatient with our African brothers and sisters. They were the quickest to condemn acts they thought to be "sin." They may have been "spiritually" sensitive, but they were obviously not very "culturally" sensitive.

As I look back I realize that what one learns in his devotional times must be demonstrated in public encounters. Keeping a good balance between our humanity and our spirituality makes a big difference in how we are perceived by others. That has important missionary implications that deserve more reflection than I will be able to give here.

A New Ministry

In the early 1980's, our Lord, through the sovereign leadership of the Holy Spirit, opened the way for me to step out into a new ministry. I responded to the encouragement of a few missionary colleagues to launch a ministry in which I could use my gifts for the wider body of Christ. Consequently, World Mission Associates was begun in June 1983 as a catalytic service organization for the benefit of missionaries, church leaders and mission executives. From then until this writing (2007) I have been concentrating on issues of dependency and self-reliance in the Christian movement. During the past twenty years I have conducted scores of seminars and consultations in the USA, Europe, Israel and Palestine but primarily in East, Central and Southern Africa. The sixteen chapters in Part One of this text are a result of that teaching on how to avoid or overcome dependency. I offer it here along with the remaining chapters in Part Two for the encouragement of those who are concerned about similar issues in the Christian movement.

In September 2005, the Board of Directors of World Mission Associates launched the World Mission Resource Center in Lancaster, Pennsylvania. This was a bold venture for an organization that existed in small and modest offices for the first twenty-three years of our ministry. The purpose of the center is to provide a place where church and mission leaders can find information, seek consultation, and share their insights with others on the worldwide mission of the church. I consider it a privilege to be part of the process of establishing the resource center. However, it is for others to develop the program and carry out its activities. My desire is to teach, write and do some travel when invited while others carry on the administration and program of the resource center.

My current ministry is rewarding and far beyond anything I anticipated when I received that call sitting on my bed reading the *Reader's Digest* more than fifty years ago. I am still following that call one step at a time.

Introduction to Part One

Sixteen Chapters on
Dependency and Self-Reliance
for Mission-Established Institutions

Introduction

In 1996 World Mission Associates produced an eight-hour video series titled *Dependency Among Mission-Established Institutions: Exploring The Issues*. It includes sixteen lessons with discussion questions and suggested readings following each lesson. Part One of this book is basically the sound track of the video series, with considerable revision. Hence, in some places it may read more like a spoken presentation than text written for publication. Part Two of the text includes articles that were written since the video series was produced.

This video series (now available in DVD format as well) has been used in more than forty countries. It is sometimes used by groups of missionaries and church leaders with discussion following. It can still be purchased for that purpose and is available in various formats and languages.[1] This text version is for those who prefer a book which they can read at random, something that is not done easily in video format.

This text, because it is transcribed from a spoken video series, is not documented, as an academic document would be. In a few places footnotes are included to help the reader find a source that may be of interest. Other more scholarly treatments of the subject are needed. For encouragement of the reader, at the time of this production two doctoral level dissertations have already been completed[2] and others are in process. As doctoral dissertations are added in this field, serious documentation will be available for the benefit of all.

---

[1] At the time of this writing the video series is available in both English and French. (Portuguese, Spanish and Swahili are still in process.) Available formats are DVD (NTSC and PAL), Audio Cassette, Audio CD and VHS (NTSC, PAL and SECAM).

[2] One dissertation by Chris Little is entitled *Mission in the Way of Paul*. At the time of this writing it is available through Peter Lang Publishers. A second by Robert Reese is entitled, *Dependency and Its Impact on Churches Related to the Baptist Convention of Zimbabwe and the Zimbabwe Christian Fellowship*. Details are in the bibliography at the end of this text.

How the Term "Dependency" is Used

It is no secret today that many mission-established churches have become dependent on foreign funding and personnel. Many leaders in mission-established churches feel they cannot exist without the subsidy they have been receiving, sometimes for a century or more. Even some recently planted churches are already dependent on foreign support. This is particularly true of the former Soviet Union

This unhealthy dependency has resulted in many Christians in mission-established churches and other institutions living well below their privileges in the Lord. Without the continuing subsidy, some churches become paralyzed and, cannot reproduce themselves through evangelism or missionary outreach of their own. Sometimes others even build their church buildings for them.

The sixteen chapters of Part One seek to describe the dependency syndrome and the underlying issues as well as how to overcome them. Many practical suggestions are given with a view to promoting the move away from unhealthy dependency toward Spirit-led self-reliance.

A word is in order about how I use the term *self-reliance* in this context. **Self-reliance, as used in this series, does not imply that Christians do not rely upon God**. Rather, my use of it has to do with breaking reliance on the resources which are at a distance (usually in North America, Europe or Korea) rather than on what God has placed close at hand where much of our world lives.

Included in this text are numerous stories of churches that have made significant progress toward self-reliance. **These churches are by no means perfect**, and many people in them admit that they have many things yet to learn about how to stand on their own two feet. However, in each case cited, some significant step in the direction of self-reliance has been taken. These stories are given for the encouragement of church and mission leaders as well as western missionaries who may feel that the situation they face is hopeless and will never change. There is ample evidence that change can and does take place.

The content of this series of lessons is primarily based on experiences and prevailing conditions in East, Central and Southern Africa. The author does not claim to speak authoritatively for the rest of the world. However, in conversation with church and mission leaders and missionaries from West Africa, Latin America and Asia, it has become clear that the problem is widespread and not confined to East, Central and Southern Africa.

For those interested in further reading, Appendix A is an Annotated Bibliography that includes descriptions of basic texts and articles on issues of dependency and self-reliance in the Christian movement. That is only a brief list, but it is a place to begin. As I describe in the introduction to that appendix, each book one picks up will have other entries in the bibliography that will show what the author of that book thinks are important. That leads to an unfolding list of readings that are available.

Notes and Suggestions for Understanding Dependency Issues

1. **The subject matter in some of these lessons will not be easy for some people to hear.** There is no intention to cause hurt or do harm to anyone in the Christian movement. However, it is clear that if progress is to be made regarding the dependency syndrome, serious attention will need to be given to root causes. Otherwise the problem will be perpetuated into future generations. The author apologizes in advance for any statement that should have been said in a more helpful and less disconcerting way.

2. **These lessons are designed to give an overview of the subject in Chapter 1.** Chapters 1-4 are designed to provide information and inspiration for those who do not want to create or perpetuate dependency with the funding they provide. Chapters 5-12 are a deeper look at the missiological issues related to dependency and self-reliance. Chapters 13-15 are intended to be a mini-course on cross-cultural issues for those who have not had such training. The author's purpose is to show how these major issues in chapters 13 to 15 are related to dependency and self-reliance. Chapter 16 was subsequently added to show the important role of business people in relation to healthy self-reliance in the Christian movement.

3. **Not all suggestions given in these lessons are applicable to all situations.** What works well in one place may not work at all in another. However, that is the nature of cross-cultural ministry. Cultures vary and so must the methods used to present the Good News of the Gospel. Those who say "we tried that and it didn't work" should remember that it may very well have worked elsewhere because times and conditions were different in one way or another.

4. **Some subjects will come up several times throughout the series.** For example, since nominality is at the heart of the dependency problem, the issue of marginal Christian conversion will surface in several different lessons. This is purposeful and in learning circles is called positive reinforcement.

5. **There is more material in this written version than in the video series.** There simply was not enough time in the video presentation to cover all of the material. A number of outlines that were not covered in the video series are included in the first sixteen chapters of this written version. Of course, other issues such as short-term missions, etc., are covered in the remaining chapters of Part Two of this text.

6. **Suggested readings are given to broaden the knowledge of those seriously interested in the subject.** It does not mean that the author agrees with everything those writers are saying. However, there is something in each suggested reading that will shed light on the problem of dependency in the Christian movement. The author's purpose is that, with the presence and guidance of the Holy Spirit, the Christian movement will benefit from giving serious attention to the subject of dependency.

7. **For the benefit of those who are not familiar with the terms used in missiology** or mission studies, Appendix B is a limited glossary of terms with definitions *as I use them*. For some, it may be helpful to read through the glossary before reading the text.

I trust that everyone who reads what follows will know the presence of the Holy Spirit and be encouraged in the work of the Kingdom of God.

CHAPTER 1

Introduction to Dependency
Among Mission-Established Institutions

The subject at hand is primarily about dependency and self-reliance throughout the Christian movement. The material and illustrations are mostly drawn from East, Central and Southern Africa. Since the launch of the video series on this subject in 1996, it has been found to be useful to some who are living and working in countries outside of East, Central and Southern Africa. The author does not claim to speak to church and mission issues beyond Africa, though an occasional illustration may be given from other parts of the world. Serious students of mission studies will find many materials on related subjects that will be informative regarding how the church was planted and is sustained in other areas of the world.

Definition of Self-Reliance

I begin with a definition of self-reliance because this creates a concern for some people. The word "self-reliance" as I am using it, does not mean that people do not rely on God. In the spread of the Gospel and the work that missionaries have done down through the years, people who have received the Gospel have often become dependent upon the missionaries who brought the Good News. They also became dependent upon the money and other resources that were brought to them. Sometimes they became dependent upon such things as foreign structures or development projects which accompanied the spread of the Gospel. Sometimes they even became attracted to shipping containers filled with used clothing and other things. Sadly, in some cases, the true meaning of the Gospel got lost in the process.[1]

So, how can those in mission-established churches learn to depend upon God to provide locally what they need in order to do His work? Why is that so important? It is important because unless people are able to use and multiply the resources that God has put

---

[1] For an in-depth treatment of this, see an article on the WMA website which I have entitled *I Believe in the Local Church*. The website is www.wmausa.org.

close at hand, they will not be able to sustain the work they have to do locally, and they will have nothing to give to those beyond their own borders. In this respect our understanding of the term self-reliance becomes critically important. All of us <u>must</u> rely upon God. The problem that many mission-established churches have is that they depend on someone else's resources at a great distance.

Historical Spread of the Christian Movement

First, let's take a look at the spread of the Christian Gospel across the world. Think about how the Gospel exploded out of Jerusalem and the Holy Land, into Asia Minor and then the Roman Empire, and then into Northern Europe and Scandinavia. It didn't stay in Jerusalem, or other parts of the Holy Land or Asia Minor. It didn't stay in Northern Europe or Scandinavia. It exploded out of Scandinavia, so much so that at one point in time the Norwegians had the reputation of sending out more missionaries per capita than any other country in the world.

The Gospel went into England, but it didn't stay there. It went out from England into North America. It went out from North America into Brazil, Korea, India and Nigeria and is now going out from those places to other regions of the world. One mission society in Nigeria sends out a thousand cross-cultural missionaries. Another mission society in India sends out 1000 Indian missionaries with Indian resources and 30,000 Indian prayer supporters.

Despite this good news about the expanding Christian movement, the Church in East, Central and Southern Africa is not keeping pace through cross-cultural evangelism in new areas. Why is this? It is evangelizing its own close neighbors, but it is doing very little in what is traditionally called E-2 or E-3 evangelism.[2]

I wish to emphasize that the Church <u>is growing</u> in East, Central and Southern Africa. We are told by missiologists that in sub-Saharan Africa the Church is growing at the rate of as many as twenty thousand new believers every day. So evangelism is being done in one form or another, but when one looks around for missionary societies that recruit, train and send missionaries into cross-cultural work, there are very few in East, Central and Southern Africa. In

---

[2] For a definition of these terms, see the glossary in Appendix B.

addition, there are also very few indigenous training institutes which prepare missionaries for cross-cultural evangelism in that part of Africa.

There are a few training institutes in East Africa and some in Southern Africa, but most of these were started and carried on by expatriate missionaries, often with a significant amount of foreign money. In some of them, teachers are still expatriate missionaries whose salaries are paid from overseas. In many cases the people who graduate from those training schools don't go into what missiologists call E-3 evangelism, or cross-cultural evangelism. Hence, for the most part, the church in that part of Africa is not reproducing itself through cross-cultural evangelism. It is not enjoying its rightful place in the globally expanding Christian movement.

At first glance, South Africa may be considered an exception to this scenario. There, mission societies such as SIM and the OMF are recruiting non-white South Africans for ministry in Asia. However, the OMF (Overseas Missionary Fellowship) or the SIM (Serving in Missions) can hardly be called indigenous mission societies in South Africa. They were born somewhere else. It was someone else's vision that brought them into being. Later on they opened offices in South Africa, and are now recruiting and sending South African missionaries.

But over all, there is a definite shortage of indigenous organizations in East, Central and Southern Africa raised up from the vision of people within Africa, funded by resources within Africa, and sending out their own people in what one would call a "locally owned and operated" missionary movement. Incidentally, *locally owned and operated* is my definition of something that is *indigenous*.

Why is the church in this part of Africa not reproducing itself through cross-cultural evangelism? Why is it not sending its own missionaries to the 10/40 window, for example? In the 10/40 window, 97% of the people do not yet know that Jesus is Lord and Savior, while in some parts of Africa there are places where the Gospel has been preached for a hundred years, sometimes much longer than that. Sadly in these same places, people are still receiving missionaries and money from the outside. They are not giving back to the Christian movement some of that which God has given to them. Someone recently said that South Africa still receives five times as many outside missionaries as it sends. So the question is, why is this happening? I suggest there are two primary reasons.

Analyzing the Nature of Christian Conversion

The first reason I believe the church is not sending out its own missionaries has to do with the quality of the Christian conversion experience that many Africans have had.[3] In 1984, I traveled through Africa, going first to West Africa, then across to East Africa and down through Central Africa, ending up on the Southern Coast of South Africa. Everywhere I went I heard pastors lamenting the fact that their church members have a divided loyalty. It is what missiologists call *dualism*. They hold two worldviews at the same time. They hold the Christian worldview which represents the church they attend and certain aspects of their schooling. However, in times of crisis they often turn to their original paradigm, the traditional worldview. This occurs, for example, when there is a death in the family or a terminal illness. It occurs when a woman cannot conceive or when a university graduate cannot find a job. Those pastors and church leaders were saying to me then — and many have done so since — that their people turn to the local traditional practitioner of religion, sometimes called the witchdoctor, in times of real crisis. Many do not feel that what they are getting at church is sufficient for the really deep issues of life.

Dr. Aylward Shorter explains dualism this way:[4]

> *During the past hundred years African Traditional Religion has been visibly sinking beneath the surface of modern social life in Africa, but what remains above the surface is, in fact, the tip of an iceberg. At Baptism, the African Christian repudiates remarkably little of his former non-Christian outlook. He may be obliged to turn his back upon certain traditional practices which the Church, rightly or wrongly, has condemned in his area, but he is not asked to recant a religious philosophy*

---

[3] What I say here could well be applied to Christians in many other places, including North America and Europe.

[4] This quote will be repeated and given more in-depth treatment in Chapter 13.

> . . . . *Consequently, he returns to the forbidden practices as occasion arises with remarkable ease. Conversion to Christianity is for him sheer gain, an 'extra' for which he has opted. It is an overlay on his original religious culture. Apart from the superficial condemnations, Christianity has really had little to say about African Traditional Religion in the way of serious judgments of value. Consequently, the African Christian operates with two thought systems at once, and both of them are closed to each other . . .* [5]

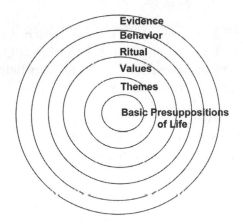

Looking at the issue of Christian conversion through anthropological eyes, it is helpful to consider the accompanying concentric circles. At the very center there are *basic presuppositions of life,* those powerful assumptions that drive our differing worldviews.[6] Too often, the change that takes place in the conversion of many Christians does not happen at the deepest presuppositional level of the concentric circles. The outside circles show the *evidence* of things going on. Then there is *behavior* that relates to the evidence. Further in toward the center one observes *rituals* which accompany the evidence and the behavior.

For example, in the Christian worldview, one may notice a church building (evidence) and watch people going in and out (behavior). Inside that church building people sometimes kneel to pray, take

---

[5] Aylward Shorter, *African Christian Theology: Adaptation or Incarnation.* (1977:10)
[6] I am indebted for Dr. Donald R. Jacobs for this illustration.

communion or perform baptisms (rituals). If one continues to follow through the concentric circles, it becomes apparent that a *value* system characterizes those who call themselves Christians. In fact, in a place where many Christians live, one can discover *themes* that run through society. For example, volunteerism and ministry-type organizations often exist (e.g., the Red Cross, the YMCA, Rotary Club or the local ambulance association). Each of these points to the theme that Christians want to be helpful to those in need. At the very center of such a worldview is a *basic presupposition of life* that says if we want to please God, we must care for others. In reality, a westerner's view of eternal life has its roots at the presuppositional level of these concentric circles.

There are hundreds of things in society which can be analyzed using this simple diagram. In Chapter 13 of Part One I deal more in depth with how these concentric circles can help us analyze a traditional African society.

Part of the problem is that many Christians have been converted at the outer edge of the circles but not seriously changed at the center. I refer to this phenomenon as "marginal Christian conversion."

This does not discount those individuals who have been thoroughly converted. Thankfully, there are many in Africa. Thank God for those who brought the Gospel to this continent and for the twenty thousand per day who are coming to the Christian faith. Our concern here is for the depth of that conversion and how that relates to the church's failure to develop a cross-cultural ministry beyond its own borders.

I maintain that though there are individuals in many churches who have been converted thoroughly at the center, a missionary movement is not built on individuals here and there who are thoroughly converted. Such a movement must be built on a *generally energized Christian church*, so filled with God's love and God's Spirit, that there is something left over to carry the Christian Gospel to places where it has not yet been preached.

Understanding the Western Christian Gospel

We must recognize, first of all, that this battle is spiritual. We are reminded in Ephesians 6:12 that "we fight not against flesh and blood but against principalities and powers." Not only that, 2 Corinthians 10:4 reminds us that the weapons of our warfare are *spiritual*. We cannot use the weapons of the world for what is a spiritual battle.

Second, we need to grasp the meaning of the very Gospel that we seek to proclaim. Understanding our own faith is the first step to learning how to understand someone else's.

Dr. Paul Heibert has helped us to understand this using the accompanying diagram.

THE CONCEPT OF THE HIGH GOD
THE EXCLUDED MIDDLE ANGELS, DEMONS, HEALINGS, SIGNS, WONDERS
JESUS WHO WALKS WITH ME DAY BY DAY

Those of us who are westerners have a well-developed concept of the high God. He is "Our Father who is in Heaven." We also have a well-developed concept of Jesus who "walks with me day by day." We enjoy singing, "What a Friend we have in Jesus." However, there is a significant area in the middle that westerners tend to avoid. Dr. Heibert calls this the "excluded middle." This is the area where angels, demons, healings, signs and wonders exist. Many westerners have traditionally written off this area as not being valid. With our predominantly scientific assumptions, we don't know much about such things and, in fact, find them rather unsettling and baffling. Yet this is the very area in which many non-westerners live their lives. It is part of what they confront on a daily basis. This area makes some of us so uncomfortable that we have rationalized it out of our theology, concluding that it belonged to a different dispensation, not the one in which we live.

What can we learn from this? Unless people are thoroughly convinced that the Christian Gospel is the best news they've ever heard, and that it has the answer to major questions in their lives, they are hardly candidates to carry the Gospel to other parts of the world.

The Nature of an Imported Structure

The second reason why I think the Church in East and Southern Africa has difficulty reproducing itself cross-culturally has to do with the structure that was imported along with the Gospel. Too often that structure was not only expensive, but also foreign in nature.

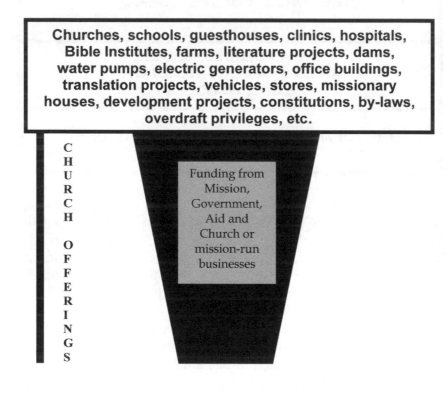

Churches, schools, guesthouses, clinics, hospitals, Bible Institutes, farms, literature projects, dams, water pumps, electric generators, office buildings, translation projects, vehicles, stores, missionary houses, development projects, constitutions, by-laws, overdraft privileges, etc.

CHURCH OFFERINGS

Funding from Mission, Government, Aid and Church or mission-run businesses

The structure that some western missionaries brought to Central Africa was a very expensive form of church government. The accompanying diagram shows that the missionaries built a very large "box" which included many wonderful things. Thankfully, they included over-draft privileges, because these would be needed later on to help sustain the system when the mission establishment withdrew the outside funding. A large post holds up this box, representing government, mission and aid funding. During the missionary period, this was sustained by government grants, money from overseas, and sometimes aid funding from World Vision, Bread for the World or TEAR Fund. All went into helping build and maintain this very large box. Sometimes, a portion of missionary salaries from the government or from overseas contributed to holding up the box. On the left hand side of the diagram I show a very thin post called "local church offerings."

The Role of Local Church Offerings

By comparison to the large central post, local church offerings were often small. In East, Central and Southern Africa there was sometimes a unique mentality behind local church offerings. People put a very small amount into the church collection, partly because they saw very little relationship between what they were giving and the enormous size and cost of the box and the cost of it.

There was a device throughout East, Central and Southern Africa in various churches called the "ticket" system. An individual would put a small amount of money into the church collection. It was then marked off on the ticket which all church members had in their possession. A man in one area, for example, might be encouraged to give two shillings and sixpence each month; a woman, two shillings; and a child, sixpence. Each time it would be marked off on the ticket.[7] The problem with the ticket system in Africa, however, was that even though a man might have a hundred bags of maize from his harvest in a given year, his obligation to the church might be only two shillings and six pence per month.

This system was seriously abused in some places. There were places in which it was decided that if a man's ticket was not marked up to date, he was not allowed to take communion. In some places, if a man died and his tickets were paid up to date, they were put on a stack on top of the coffin to show that he was ready to go to heaven.

---

[7] This system was actually imported from England where, I understand, John Wesley introduced it. In fact, there are Methodists in England today who are still using some form of the ticket system. But in Africa many churches used it—not just the Methodist church—and some are still using it today.

We all know that this was a misunderstanding of how one gets ready for heaven, but this mentality was communicated in some parts of the Christian movement.

What is "Church Money"?

In some places the penny became known as "church money." In the Sindebele language of Zimbabwe it was known as *Imali esonto* ("Sunday money"), or in Zulu, *Imali ecawe* ("Church money"). As a result, the penny was sometimes seen as what belonged to the church. Even non-Christian businessmen and women knew that a penny was called church money. One might go into a shop to buy something which cost two shillings and seven pence. If one paid with two shillings and six pence, the non-Christian shop owner, who may have been a Hindu Indian trader, would say, "*Ngifuna imali esonto* — I still need one piece of Sunday money."

The thin post of church offerings shown in my diagram often bore little relationship to the cost of operating the huge box. Eventually when the box had become very heavy, missionaries decided something needed to be done. So, beginning in the middle of the 20th century, missionaries began to say, "We must indigenize." So they looked into the box and began to fill positions with local leaders, one after the other. When the positions were filled with local people, some felt, "Now we have indigenized because we have local leadership." But that was **not** true *indigenization*; it was more like *nationalization* — filling the positions with local leaders.

The local people who took over this "box" were typically those most loyal to the missionary. They exhibited traits that missionaries appreciated (like coming to meetings on time, speaking English and dressing in appropriate western clothes). In some cases, the missionaries set up a scheme to reduce the outside funding, perhaps ten percent each year, assuming that the local people would take full financial responsibility at the end of the specified time period.

The problem was, however, that those "ten percent per year" reducing schemes often did not produce an indigenous church. In fact, a church doesn't usually become indigenous ten percent at a time. A church becomes indigenous when local people take responsibility and say, "This is ours — it belongs to us. We are going to take charge of it and make it work. We're going to manage it with our own decisions, structures and resources." That is when a church or other institution becomes independent or indigenous, not necessarily when someone else sets up a ten-year plan to make it happen.

I've sometimes said — rather facetiously — that when the missionaries decided they would reduce that support ten percent each year, they were honorable people and faithful to their promise. It does not mean, however, that the small post on the left automatically moved over to take the place of the former subsidy.

As I intimated above, there were other implications to this. When missionaries began to remove themselves from the situation, some of them had been earning salaries of which a portion was used to hold up the box. A missionary may have been earning a hundred pounds a month from the government for a position as a teacher. Since a missionary could live on fifty pounds a month (in the good old days), the other fifty pounds went to help hold up the box. That was just one of the ramifications, and one of the ways the support was removed when missionaries moved off the scene.

How did Western Missionaries Maintain "The Box"?

The missionaries themselves often could not manage the box without outside help; but they still hoped their scheme to reduce the funding they were bringing in would allow local church leaders to manage the box with local offerings. However, when the outside support was taken away and local support did not take its place, local church leaders looked around for something inside the box that might help them. That turned out to be the "overdraft privileges"! In some cases, church leaders such as bishops, moderators and superintendents began to borrow money at the bank just to maintain the box. Several years ago I knew of three churches that had overdrafts in the range of a million units of currency which they borrowed to hold up the box. In the early 1990s a million units of currency in Central Africa was still quite a large sum of money. Today a million doesn't buy what it used to buy. But at that time it was significant.

I have come to believe that it is immoral to create an unmanageable situation such as "the box", turn it over to local leaders, and then blame them when they fail to manage it successfully.

What is the Alternative?

The alternative is for a complete transfer of ownership and an eventual restructuring of the box. What would that include? It is not just turning over the paperwork; that's <u>legal</u> ownership. It's also not just filling the positions with local people; that's <u>functional</u> ownership. There is a third type which I call **psychological** ownership. This occurs when local people say, "This is our church, and we are going to make our own decisions and support it with our own resources!"

The good news is that there are churches which at one time were heavily dependent on outside funding, but which have moved toward self-reliance.[8] Let me tell you briefly about two such churches.

The Presbyterian Church in East Africa

One church that made progress toward self-reliance is the Presbyterian Church in East Africa. They originally received substantial support from the mission society in Scotland. However, in the early 1970's they made the decision to ask the people in Scotland to do the following:

1) Keep their money
2) Keep their missionaries and
3) Keep their missionary decision-making – all for a period of at least five years, to begin with.

They were asking for an opportunity for their church to get on its own two feet. The PCEA very quickly began to pay their own pastors, build their own church buildings, and buy their own vehicles. They planted new churches; several years ago they planted nine new congregations in one year. They started a pension fund for their pastors, something missionaries told them could not be done. And then one day they heard that there were homeless children in Edinburgh, Scotland. So they took a collection of 200,000 Kenya Shillings (roughly US$30,000 at the time) to help those caring for

---

[8] I use the word "toward" self-reliance, because finding perfect churches is not very likely. However, in each illustration I give, some progress toward self-reliance was made. Perfection? No. Progress? Yes.

homeless children from the streets of Edinburgh—the place from where their money previously came.[9] One might well conclude that <u>psychological ownership</u> had begun to transfer to the church in East Africa.

The Assemblies of God in South Africa

In South Africa there is a church called the Assemblies of God.[10] Every year one of their senior ministers by the name of Rev. Nicholas Bhengu went to North America to raise money for his church. Once while he was in North America God spoke to him and said, "Go back home and get the money from your own people." Rev. Bhengu replied, "But, Lord, how can I do that? The only people in my church are women and children; the women are unemployed, and the men don't come. How am I supposed to get the money from them?"

God spoke to Rev. Bhengu very directly and said these four things:

1) Go home and teach the women how to care for their families.
2) Teach them how to bring their husbands to the Lord.
3) Teach them how to make something with their hands so they can earn a living.
4) Teach them to give some of it back to God in thanksgiving— in other words, to tithe.

That is not the end of the story. Every year the people from this denomination—now whole families—gather for a weekend conference at a place called Thaba Nchu in South Africa. Several years ago they met for that conference and took a collection of nearly four million South African Rand—in one weekend! At the exchange rate at that time, that was nearly <u>one million US Dollars</u> in one collection. It was from the same church that at one time was comprised of unemployed women and children!

---

[9] Some in the church in East Africa have differing opinions as to how that gift for Scotland was handled. Suffice it to say, the initiative for the collection was generated from among those who were primarily receivers and now found they can be givers.

[10] There are at least three denominations called the Assemblies of God in South Africa.

I asked one of their church leaders how this kind of offering was possible. He said, "When a woman makes dresses, she knows as she sews them that one out of ten belongs to the Lord. When she weaves twenty baskets, two belong to the Lord. And if she makes thirty grass mats, three belong to the Lord." In this way, <u>the concept of stewardship is built into the earning process</u>. That could well be the most important principle as we seek to understand how people can move successfully from dependency toward self-reliance.

Conclusion

The following are a few characteristics of the dependency syndrome. More will be given in later chapters.

1) **Two forms of fatalism are at work** in the process that creates and perpetuates the dependency syndrome. One form of fatalism is seen among local people who say, "We are poor, and that is the way it always will be. You may as well help us because nothing can be done about it." This fatalism fits hand in glove with the basic paradigm of African spiritism which concludes that one is at the mercy of things that cannot be controlled. In short, it is assumed that we are all victims of things beyond our control.

   The other is *western fatalism*. It concludes: "Those people are poor, they will always be that way, and we will have to help them — perhaps for a hundred or a thousand years."

   Both of these forms of fatalism must be confronted with the positive message of the Christian Gospel. There is good news in the Gospel for both.

2) **Not all dependent churches are poor.** There **are** poor people in this region of Africa, and someone must be prepared to help them. Jesus commands it. However, many *dependent* churches are not poor. It is dependent churches — not poor churches — which I am seeking to address in this study. In fact, church leaders in both Tanzania and Malawi said that the poorest synods of their churches are more likely to support their pastors one hundred per cent than wealthy synods in urban areas. Therefore one might well conclude **that the dependency syndrome has little to do with wealth or poverty**. It has to do with a mentality on the part of both local people and the outsiders who try to help.

3) **Foreign funding can be like a poison or pollutant.** One problem with foreign funding is that it distorts reality and makes people think that the situation is not like it really is. It causes local people to conclude that what they have is too little and not worth giving back to God. In this case, if they give nothing, God cannot multiply it. As one church leader in East Africa said, "If you give nothing to God, He can multiply it and it will still be nothing!"

4) **Finally, the good news is that dependency does not need to be considered a terminal illness.** Churches do not need to die from it or be handicapped all their lives. For further information on this positive way of looking at it, see the article on the WMA website entitled *Is there a Cure for Dependency Among Mission-Established Institutions?*

QUESTIONS FOR DISCUSSION
Chapter 1

1. *Reflect on your own conversion experience. How near to the center of the concentric circles has change occurred? As part of your Christian growth are things still changing at the center?*

2. *Do you agree with the illustration about the excluded middle? Explain.*

3. *Does your church have a heavy box which it is carrying? What kinds of things are in it? Who is paying for it? What do you think should be done about it?*

4. *What level of ownership do the people in your church have: legal, functional or full psychological ownership?*

5. *Do you accept that many dependent churches are not poor? Why or why not?*

6. *Discuss the ways that outside funding distorts reality in church or community finances.*

SUGGESTED READING

McGavran, Donald A. *Bridges of God*. New York: Friendship Press, 1955.

McGavran, Donald A. *Understanding Church Growth*. Grand Rapids: Wm. B. Eerdmans, 1970.

Shorter, Aylward. *African Christian Theology: Adaptation or Incarnation*. Maryknoll: Orbis Books, 1977.

Wakatama, Pius. *Independence for the Third World Church: An African Perspective on Missionary Work*. Downers Grove: InterVarsity Press, 1976.

CHAPTER 2

STORIES OF CHURCHES WHICH MADE SOME PROGRESS TOWARD SELF-RELIANCE

Introduction

In this lesson we will look at some of the churches which have successfully made a transition toward self-reliance. I am not saying that they have become totally self-reliant, but they are churches that recognized they had an unhealthy dependency on someone else's resources. They made a conscious decision to do something about it, and a change took place. It was as if they said, "We believe we can do more for ourselves than we are now doing."

Are these churches perfect? No, many of their leaders will admit that. Have they solved all of their problems? No, they will also admit that. Are their leaders perfect? No, some of them disappoint themselves and their own people. In some cases, thank God, that is admitted and the church moves forward.

Are some church leaders in Christian ministry for personal gain? Yes, just as in North America and elsewhere where televangelists and others sometimes benefit unscrupulously from Christian ministry. Does self-reliance touch every area of their lives? Not necessarily. Sometimes it touches church life, but it doesn't necessarily touch the development projects in which they are involved.

Another important observation is that what we are dealing with differs significantly in different areas. For example, what worked successfully among the Assemblies of God in South Africa isn't the same as what worked among the Presbyterian Church in East Africa. Remember that Africa is a vast area. Geographically, it is huge; culturally, it is diverse. So one cannot expect that what works in one place will automatically work elsewhere. However, my purpose here is to share the good news that *the dependency syndrome does not need to be considered a terminal illness.* Churches which suffer from this syndrome can recover and move toward local sustainability.

The Presbyterian Church in East Africa (PCEA)

I mentioned this church in the previous chapter. However, it is such an important example of what I am dealing with that I feel I should add more details. One significant factor that accompanied the PCEA transformation was the preparation of the Holy Spirit through the East African Revival. God went before the church in this movement that began about 1930 in East Africa. This movement of the Holy Spirit touched the lives of many local church leaders as well as expatriate missionaries. One Presbyterian church leader in East Africa said, "Thank God that the East African Revival went first. Because when we set about to restructure our church, we often had to look each other in the eye and say, 'Brother, under the direction of the Holy Spirit we believe this is what God wants us to do. Let's pray and ask God's guidance as we go through this."

The Presbyterian Church in East Africa decided to restructure "the box" which I mentioned in the previous chapter. When they set about to do so, it meant some positions were eliminated and new ones were created. Sometimes church leaders were asked to take jobs for which they did not feel prepared or, sometimes, jobs they didn't want to do. Some were asked to take early retirement. As you can imagine, without the presence of the Holy Spirit, this could have been a very difficult transition. So the preparation of the Holy Spirit through the Revival was central to the change that was on the way.

When the PCEA addressed the matter of restructuring, church leaders decided there were two kinds of things in their box. First, there were churches, congregations and synods. These involved theological education, evangelism, baptism and so on. Leaders decided that these were the work of the church. But they also found other things in the box which were inherited from the missionaries. These included guesthouses, clinics, bookstores, secondary schools, etc. They decided these were like businesses which function on a profit and loss paradigm. The church, on the other hand, exists by contributions – tithes and offerings. So when they began the process of restructuring, they put churchmen in charge of the church and business people in charge of the "businesses."

The problem with the "box" as I described earlier is that a bishop or a moderator (or whoever is at the top of the ecclesiastical pyramid), often becomes responsible for the profit or loss in the development projects, guesthouses, schools, hospitals and clinics. When that happens, bishops or moderators find themselves unable to think about church planting, evangelism, discipling new believers or counseling their pastors. They may simply be preoccupied with a bank overdraft caused by a failing church-run business.

The Presbyterians consciously and deliberately sought to deal with this. In addition to separating out the businesses and putting businessmen in charge, they started what they called the "Presbyterian Foundation." Through this they invited church members to make investments in the foundation, to keep a clear distinction between the issues of church and business.

Another thing that happened was that PCEA leaders became aware that God would bless their efforts if they managed His resources well. So they began to train church treasurers. A man from another church in East Africa said this about the Presbyterians: "Do you know why God has trusted them with so much money? It's because they train their treasurers to act with competence and integrity." If there is any one lesson that churches could learn about the transition to self-reliance, it is that God trusts those who are faithful with the resources He provides. To put it simply, when church money is misused, or when it is hidden from church members, it affects how much is given through tithes and offerings.

If one meets a Presbyterian minister in East Africa he will likely be found wearing a small pendant on a chain around his neck. On the one side it says "jitegemea", the Swahili word for self-reliance. (Their church magazine is also called "Jitegemea.") Their people have accepted the theme of self-reliance and it now runs throughout the church. In fact, they sing a song about a small bird that emphasizes their belief in the concept of self-reliance. By admission of their own people this church is not perfect and those who look on will be able to find things wrong just as in many other churches. But this church has taken a major step from severe dependency toward healthy, Spirit-led self-reliance. For a reminder of how that transition took place, have another look at the illustration I gave in Chapter 1.

The Assemblies of God in South Africa

I also mentioned this church in Chapter 1. As with the PCEA, the Assemblies of God in South Africa discovered the *joy of giving*, not just the *law of tithing*. (I will deal with that distinction in Chapter 11.)

If I am doing a seminar anywhere in South Africa, and I begin talking about the Assemblies of God,[1] mentioning the name of Rev. Nicholas Bhengu, I can tell almost immediately if a member of that church is in the audience. They are usually smiling from ear to ear.[2] Their transformation has brought such a major benefit to the people involved in that church that they are radiant when they talk about it. Who would ever want such people to remain dependent on outside resources all their lives when they can experience the joy of looking to God for His provision which is close at hand? Remember that they went from being a church of unemployed women and children to putting nearly one million dollars worth of South African Rand in the collection on one weekend.

The Lutheran Church in Tanzania

The Lutheran Church in Tanzania is another interesting study in the transition toward local sustainability. Again, while not a perfect church, I learned that they use at least three different kinds of offerings:

- One is the collection plate which is passed every Sunday. People put money into that collection for the poor.

- The second is the tithe.

- The third is the "thank-offering."

The collection for the poor is rather straightforward. But the tithe is handled in a unique manner. In some places the treasurer of

---

[1] I mentioned before that there are several denominations by this name in South Africa. Unfortunately not all of them know the joy of mobilizing local resources the way this church is doing.

[2] I recently spoke to a congregation of all Africans in London, England and found a half dozen people from Rev. Bhengu's church sitting in the back row smiling when I mentioned his name. After the service one of the women said, "Yes, that is the way he was. He taught us to tithe."

the church has been known to approach each church member individually to talk about their income and how their tithe will be paid to the church. He begins by asking, "What do you do for a living?"

"I teach in the school."

"How much is your salary?"

"I get 1000 per month."[3]

"Right, that means that you will be giving 100 shillings each month to the church. Is that right?"

"Yes."

The treasurer then goes to another person and asks, "What do you do for a living?"

"I work for the government."

"How much do you earn?"

"I earn 2,500 a month."

"So then, you'll be bringing 250 to the church each month in tithe. Is that correct?"

"Yes."

"We can then write that down", says the treasurer.

Another person is approached and the treasurer asks, "What do you do for a living?"

"I raise maize," she says.

"How many bags do you expect in this year's harvest?"

"I expect to get 50 bags of maize this year."

---

[3] These numbers are not intended to be realistic; rather they are for illustration purposes only.

"Right, then the church can expect that you will bring 5 bags at harvest time. Is that right?"

"Yes." And the treasurer writes that down.

The treasurer may then turn to a fourth person and ask, "What do you do for a living?"

"I'm a farmer."

"And what do you raise?"

"I raise cattle."

And the treasurer asks, "And how many cows do you expect to sell this year?"

"I expect to sell thirty cows this year."

"Oh, thirty cows; that's good. So that means that three will be given to the church, is that right?"

"Yes."

The treasurer then asks, "And when will you bring these cows to the church?"

"I will bring them in August."

But the treasurer says, "No, I'm sorry you can't bring them in August; you must bring them in January because the price is too low in August. January is a better time." And so negotiation goes on between the treasurer and the individual church members in this way.

The **third** kind of offering among the Lutherans of Tanzania is what they call the "thank offering." The thank offering takes place on an occasion when something good happens and a church member simply wants to say "thank you" to God. In addition to testifying before the congregation, he or she will put some money in the collection.

For example, let's assume that I go to Dar es Salaam by train. When I get off the train I am waiting for a taxi, and I notice that my briefcase is missing. In a panic I wonder what happened? My briefcase with my money, passport, and the papers for my meeting are all gone!

So right on the spot I bow my head and pray, "Lord, please help me to find that briefcase. Thank you. In the name of Jesus. Amen." And when I open my eyes, I am astonished to see a man standing in front of me with my briefcase in his hands. He holds it out to me and asks, "Sir, is this yours? You left it on the platform when you got off the train." I thank him and give praise to the Lord for answering my prayer so quickly.

When I look inside, everything is still there – a miracle indeed! When my time in Dar es Salaam is finished I return home and rush to the pastor and say, "Pastor, I want to tell you what happened. I lost my briefcase, and I prayed; and when I opened my eyes there it was. In the service on Sunday I want to thank God in front of the people for getting my briefcase back with everything in it."

But the pastor says, "No, I'm sorry, my brother, you can't say 'thank you' to God this Sunday." So the pastor takes out his calendar and says, "This week we have other people who want to say 'thank you' to God; you will have to wait." He turns a few pages and says, "In three weeks you will be able to say 'thank you' to God." And I say, "That's fine; I'll wait."

In three weeks, the pastor tells the congregation, "Now it's time for those who want to say 'thank you' to God, and Brother Glenn has something he wants to say."

So he calls me forward, and I tell the story of what happened when I lost my briefcase and how it was returned to me instantly. Then I say, "I am so thankful to God for helping me to find it that today I am going to put 5000 shillings into the collection just to say 'thank you' to God. And I have arranged with my brothers, James and Elias, to each put 2000 shillings into the collection to join me in saying thanks to God. If I had not recovered my briefcase, there is no way to estimate how much it would have cost me."

And the Lutherans in Tanzania say, "Sometimes when a very dramatic testimony is given (such as a miraculous healing), the whole congregation will say, 'Pass the offering plate; we all want to say 'thank you' to God for what he has done.'"

That is an example of what one might call "thanks-giving"! It is giving back to God out of gratitude for what God has done for them. In such a service no one is being forced to tithe. The tithe is taken care of in other ways as I mentioned above. This kind of giving flows from a full heart.

An Anglican District in Zimbabwe

I once met a priest from an Anglican district in Zimbabwe. When he heard that I do seminars on self-reliance, he said, "Let me tell you my story. I took over a district of sixty-five churches that had unhealthy dependency. The first thing that I did was to call the people together for five days of prayer, fasting and teaching. About five hundred people came. We slept in a boarding school, and for the first two days we didn't eat. We only prayed from morning to night — no eating, only praying. On the second day the same thing: only praying, no eating. The third day I began to teach them everything I knew about discipleship and stewardship. This continued through the fourth and fifth day. At the end of the fifth day I told them they could go home.

"After six months, I called them back. Once again, we began with two days of praying and fasting, and then three more days of teaching. Very soon the sixty-five churches in our district became self-reliant. I was the envy of other district ministers. They wanted to take over my district because it was now so different."

Stories such as these remind us that spiritual renewal is essential in the move toward self-reliance. There is no other place to begin. As with the concentric circles mentioned in Chapter 1, something needs to happen deep down inside. This Anglican priest discovered the importance of beginning with spiritual renewal.

Another Church in South Africa

A church in the Western Cape Province of South Africa was operating on the ticket system that I mentioned in Chapter 1. Members gave only small amounts of money and had their gifts marked off on "the ticket."

This diocese had an elderly bishop who passed away, unfortunately leaving the district with a debt of 600,000 South African Rand. A young bishop was chosen to take his place. Imagine a young bishop taking over a district which had a debt of 600,000 Rand! The first thing he did was to abolish the ticket system in the churches. He said, "The ticket system is not God's way for people to give to the church. Rather, we must give out of love for God; tithes and offerings must come from a full heart." Within two years they had cleared the 600,000 Rand debt which was about US$150,000 at the time. The mentality of the ticket system was set aside in favor of giving back to God from a full heart.

The Seventh Day Adventists in Zambia

The Seventh Day Adventists in Zambia learned something about giving back to God. Of course, they take seriously what the Old Testament says about tithing. One of their leaders said that sometimes the pastor goes into the cattle kraal with a farmer to help pick out 10% of the cows which will be given to the church. When I told this story in South Africa there were several South African pastors who would have been delighted to go onto some of the farms in their country where there are three or four thousand head of cattle. Imagine 10% of that herd being given to the church!

The Apostolic Faith Mission in Zimbabwe

At one point in time the Apostolic Faith Mission in Zimbabwe was planting about two churches each year. Then the missionaries decided to "indigenize" and move back to their homes in South Africa. Their churches in Zimbabwe would be on their own. At first, all church planting stopped and some people said, "You see what happens? The church planting stopped when the missionaries left."

For two years no new churches were planted. In the third year, however, when true psychological ownership transferred, local people recognized the privilege that was theirs. They began to plant new churches and in the first year after that they planted eight new congregations. This was after they decided that the work was "theirs." Just when some thought nothing was happening (during those two years), preparations were being made for the transfer of psychological ownership. For some people – especially missionaries

– that may seem like a long time to wait. Those with vision and patience, however, will rejoice in what the Lord is doing.

A Self-Help Project in Transkei

In Transkei, South Africa, one of those controversial areas formerly called a "homeland", local people decided to move towards self-reliance in church and community. Christians came together and began to rebuild the infrastructure in their own community. They began not only to build churches, but libraries and roads as well. Later on, they made a video to show other people what they had done. When psychological ownership transferred, the whole community benefited. They were proud of their accomplishment. Even though all of the leaders spoke English, they produced a video in their own language because they wanted to demonstrate their local ownership.

Don't Chase Buffaloes

Several years ago I did a seminar in Capetown, and a pastor shared his story. Several years before, he had been in North America preaching in various churches. On one occasion he phoned home to find out how his family was doing. His wife was not there, but his sister-in-law answered the phone. Her first words were, "Oh pastor, I'm glad you called. I have a message for you. By the way, your family is fine, everything's fine here; but I have a message for you. I had a dream the other night, and God told me to give you this message: 'While you are in America, don't chase buffaloes'."

This was a rather strange message, so the pastor hung up the telephone and said, "Thank you Lord for the message; but I have no idea what it means." He went on preaching. One Sunday evening he preached in a church in which he was given the collection as his honorarium. They simply gave him the money that came in rather than writing out a check. He took this money back to the place where he was staying and began to count it. In the process, he came to a five-cent piece which in America is called a "buffalo nickel." He looked at the buffalo and said, "That is the meaning of the message. I am not here to get money."

So he said, "Thank you, Lord. I got the message." Little did he know the importance of that message, because the very next morning he was taken to breakfast by a wealthy businessman. The pastor said, "I don't know how wealthy that man was, but he owned four airplanes."

As they were having breakfast, the businessman said, "Pastor, I liked the things I heard you saying in church last night. I have a lot of money, and I would like to give you some. How much do you want? Just name the amount and I will write the check for any amount you say."

At this point the pastor was being tested; he knew he was not supposed to "chase buffaloes." So he turned to the businessman and said, "Thank you very much, but God in His providence cares for me and my people in His own way." The pastor then said, "I didn't get any money from that man."

He finished preaching in North America and went to England where he boarded a flight for Johannesburg. On the plane he found himself sitting beside a white South African businessman. The businessman asked the pastor what he did and he said, "I'm a pastor of a small congregation in Capetown." At this the businessman replied, "I am a member of a church which supports apartheid. I do not agree with the policy of my church or my government, so I won't give my money to my church. I would rather give it to you. How much do you want? Just name the amount, and I will write the check."

Again the pastor said, "Thank you very much; but God takes care of me and my people in His own way." The pastor said he didn't get any money from that man either. Instead, he went back to Capetown, and the small congregation he was pastoring decided to build a new sanctuary. They gave all the money necessary to build their new building. Then he said as he smiled, "And we found that we didn't need any 'buffaloes' from America to do it." One can only imagine what would have happened to that congregation if he had presented them with two checks representing hundreds of thousands of dollars from those well-meaning businessmen. All too often such "goodness of the heart" has destroyed local giving initiative in many parts of the world.

An Observation

Consider the following observation: *Missionaries and mission executives must be careful not to resent the transition of mission-established churches toward self-reliance.* Those with a tendency toward such resentment should lay at the foot of the cross all the work they have done in the past and then look forward to a new day in missions. Remember, self-supporting churches are possible, despite the long history of dependency which has so often held them back.

Missiological Principles from Irian Jaya

I will finish this chapter by listing a series of principles from the book *Torches of Joy* by missionary John Dekker. These are lessons from Irian Jaya showing how missionaries were able to plant churches that were not dependent.[4]

1. *No foreign funds were used in the development of local churches.*

2. *The mission employed no paid evangelists.*

3. *Missionaries did not burden the churches with a structure they could not afford.*

4. *Church members paid their pastors by cultivating their fields for them.*

5. *The principle of self-support was practiced in both church and community life.*

6. *To avoid the development of "rice Christians", no preferential treatment was given to believers in medical or community work.*

7. *Stewardship was taught from the very beginning.*

Within ten years of planting those churches, the Dani people began to send out their own cross-cultural missionaries to other parts of Indonesia. One could also add that the missionaries who went there had cross-cultural training and sensitivity, a theme that will come up again and again later on in the following chapters.

---

[4] *Torches of Joy,* Dekker, John. Westchester (Illinois): Crossways Books, 1985

QUESTIONS FOR DISCUSSION
Chapter 2

1. *What is your attitude toward churches that declare their financial independence such as the Presbyterian Church in East Africa?*

2. *Which of the giving practices mentioned in these stories inspires you most and could help your church in its giving?*

3. *Do churches have to be perfect before they can move toward self-reliance? Discuss.*

4. *What would you say to a missionary who resents people disregarding the work he or she did because it was inappropriate or too expensive to maintain?*

SUGGESTED READING

Cotterell, Peter. *Born at Midnight.* Chicago: Moody Bible Institute, 1973.

Dekker, John. *Torches of Joy.* Westchester: Crossways Books, 1985.

Schwartz, Glenn J. *"From Dependency to Fulfillment."* Evangelical Missions Quarterly, July 1991.

Schwartz, Glenn J. *"It's Time to Get Serious About the Cycle of Dependence in Africa."* Evangelical Missions Quarterly, April 1993.

Schwartz, Glenn J. *"Cutting the Apron Strings. "* Evangelical Missions Quarterly, January 1994.

CHAPTER 3

Characteristics of the Syndrome of Dependency

I will now introduce some of the characteristics of the syndrome of dependency. This is not an exhaustive list of characteristics because there are as many as the various cultural conditions in which dependency is found. Nevertheless, the following are some of the more important characteristics that I have been able to identify since collecting information on the syndrome.

Dependency Affects Almost Every Aspect of Mission-Established Institutions

The first characteristic of the dependency syndrome is that it is very pervasive. It touches many areas of church and mission life in the part of Africa to which I have been referring. It not only affects churches and the support of pastors, it affects the building of church buildings, development projects, medical projects and church planting. It especially affects the production and distribution of Bibles.[1] Dependency affects food aid and literacy projects. It also adversely affects governments when they become dependent on the International Monetary Fund (IMF) or the World Bank. Governments end up not being able to pay their own way because there is not enough locally generated income to support their own economies.

The Problem is Long Standing

The problem of dependency did not begin yesterday, and it won't be resolved overnight. Thankfully there are some happy exceptions to this. Sometime ago I was in Zimbabwe, staying in the home of a church leader. I pulled a book from his shelf which was written by Robert Speer, the famous missiologist in the early part of the twentieth century. It is called *Christianity and the Nations*. Speer was doing an analysis following the 1910 missionary conference in Edinburgh, Scotland. At one point in the book he quotes Bishop

---

[1] See Chapter 22 for a description of how Bible production and distribution are affected by issues of dependency.

Tucker, the famous Anglican who served in Uganda at the beginning of the 20th century. Bishop Tucker, speaking at a missionary conference in Brighton, England in 1901, made this remark:

> *I have already spoken of the 2,000 native evangelists at work in the country. These are all maintained by the native church. The same is true of the 27 native clergy. Nor is this all. The churches and schools of the country – some 700 in number – are built, repaired and maintained by the natives themselves. In one word, the whole work of the native Church – its educational, pastoral, and missionary work – is maintained entirely from native resources. Not one single halfpenny of English money is employed in its maintenance.[2]*

I use this, acknowledging the outdated language, but it demonstrates that as long ago as 1901 someone learned how to avoid the problem of dependency in cross-cultural church planting.

In the case of the Dani people in Irian Jaya, referred to in *Torches of Joy* by John Dekker, within ten years of receiving the Gospel they were sending out their own missionaries! This stands in sharp contrast to the long-standing problem of dependency that we have known in East, Central and Southern Africa, and shows that this syndrome does not have to cripple mission efforts around the world.

In India there is the positive example of the Friends Missionary Prayer Band – 1000 missionaries supported by 30,000 praying supporters – who decline offers of outside funding because they are afraid it will negatively affect the 30,000 people who pray for the 1000 missionaries they send out.

It is encouraging to note these positive exceptions to the long-term problem of dependency.

This Problem is Not Confined to One Geographical Area

In East, Central and Southern Africa the dependency syndrome affects every country in the region. When we began to identify

---

[2] *Christianity and the Nations*, Robert E. Speer, Fleming H. Revell, New York 1910:136

this syndrome missionaries would say: "Yes, but this is not just a problem in our mission. The Methodists have this problem, and so do the Anglicans and the Wesleyans." Unfortunately, that was true. The dependency syndrome does affect many different churches in many different geographical areas. I have learned since beginning to speak about this that it has serious consequences in Vietnam, Cambodia, India, and in other parts of the world.

The Problem is Contemporary

Unfortunately, the dependency problem still exists today, even though some would like to believe otherwise. This isn't a problem that only happened 30, 40, or 50 years ago. No missionary today can say, "Well, you are talking about something that happened in the past, and is no longer in existence." In fact, there is some evidence that because of the new interest in short-term missions, the problem is on the increase. Many involved in contemporary mission efforts do not even know about the basic concept of self-supporting churches in cross-cultural ministry. In fact, some find it repulsive to think that our western funding is not the key to cross-cultural church planting. They rationalize that the western church has so much wealth and the rest of the world has the labor.

In 1990 I learned that one church in East Africa with five districts of that denomination still had their funds <u>managed</u> by an outsider — an expatriate missionary from overseas. There are other churches today that look to outsiders for management of their finances.

Some churches, unfortunately, have been so frustrated trying to support themselves that they have <u>reverted</u> to getting money and personnel from overseas. In one case, a church in Zimbabwe returned to missionary leadership after almost one hundred years of existence, twenty-five of which were under the leadership of local bishops. One might well ask how this could happen? One reason is that the unrestructured "box" is still so massive that local leaders are being crushed by the mere weight of it. Instead of restructuring the box and making it manageable, they chose to place a missionary into the top administrative post – in the mid 1990s!

I learned some time ago about three churches and mission societies that were before the secular courts trying to solve their financial problems: one in Tanzania, one in South Africa, one in Zimbabwe.

Imagine, the church going before the secular courts trying to solve their money problems! It is just one more evidence that the problem is contemporary. When "glasnost"[3] allowed an outside missionary presence to once again enter what is now the Former Soviet Union, it took only a matter of three to five years for some groups to create a serious dependency problem.

This Issue is Emotionally Charged

There are two groups of people who are most likely to react negatively to what I am saying about unhealthy dependency. **First** are the older missionaries who built the system—the box to which I have been referring. Though we thank God for their dedicated years of service, as the winds of change begin to blow, they might very well react by saying, "You don't appreciate what we did!" Actually we are trying to deal with the fact that many church leaders in mission-established institutions have an almost unmanageable legacy without sufficient local funding to carry it on. This doesn't mean that we do not appreciate some of what was done in the past, but the church now has an enormous problem to solve. Hopefully church leaders will be given the freedom and encouragement to deal creatively with the challenges before them.

One of the healthiest churches I encountered in South Africa inherited their program from the missionaries and immediately sold the properties that were accumulated. They knew instinctively that such properties had the potential to become a millstone around their necks. Today they concentrate on being the church, not managing properties. Interestingly, they requested that I conduct a one-day seminar on dependency – which I decided later they didn't really need. It should not be surprising that I was given a generous honorarium for my services that day – something not likely to happen in unrestructured and dependent mission churches.

The **second** group concerned about what I say about unhealthy dependency includes those church leaders whose salaries currently come from foreign sources. In some cases they have opened fund-raising offices in Europe or North America in order to get money for their churches. They are concerned because talk of self-support

---

[3] I am referring to the spirit of openness that spread through the former Soviet Union in the 1980s and 90s.

works against their efforts to raise money overseas for their churches and projects in Africa.

I met a man recently who said that his church opened an office in America to recruit people and money for his church in West Africa. It is my dream that we can help such church leaders to discover the joy of finding sufficient local resources not only to help their own churches, but also to become part of the globally expanding Christian movement about which I spoke earlier.

This Problem has at its Roots, Suspicion

Foreign funding often seems to be at the center of misappropriated money in Africa. If a church puts enough money in the collection to sustain itself, it is unlikely this money will be the source of contention that foreign money often is. This is partly because foreign money often comes in hidden ways. It also frequently comes in large amounts. Sometimes church members do not know how much comes in, and they aren't aware of how it is spent. When that happens, funds can easily be misappropriated. When suspicions arise among the members, they may even provide less local funding for the church.

When churches are healthy and supporting their own programs with local funding, leaders are most likely enjoying the confidence of the members. Local funding can be misused, but large amounts of outside funding represent a temptation that many church leaders find difficult to resist. There are two factors related to this: first, there is better ownership of local giving, and second, the hidden nature of foreign funding makes it difficult to exercise a watchful eye.

Unhealthy Dependency Makes it nearly Impossible For Churches to Send out their own Missionaries

This is a central theme of this series of lessons which I mention in other places. When local congregations cannot support themselves, it is unlikely that they will become excitedly involved in missionary outreach. Remember, genuine missionary outreach results from a generally energized church that not only sustains itself, but also has enough spiritual and financial energy left over for outreach. That should characterize every Spirit-filled church far and wide.

The Dependency Syndrome Cripples Inter-Denominational Efforts

Consider for a moment Evangelical Fellowships or Christian Councils present in many countries. They often struggle to get enough money to sustain themselves because they are dependent upon churches within their own country. Unfortunately some of those very churches are dependent upon someone else. If the churches do not have enough local income to sustain themselves, it stands to reason that they don't have enough to give to their Christian Council or Evangelical Fellowship.

There is another aspect to this dilemma. When there is widespread dependency, those churches that should be supporting the Evangelical Fellowship or Christian Council, are often looking to those same groups for subsidy for local church projects. The same is true of Bible societies and aid organizations. Rather than sending contributions to their national Bible society or local aid office, some churches are actually looking for free handouts of literature or funds for their development or evangelism project. Churches like that have yet to discover that they can contribute to the larger Christian movement, not only receive from it.

For Some, The Mentality of Dependency has become a Long-Term Way of Life

Sometime ago in England they reported that when a person is unemployed for a period of three to five years, it is very difficult for him or her to get back into employment again. Something happens to them psychologically, and re-training or reprogramming the person to go back into full-time employment can be very difficult. Think about churches that have been dependent on outside assistance for a hundred or two hundred years. They have become convinced that they are poor. "That's the way we are. It can't be changed, so you may as well help us," is their philosophy. This sense of fatalism becomes a long-term way of life.

One day I was involved in a meeting regarding a Bible concordance project in Zambia. In that particular meeting, the leaders were saying, "Yes, we want a Bible concordance." Then they asked me, "Can you get a grant from overseas to help us?" So I asked, "Why do you always ask for a grant from overseas?" I was given a classic response: "We always ask first, and we are usually given." Such statements reflect the reality of long-term dependency: "We always ask, and we are usually given."

This Mentality Sometimes Presents Itself in Very Attractive Clothing

There are now funding agencies from North America that have opened offices in African cities for the purpose of giving away money to churches who ask for it. Likewise, there are people in North America who have accepted the idea that supporting "nationals"[4] is better than sending North American missionaries, because "nationals" are cheaper and because they already speak the language. It sounds impressive as we are told that one can make an impact for only $50 a month! This idea sounds very attractive.

Why is it not as attractive as it sounds? Local people who could support their own local evangelists are being deprived of the privilege of doing so. Not only that — the local evangelist who is paid from the outside is sometimes perceived as a paid "foreign agent" of those overseas who provide the funding. Some local people have been known to say, "I can't be a evangelist; I don't get money from overseas. Those other people, it's their job. Let them do it. They get paid from overseas."[5] This is such a significant problem in places like India that nonbelievers assume that if one is even a Christian, they are being paid from overseas.

Sometimes there are linkages between institutions that perpetuate this problem. Some time ago, a Board of Directors of an educational institution in East Africa was promoting the importance of raising local funding for their institution. It was a well-established institution, doing a good job on the local scene. To their credit they were trying to raise money locally, but suddenly a grant of ten thousand dollars arrived unsolicited from an organization in Europe. The Board of Directors looked at the size of the grant and

---

[4] I put this term in quotes because I do not use it to refer to church leaders in other countries. More than once, I have been reminded by some of my African brothers and sisters that as an American, I am a "national" in the country from which I come.

[5] For a further discussion of this, see Chapter 5 under the heading A CALL FOR PARTNERSHIP.

how easy it was to get, and asked themselves: "Why do we work so hard to raise money locally when it is that easy to get overseas?" This was a case in which linkages between two institutions affected the initiative of a local board of directors to raise money among their own people.

Another way that the new philosophy portrays itself is reflected in the use of such terms as "partnership" or "interdependence." One can be justifiably suspicious of terms like these. Often those using these terms mean western money and local labor in the non-western world. This is usually an unequal partnership at best, because those who have the money often decide how it should be used. There are frequently strings attached to the funds being given. The way to test a true partnership is to ask how many ways resources flow. If resources flow in only one direction, then the better word might be "sponsorship" rather than "partnership."

A healthy partnership is one in which everyone contributes meaningfully to a project, and the best are ones in which money is not the central issue. One positive example of the use of the term partnership is the way it was developed by an organization called InterDev. During the 1990s they established partnerships in West Africa, Mongolia and the former Soviet Union, among other places. The purpose was to bring together churches, mission societies, Bible translators and aid agencies. Each one brought to the table their particular strength. Money was not the thing that made those partnerships work. In fact, one of their people observed that when money entered the picture, as it sometimes did, the partnership lost it effectiveness. Partnerships that successfully leave money out of the picture are a credit to the term.

Interdependence has its own set of problems. Interdependence works among those who are relatively equal. Churches in a very poor area of Nairobi have very little in common with a large suburban church in North America. How is "inter"-dependence applicable there? In East Africa, one of the church leaders promoted what he called local-local interdependence. He explained that the kind he believed in was interdependence between Presbyterians, Anglicans, Methodists or the African Inland Church in East Africa. When churches like that learn to work together — to share resources — that could logically be called true "interdependence." International interdependence might well have financial overtones.

The Dependency Syndrome Sometimes Makes Local Church Leaders Look like Poor Managers

I believe it is immoral to create an impossible administrative and financial structure and then blame local leaders for not being able to manage it. When "the box" is simply turned over and subsidy is removed, it might well place an impossible burden on local church leaders. It is wrong to place the blame on local church leaders who did not create the problem in the first place. After all, the missionary administration could not manage it without outside assistance. The solution is not the continuation of outside resources, but rather restructuring so that it becomes manageable with local resources.

The Problem of Dependency is Risky to Deal With

If one is not prepared to be criticized, then he or she should not try to resolve the problem of dependency in mission-established churches. There are two ways one may suffer in the process. First, this challenge has a way of affecting one's own reputation. People may begin to think of such a person as one who is simply agitating for change. Those who successfully bring about change follow a vision; they call people around them, and give leadership to the process of change. If there is no anticipation for change in the hearts of the people, then those who call for it may well be victimized, encapsulated, criticized and risk having their reputations destroyed. Sometimes such a person is before his or her time, and then the vision for change will not be effective.

A second risk is that one's own salary might be affected. The man in East Africa who told the mission in Scotland to keep their money was saying, "no, thank you" to his own salary. I often wondered what happened when he went home and said to his wife, "My dear, I just told the people overseas to keep the money which has been coming to pay our salary. How do you feel about that?" I once spoke to his wife and asked her about it. She gave a wonderful testimony of how God provided for them when they took that step of faith. So, when foreign money is used for local salaries, and church leaders become comfortable with it, challenging that system could mean a personal loss of income for a period of time.

A third risk relates to losing potentially good leaders. The fear of losing one's reputation is one of the reasons why church leaders leave mission-established churches to establish or join independent churches. One may find that the only way to preserve his or her personal dignity is to get out of the system and go somewhere else to carry on ministry. There are tens of thousands of African Independent Churches (AIC's) founded by people who came to know the Lord in mission-established churches but did not find those churches a place to feel at home. This is a huge and complex question and cannot be dealt with adequately here.

For Some, the Time to Deal With this Problem is Now

I'm pleased that in the decade of the 1990s, a new local missionary vision was developing in Africa, particularly in South Africa. Churches became aware of the unreached world and decided to send their own people to the 10/40 Window. Hopefully, they won't carry the problem of dependency to the new places where they are going. There are some indications that this new missionary enthusiasm is perpetuating the problem. But there is also a growing awareness that we cannot go on doing what we have been doing in the past.

The time to change things is **now**. I have met one African leader after another who has said, "Yes, we are tired of asking for money from overseas." I have met many church leaders who have talked at length about how to break the dependency syndrome. Many want to know how to get the idea of local support across to their people, because they know that prolonged dependency is not good for their churches.

What about African governments? In a book called *What is Africa's Problem?*, President Museveni of Uganda, heartily endorses the concept of self-reliance for the nation. On many pages of that book he promotes self-reliance saying such things as, "Uganda should never import another safety pin, only machines to make safety pins." Obviously governments like that are not perfect, just like many of the churches that I mentioned earlier. But clearly there is something to be learned from the mentality of local sustainability that President Museveni is promoting in that book.

It is a Blessing When the Problem of Dependency is Resolved

The smiles on the faces of church leaders who say, "Yes, we used to be like that, but we no longer are" give testimony to the importance of resolving the problem of dependency. I once met a Lutheran layman from Tanzania who worked for the railways. He excitedly told me how they built their own church building in an urban area. They were in the process of building a fence around the property. He said, "When that is completed we will put in electricity, and it's OURS!"

One Bible Society director in Africa decided to use local currency to print a Bible in his own country. When it was complete he said, "This was very difficult—but we did it and it is OURS!" It is this kind of satisfaction that encourages anyone who is promoting local sustainability.

Many Successful Transitions toward Self-Reliance Include a Direct Revelation from the Lord

I have met or heard about no less than five South African church leaders who said that the Lord spoke directly to them and told them not to get money from overseas. Instead, they were told by the Lord to go back home and get the funding from their own people. Several examples follow.

One non-white pastor from Capetown went to the USA to look for funding for his ministry. (This is not the "Don't Chase Buffaloes" pastor mentioned in chapter 2.) This pastor began with what he thought was a noble principle of going to non-white churches in America for the help he wanted. As he visited one American congregation after another, the Lord spoke to him and said, "Don't ask these people for any money. Instead, put something into their collection." He said he found this happening again and again as he put in $20 here and $50 there. In the end, he returned to South Africa without having raised any money in America.

After he returned home, his small congregation decided to buy an old cinema building to use as a church and Christian center. The congregation bought the building by faith and, at the time he told me the story, they had already raised 40% of the funds from among their own people. God blessed them by not letting someone else take away the privilege of giving.

The story entitled *Don't Chase Buffaloes* to which I referred earlier is another example of direct revelation from the Lord. A third example is the Rev. Nicholas Bhengu of the Assemblies of God in South Africa who received a direct message from the Lord while he was in America. I told his story in Chapter 1.

It is almost Impossible for Westerners to Accept that their Giving (their Altruism) Could be at the Root of the Dependency Problem

Part of the dependency syndrome has to do with the way we as westerners solve problems. We solve problems with money. We assume that the problems of the poor will be solved if we simply give them money or used clothing, etc. A second reality is that many westerners have discovered the joy of giving. Recently I chatted with my dental hygienist who told what joy she found in going to a supermarket to buy things to be put into a container for shipment overseas. It is very difficult for a person like that to accept that the joy she receives in giving might be related to creating dependency on the receiving end. Obviously not all such giving is wrong or ends up creating dependency. As I have said before, Jesus commands that we help the poor. The problem is that we as westerners are often unable to separate the joy we get from giving, from the unhealthy dependency that can result on the receiving end.

Westerners Can't Have it Both Ways

The primary purpose of many Western mission agencies is to plant indigenous churches. Some of them hope that the churches they plant will become self-supporting, self-propagating and self-governing. They may not have a written goal toward that end, but it is in their thinking. However, in some cases they still have a system which includes providing funding for those churches, sometimes a century after they were started. In some cases, they still send people from overseas to manage the money coming from the outside. A characteristic of the dependency syndrome is that outsiders often cannot see the inconsistency of their actions.

Breaking Dependency is a Spiritual Battle

We should not minimize the spiritual nature of this battle. For the Biblical perspective on this see Ephesians 6:12 and 2 Corinthians 10:4. I mentioned these passages earlier, but they bear repeating.

No one should use any other weapons than those of a spiritual nature when seeking to deal with the dependency syndrome. These include prayer, sound teaching, discipleship and spiritual decision-making, among other things. There is no place in the process for self-interest, greed, manipulation, intrigue and similar things. As the Presbyterian Church in East Africa said, "Thank God the Revival came first." If there is one thing I learned over the past several decades of dealing with this issue, it is that without spiritual renewal, progress toward healthy self-reliance will be illusive. Everything, including the move toward local sustainability, must be done for the right reason, in the right way, and with genuine spiritual motivation and methods.

QUESTIONS FOR DISCUSSION
Chapter 3

1. *In your estimation, how widespread is the problem of dependency in mission-established churches?*

2. *How many other problems are associated with the problem of dependency?*

3. *What can be done to deal with the long-term effects of dependency among unemployed people? Poor people? Dependent churches?*

4. *Do you agree/disagree that those helping to perpetuate dependency sometimes go around in "attractive clothing"?*

5. *Do you know any church leaders who have been made to look like bad managers because of unmanageable church structures?*

6. *"Wealth or poverty have little to do with self-reliance." Do you agree/disagree?*

SUGGESTED READING

Museveni, Yoweri K. *What is Africa's Problem?* Kampala: NRM Publications, 1992.

Schwartz, Glenn J. *"Church and Mission in Central Africa: A Missiological Study in Indigenization."* (Available on the WMA website at www.wmausa.org)

CHAPTER 4

What Should Wealthy Churches do with their Money?

Introduction

A word of explanation is in order about my choice of terms. I have been asked if the word "wealthy" is really the right word for this discussion. Many American Christians, for example, don't think of themselves as being wealthy. Someone suggested that I should use the term "Western" churches, not wealthy churches. But that doesn't necessarily solve the problem because there are churches in many parts of the world—not just the West—that have more than they need to live on. The question is: How will they use their resources for the Kingdom of God without creating or perpetuating the problem of dependency?

For example, some churches in South Africa face the problem because many of their members have access to more resources for doing God's work than they need for themselves. Churches in Korea have found that they have access to considerable funds which they can use for missionary outreach. The danger is that churches such as these will engage in either creating or perpetuating dependency unless they become aware of how the syndrome works. To say Western churches isn't quite accurate, and to say wealthy churches may be misunderstood. But the problem potentially occurs wherever people seek to help others with the resources God has given them.

The first question that we must ask is: Where does excess spendable income come from? In other words, how do Christians and others acquire what they want to give away? Sometimes Western Christians, and perhaps others, have as much as they do because it was gained in a questionable way. In other words, someone else may not have received a fair price for the raw materials that were sold to those who manufactured them into items for sale.

I refer again to the book which I mentioned earlier by President Museveni of Uganda. In that book he tells an interesting story about the relationship between the sale of coffee beans from Uganda and the purchase and importation of tractors from Western countries into Uganda. He makes the point that "in 1986 we needed four-and-a-half tonnes of coffee to buy one Massey Ferguson tractor, in 1989 we needed 16 tonnes to buy the same tractor."[1] And so, in three short years a Ugandan farmer had to work much harder for the tractor he needed because tractor makers in the West were demanding so many more bags of coffee beans for each tractor they sold.

A similar thing happened in Zambia some years ago with oil and copper. The imbalance was so great that more and more copper had to be shipped out of Zambia in order to bring in less and less oil. The result is that the people who dig copper from the soil are earning less because those selling the oil are constantly demanding more and more for their product. One has only to look at the affluence of those in oil producing countries to see the effects of the imbalance.

Those who are benefiting from this imbalance end up with more than they need to live on (excess spendable income) which they then decide to give back in the form of charity. This may be from western countries or in the form of petrodollars from the Middle East. Consider this question: Would Ugandan farmers prefer the charitable handout, or would they rather have a fair price for their raw materials? Some defend this practice by saying that it is simply market forces at work; if the Ugandan wants too much for his product, the buyer will simply go to another supplier. My point is that charitable handouts are not a fair exchange for economic imbalance or injustice.

This is not a lesson on economic justice, and indeed I am not qualified to speak to those issues. But there **are** Christian economists who can speak to this, and there is a lot of reading one can do on the subject. What I **am** saying is that all of us should look at the income we get and ask, "Has it been gained in a fair way?"

Historically, one of the most dramatic examples of such inequities occurred in South Africa under the apartheid system. White South Africans were paid as much as four times more than their non-white counterparts for doing the same work. Eventually, some of

---

[1] From *What is Africa's Problem*, Yoweri Museveni, page 287.

them became conscious of the fact that they had too much wealth, so they used their excess spendable income to provide support for non-white pastors and churches. How much better it would have been if fair wages had been paid and the non-white churches had engaged in sound Christian stewardship, supporting themselves from the fair wages they should have been receiving.

So the first issue in relation to people who have money to give away is to ask: Where did the excess come from? Was it gained through exorbitant interest rates in international markets so that someone got less while others got much more? These are not comfortable questions for many westerners, but until we resolve the matter of economic justice, we will not get a proper handle on one of the ramifications of the dependency syndrome.

The following are a few suggestions regarding the appropriate use of our excess spendable income.

Preach the Gospel Where it has not been Preached

Invest missionary funding in the proclamation of the Gospel where it has not yet been preached. In many parts of Africa funds for missionary outreach are still sent to those in places where the Gospel has been preached for 100 or 200 years or more.

Some years ago I conducted a seminar in western Tanzania not far from where David Livingstone met Henry Stanley at a village called Ugigi about 150 years ago. The Gospel has been know in that area ever since. In the seminar some of the church leaders admitted that, after all this time, they were still waiting for people to send them missionaries and financial assistance.

Where has the Gospel not yet been preached? Consider the 10/40 Window — North Africa, the Middle East, Southeast Asia and parts of East Asia. Missiologists tell us that 97% of the people living in the 10/40 Window have yet to hear and understand the Christian Gospel for the first time. The unreached part of the world where people are waiting to hear the Gospel for the first time is a valid investment of missionary funding.

A word of caution is in order about carrying money into the 10/40 Window to plant churches. Some who are doing this have created dependency in a very short time. One American pastor confessed that in less than three years he and his colleagues created serious dependency in the Former Soviet Union. He acknowledged that he was not aware of the dynamics of the dependency syndrome. In cases such as these, it is important to learn how to avoid dependency before it gains a foothold.

Consider Providing Full Missionary Support for a Missionary Family

Congregations should consider providing full missionary support for the people that God calls from among them. In places like North America, England or Korea, God speaks and people are called to missionary service. Sometimes the church leaders tell them, "Now go and find your support." Some frustrated missionary candidates travel hundreds of miles—even thousands—looking for churches that will support them. While there are some benefits to spreading one's prayer support base far and wide, there are also disadvantages because so much time and effort is given to the cost of raising support. Churches with the resources could support a smaller number of missionaries with full support rather than sending out their own members to other churches to raise support.

Sometime ago I met a frustrated missionary who came into the area of Pennsylvania where I live. He had driven all the way from the southern part of the United States—more than a thousand miles – to speak in a church in Pennsylvania. Unfortunately, when he got to Pennsylvania, the church was not prepared to receive him. They said, "Didn't you get our message? We told you not to come." While he had driven more than a thousand miles to preach in that church, his next appointment was more than fifteen hundred miles away in Alabama. What I am suggesting here would help to avoid that kind of thing happening.

Congregations which feel they cannot take on the full support of one of their own can actively look for other similar congregations in their area and join with them in finding the support that is required. This concept is sometimes referred to in missionary circles as a "consortium of churches" for missionary support. A missionary candidate might end up having five or six churches to which he or she is accountable, and they are not likely to be fifteen hundred miles apart. When on missionary furlough, the missionary can concentrate on a smaller number of churches rather than being spread thin over many parts of the country.

Invest in Cross-Cultural Training for Missionaries

Frequently missionaries are well-meaning people who have not had cross-cultural training. They may have two or three weeks of orientation in a candidate program, but many do not have the kind of cross-cultural training which seriously prepares them to understand their own worldview and that of others. Some are so ill prepared that they don't know the *questions* to ask in another culture, let alone the *answers*. How many of us would want to have serious surgery from a medical doctor or surgeon who is a well-meaning person but who has not had professional medical training? If a surgeon operated on me—and his only qualification was that he was a good man and that his "heart was in the right place" — by the time he finished working on me, *my* heart might not be in the right place! Indeed, people have been prosecuted for practicing medicine without proper credentials. Unfortunately, missionaries often serve with little or no cross-cultural training. We may think that sincerity is sufficient to carry them through complex cross-cultural experiences. Is understanding the soul that much less important than understanding the body?[2]

Investing in cross-cultural training is a valid use of mission funds and will make missionaries more effective. It will also help to cut down the number of missionary casualties.

One ramification of cross-cultural training is the cost of college and seminary debt. That is one of the major problems that prevents called and committed people from becoming missionaries. They end up with so much debt to repay that by the time they accomplish that, they have a house mortgage, children, and a secure profession. Sadly, some never get to the field of service to which they once felt called. Sometimes by the time they get their debts paid, they

---

[2] Dr. Ralph Winter used to say that adding cultural issues to preaching the gospel was like moving from being a medical doctor to being a veterinarian. The mono-cultural minister has a much easier task than the cross-cultural minister. As with the veterinarian, the number of variables greatly increases in cross-cultural ministry. For one thing, the medical doctor can speak to his patient; the veterinarian can't.

are considered too old to be accepted by the mission societies or too burdened by a growing family's needs to make the change. Helping missionary candidates overcome college debt is one valid use of missionary funding. There are too many ramifications of this to be dealt with adequately here. Among those is developing the criteria for who should be helped. But helping to overcome debt related to missionary training is worthy of consideration.

Invest in Mobilization Efforts

The original recording of the WMA series on dependency was done at the US Center for World Mission in Pasadena, California where mobilization is a high priority. Mobilization is one of the things that Western churches and wealthy churches and individuals with money can do to promote the cause of Christ. There are many ways to engage in mobilization.

Consider, for example, the work I have been doing with churches in East, Central and Southern Africa. What is the justification for going back to places where the Gospel has been preached for two hundred years or more? One of my purposes is to help awaken a sleeping giant called the Church in Africa and to make it aware of the privilege of carrying the Good News of the Gospel to the 10/40 Window where it has not yet been preached. That's mobilization. Otherwise, I and others should be going to the 10/40 Window ourselves.

Wherever there are sleeping Christians, waking them up and motivating them to make the Kingdom of God their highest priority is a worthwhile investment of time and energy. Mobilization efforts require resources, but it is one way to multiply efforts for the wider purposes of the Kingdom of God. Remember, former missionaries can be effective mobilizers – either after they return to their homes or among the people with whom they lived and worked during their time of service.

Invest in Ministries that do not have a Natural Constituency

Radio broadcasting is an example of a ministry without a natural giving constituency. Unfortunately, often funds are invested in churches that ought to have their own giving constituency. Once again the challenge in radio ministry is to promote the spread of the Gospel and the planting of churches in a way that local self-supporting churches will emerge, free of outside support.[3]

I suggest investing in **campus organizations, radio broadcasting, Bible translation** and similar projects which do not have a natural constituency the way a church has — or should have. Remember, that even among these, whenever possible, local people should be encouraged to support such ministries if they are close at hand.

Help Refugees

There are more refugees in the world than at any previous time in history. They deserve to be helped. However, remember that indiscriminate handouts are not the only way to help refugees.

Refugees have a sense of dignity which ought to be preserved whenever possible. In fact, their fragile sense of dignity might be one of the few things they have left. If that is the case, then care should be taken that one does not destroy that along with the other things that have been lost.

Many years ago I read a story about the devastation following the Indo-China war in the 1940's and 1950's. Church property was devastated and pastors' homes were destroyed. After the war ended, missionaries rushed back in with the desire to help rebuild. But the local church members said, "Please don't help us. It is our privilege to re-build the houses of our own pastors." Conclusion? Even in the midst of devastation it is important to preserve the dignity of those who are already suffering for other reasons.

Those who do community development tell us that there is a way of charging a "social price" for food or other things they distribute. It may be only 10% of the going price, but something can be charged so that those who receive are not made to feel that they are totally helpless. Here again the distinction between relative and absolute poverty becomes important.

---

[3] For an in-depth discussion of the importance of this, see the article on the WMA website, which I have titled *I Believe in the Local Church*.

Invest in Preventive Health Programs

Western medicine has often concentrated on curative medicine. Thankfully now there is a move toward preventive medicine. This is a valid place for those who are concerned to use their resources. I do not have time to go into it now, but there are programs where African storytelling is being used to promote preventive medicine so that the number of people needing crisis medicine is reduced.[4] What other solution is there for the massive pandemic of AIDS, than for education about the moral implications of human behavior? Yet here again, the best resources are those close at hand.

Even in the area of preventive health, it's important to realize that if people can do something to help themselves, they should be encouraged to do so. Investments into improving health care, nutrition and literacy will pay long-term dividends for overall community development.

Invest in Breaking Dependency — not in Creating it

Breaking or avoiding dependency means investing in such things as **employment projects, job creation schemes and revolving loan funds.** These are the kinds of programs that help people stand on their own two feet and do something for themselves. When successful, such programs bring a personal reward that helps people avoid or move beyond the state of dependency.

Considering the global economic scene, it is apparent that the World Bank and the International Monetary Fund (IMF), for example, make their greatest contribution when they help a country to establish an infrastructure such as roads, water supplies, or electricity. It is then that job creation follows. This is much to be preferred to simply handing out aid because it creates an infrastructure that benefits the nation long term. This is a complex area. But there are places in the world where infrastructure was re-built, and people benefited without acquiring a long-term welfare mentality. I do not mean by this that all investment programs of the World Bank or IMF have

---

[4] For more information on this see Contact 41, a publication entitled *The Lardin Gabis Plan of Preventive Health Care* prepared many years ago by the World Council of Churches.

been healthy, but providing employment is preferred to simply giving handouts.

Never do for Others what They Can and Should Do for Themselves

Avoid unhealthy dependency like the plague which it can become. Here again is where the question of preserving dignity enters the picture. Destroy someone's self-respect and many other problems follow.

Several years ago I met someone who worked with Bread for the World in East Africa. He told me his view of how to help others. He said in one area people asked their organization for tables which would be used for some purpose in the community. The aid worker asked them if there was no wood in the community to make into tables. They assured him that there was. He then asked them if there were no carpenters in the community who could make tables. They assured him that carpenters were there. He then asked if there were no nails in the community with which to put the tables together. They scoffed, saying that there were nails and that they are cheap. He then asked why they could not make their own tables. They said they lacked a carpenter's plane to prepare the boards for making the table. He then said to them, "If it is only a plane that you need to make the tables that is what you should be asking me for." In that way he would not be doing for them what they could and should do for themselves.

Don't Forget about Outreach in Your Own Community

In Chapter 1, I mentioned the revolution that took place in the Presbyterian Church in East Africa. One of the things they said during that transition toward self-reliance was this: "People overseas are sending us money. They are sacrificially putting five or ten dollars or pounds into the collection to send to us here in Africa, and then they are satisfied that they have done God's work. Unfortunately, the people next door to them don't know the Gospel." Those church leaders in East Africa were calling for was a period of time in which everyone should take a good hard look at how we do God's work. They were saying, "We here in Africa need to look at how we do the work of the Church, and the people overseas need to look at how they do it. People in England and

North America should not abandon the people on their own streets in favor of putting money in the collection and then conclude that they have done God's work."

There are a few things about which we should exercise care.

We should **be cautious about child sponsorship programs** where there are extended families intact to care for their own children. Consider this: God in His providence ordained extended families to care for children, the infirm, the elderly, widows, orphans, and the unemployed. If outside child sponsorship is used in a place where the extended family could and should be doing such things, the outside funding becomes a substitute for the family. It is here that the seeds of dependency can easily be sown. I am not saying that all child sponsorship programs should be abandoned — only that care should be taken not to replace God-given resources that are close at hand.[5]

Recently I spoke with someone involved in a child sponsorship program in Southern Africa. This is what he said: "What we are doing here is what local families should be doing for their own children? But it is one of the ways that funds are raised in North America because we appeal to people to sponsor a child for ten or twenty dollars a month." The danger is that we may be nibbling away at the foundation God put there, in this case the extended family, to care for its own people. I wish to repeat that I am not opposed to all child sponsorship programs because Jesus told us to help the poor. However, in places where people are simply dependent and not poor, child sponsorship is one of those things that should be looked at carefully.

Don't send money to individual church leaders. Frequently when individual church leaders get outside funding, their own church members don't know how much has been received or how it is used. If local believers suspect that funds are coming in from the outside, it can easily destroy local initiative for giving. Local church members may not put money in the collection simply because they see the quality of clothes their church leaders are wearing, or they see that school fees for the pastor's children are all miraculously paid from

---

[5] I have dealt with this in-depth under the subject of "geographical proximity" in chapter 10.

some unknown source. They may then conclude, "Such a pastor obviously doesn't need my money." Conclusion: Be exceptionally careful about sending money to individual church leaders.

Don't subsidize literature which reduces its value in the eyes of those who buy it. This principle has to do with Bibles and other Christian literature. Some years ago a person who was becoming aware of the dependency problem said, "But our whole ministry is to give away literature." Without realizing it, they were re-enforcing the idea that people are too poor to pay for what they want; in that way, free literature exacerbates the problem of dependency. The end result is that eventually people begin to think that Bibles and other Christian literature should be **free of charge,** not realizing that somewhere, someone is spending a lot of money to produce it. A commonly heard phrase in some parts of Africa is, "How can you charge for this Bible? It is God's Word." That mentality results from the long history of giving away Bibles free of charge, even to those who could pay something for them.[6]

Be careful about providing scholarships for people to be trained outside of their cultural context. Sometimes those who have been educated outside of their cultural context find it difficult or impossible to go back and minister among their own people. In Pius Wakatama's book *Independence for the Third World Church: An African's Perspective on Missionary Work* there is an interesting section on the motivation for overseas study (Chapter 7). It is most enlightening and highlights some of the dangers in providing overseas scholarships.

Avoid building church buildings for people who can build them for themselves. Building church buildings is one of the biggest areas of abuse in the dependency syndrome. Sometime ago I did a seminar in Israel, and there was an American missionary sitting in the back of the room. He said, "I know what you are talking about. Sometime ago, we took thirty-six young people from North America to the country of Guyana in South America. There we built a church building and gave it to the people. We had a ceremony, turned it over to them, and then went back home. Two

---

[6] For more on how dependency affects the production and distribution of Bibles, see Chapter 22.

years later we received a letter from the people in Guyana saying: 'Dear friends, the roof on **your** church building is leaking. Please come and fix it.'"

Once while in Capetown, South Africa, I was doing a seminar, and a man stood up and said, "I know what you are talking about. We went over to Namibia, built a church building and gave it to the local people. We had taken enough money and people from Capetown to complete the project. We gave the building to the people assuming they would use it as a church. After we left, the people divided the building into four parts and four families moved in and used it as a place to live."

Consider this: If local people had built that building in Namibia with their own hands and with their own resources, is it conceivable that it would have been divided up and used as a place for several families to live? It is most unlikely.

I recently learned about a short-term mission group that went out to build a church building for those whom they thought were deserving. Not having gone about it in the right way, when all was said and done, they were told to tear down the building. It was neither what they wanted nor where they wanted it. Sound principles can be used to avoid this kind of unfortunate incident.

Regarding church buildings, remember this principle: **People can have a church building equal to the houses in which they live**. If they live in a house that is made of sun-dried bricks with a grass roof, they can have a church of sun-dried bricks and a grass roof. If they live in a house with burnt bricks and an iron roof, they can have a church with burnt bricks and an iron roof. If they live in a house with carpet and air conditioning, they can most likely afford a church like that.

The problem is that many of us as westerners look upon people who live in modest houses and conclude, "You shouldn't have to worship in a church that looks like the house you live in" — and then the problem of dependency gets a foothold and is perpetuated.

Avoid glittering projects such as satellite dishes, etc. Sometime ago I heard about some well-meaning westerners who gave a satellite dish to a bishop in Central Africa. While the pastors for whom he was responsible were hardly getting any salary, he had something that was very much out of character in his community.

Be careful about food aid projects which may have the potential to affect local prices. Several years ago in West Africa a shipment of food aid arrived simultaneously with a 110% local harvest. As a result, the price of locally produced products dropped 90% because of the presence of the foreign shipment of food. Farmers threw up their hands and said, "We can't afford to plant next year if we can only get 10% on the value of the crops we produce." One of the dynamics of a situation like this is the long time between the identification of the need and the delivery of the food aid. In this case it arrived during the next growing season.

Conclusion

There is no simple answer to the question of how resources should be used in the Christian movement. The challenge is to keep the love of money which is the root of all evil, from looking like the Good News of the Gospel. Another challenge is to use resources in a way that does not create or perpetuate a dependency mentality.

QUESTIONS FOR DISCUSSION
Chapter 4

1. *What part do global economics play in third world dependency?*

2. *"A Western standard of living is a luxury that the non-western world cannot afford to support." Discuss the implications of life-style.*

3. *Do you personally know any missionaries who are ministering in the 10/40 Window? Name them if you can.*

4. *What importance do you attach to cross-cultural training for westerners or other missionaries? Do non-western missionaries need cross-cultural training?*

5. *Discuss the relationship between preventive and curative approaches to medical care.*

6. Do you agree that <u>people can have churches equal to the houses they live in</u>? Discuss the implications.

7. Who gave the money for the church building in which you are worshipping? Where does the money come from for salaries in your church? Is the primary source from outsiders?

8. Discuss the implications of having paid professional employees in the church.

SUGGESTED READING

Allen, Roland. *Missionary Methods: St Paul's or Ours?* London: World Dominion Press, 1960.

Bonk, Jonathan J. *Missions and Money: Affluence as a Western Missionary Problem.* Maryknoll: Orbis Books, 1991.

Wagner, C. Peter, et al, Eds. *Praying Through the 100 Gateway Cities of the 10/40 Window.* Seattle: YWAM Publishing, 1995.

Stearns, Bill and Amy. *Catch the Vision 2000.* Minneapolis: Bethany House Publishers, 1991.

CHAPTER 5

Historical Development of the Syndrome of Dependency

My purpose here is to look at the syndrome of dependency in historical perspective. Why has this caused so many concerns over the last century in Africa and elsewhere? Interestingly, there were missiologists well before the twentieth century who knew about this problem and spoke out about it. I am referring to what one might call the birth of indigenous thinking — the three-self principle is one example. This happened in the middle of the 19th century, and a lot more has been learned about indigeneity since then.

What Do We Mean by the Indigenous Principle

The three-self principle simply says that mission-established churches can be (and *should* be) self-supporting, self-governing and self-propagating. This was promoted by missiologists like Henry Venn, Rufus Anderson, John Nevius and others who said that indigenous churches should be able to support and manage their own affairs.

Many missiologists today think that the three-self principle is too simplistic — that a church isn't necessarily indigenous just because it is self-supporting, self-governing and self-propagating. For those who are interested in learning more about this, there is a book called *Readings in Dynamic Indigeneity* edited by Dr. Charles Kraft. In this book the problem of the three-self's is exposed and criticized rather severely. One of the best chapters is by Dr. Hans Kasdorf in which he traces the development of the three-self concept and explains why that definition of indigeneity is of concern to missiologists. For our purposes here, it is important to acknowledge that in the last century many people became conscious of the need for churches to stand on their own two feet, whatever else one thinks of the three-self principle.

A fair conclusion one could draw is that healthy churches are not dependent on outside resources. The extent to which the three-self's are present in a congregation or denomination, to that extent the church becomes stronger in both self-image and community image. It does not necessarily mean that the church has an indigenous theology or hymnology which is one of the criteria which missiologists prefer to use. But neither could one say that a church is truly indigenous if it cannot support, govern or propagate itself.

From my perspective, the three-self principle represents a minimum, not all there is to the concept of a healthy indigenous church. Think for a moment about the germ theory of sickness. It is basic and fundamental to the treatment of those who are ill. Of course, it is not all there is to know about medicine. Since the discovery of the germ theory, medical people have learned far more complex things such as nuclear medicine, antibiotics and chemotherapy. Having learned those things, no one is advocating discarding the fundamental germ theory of sickness. In a similar way, while the three-self principle doesn't deal will all the sophisticated things that we now know, it does not mean that it is invalid, however much some might wish to explain it away by missiological sophistication.

The indigenous principle was understood, promoted, debated and written about by people like Robert Speer (in *Christianity and the Nations*) and others that I mentioned above. Those writers made many points about the importance of churches standing on their own two feet, yet for almost all of the twentieth century, many churches in Africa did not come to know the joy associated with being self-supporting, self-governing and self-propagating. Self-propagation, particularly, suffered because dependent churches feel they could not afford to reach beyond themselves.

While the indigenous concept is not new, we should ask ourselves the question: Why have missionaries today so systematically avoided making principles like self-support a priority in their ministries? Or why has it been a priority only in word but not in practice? It is interesting to reflect on that conundrum.

Another person writing on the subject of indigenous churches was Roland Allen. He contributed several books to help us understand the missionary movement. The first was *Missionary Methods: St Paul's or Ours?* The second was *The Spontaneous Expansion of the Church and the Causes which Hinder it*. A third he called *The Missionary Principle* in which he emphasized the importance of the Holy Spirit in missionary activity.

Missionary Methods – St. Paul's or Ours? is a severe analysis of the way traditional missionary work has been done. Allen outlines serious reservations regarding the use of money in planting mission churches. His second book, *The Spontaneous Expansion of the Church* deals with how the Church multiplies, how it goes from the introduction of the Gospel to a state of growth and, finally, to expansion outward. Interestingly, on page 19 in this book, Allen, referring to missionaries, writes, "A thousand, thousand would not suffice and a dozen might be too many." He conveys the meaning that it isn't the proliferation of missionaries that produces the healthiest churches. It is the quality of the missionary and the soundness of his or her practice which determines the outcome. What he says has been proven right again and again in the intervening years.

In about 1970 there was a study done on Latin America called *Latin American Church Growth*, by authors Read, Monterosso and Johnson. One of the conclusions they came to was that the Church grew faster in numbers where there were the fewest missionaries. That would support Roland Allen's claim that "a thousand thousand cannot do the job and a dozen might be too many"! *Latin American Church Growth* is now more than thirty-five years old but well worth reading if one can secure a copy of it.

What Happens when Western Missionaries are forced to Withdraw?

Recently I learned about a place in Northern Mozambique where, when missionaries were forced out of the area, the local churches came alive. In the early 1950's when all western missionaries were forced out of China they left behind roughly one million believers. More than fifty years later we find that the church in China grew from one million to possibly 80 million believers (some say as many as 120 million) without the presence of western missionaries or outside support.

Does this mean that western missionaries are not needed? Of course they're needed. But they need to do what God wants them to do and then, by God's help, move on. Someone observed that the apostle Paul's greatest problems, as described in his New Testament letters, occurred where he stayed the longest. This is not to disparage the life-long work of long-term missionaries. Some of them have lived and modeled a spirit that produced healthy indigenous churches.

Others have sown seeds that will produce fruit only in the next generation.

The problem of unhealthy dependency often results from missionaries entrenching themselves and establishing huge foreign institutions. Local people become dependent on the institutions and what they represent – employment, education, medical care, used clothing, etc. Sometimes they simply become dependent on the missionaries and the foreign money. Sometimes because of getting bogged down, missionaries see no way of moving on. It is helpful to remember that a mission society is like scaffolding used to build a building. At some point, it should be taken down and moved to another place. If left in place too long, it virtually becomes part of the structure. Sometimes, if it were to be removed, the building would collapse!

I referred in a previous lesson to Bishop Tucker of Uganda. He knew back in 1901 that churches could be planted, evangelists could be trained, and clergy could be ordained without money from the outside. I will restate what he said for emphasis: " . . . not one half-penny of English money is used in support of it all." What a profound lesson he had learned!

There is another example from history of someone who understood the importance of churches becoming self-supporting. The story of J.O. Fraser of the China Inland Mission can be found in a book called *Behind the Ranges*. It tells the story of his ministry among the Lisu people of China. Fraser knew instinctively that he should not use money to entice people into Christianity. Therefore, he did not pay the people who carried his bags as he marched up the mountains. He felt that the people were not mercenary at heart, and he did not want to teach them to be mercenary — to expect to be rewarded for participating in the spread of the Gospel. He decided that if they wanted a hymnbook, a notebook or a pencil they should buy it, because he did not want money or things to become the "good news" that might mistakenly become associated with the Gospel.

The Gospel Came to Southern Africa Several Centuries Ago

There are many stories about the coming of westerners to East, Central and Southern Africa. One of them concerns a group of American missionaries who went to Southern Africa, at the end of the 19ᵗʰ century. They went to Cecil John Rhodes, head of the British South Africa Company, since he was responsible for land in Central Africa and the development of the Rhodesias, as they were then known.[1] It took the missionaries about six months to get an appointment with Cecil John Rhodes, but eventually he agreed to see them. During the meeting they asked for a place in Central Africa where they could "do missionary work." In response to the missionaries' request Rhodes gave instructions to his assistant as follows: "I think you might grant a farm of fifteen hundred morgen[2] in the middle of natives, title to be given after proof of work, . . . This class I think is better than policemen and cheaper." [3]

Ian Smith, as head of Zimbabwe's white minority government in the 1960s and 70s, made his contribution to the colonial spirit by saying "never in a thousand years would he agree to majority rule." He was verbalizing one of the presuppositions of the colonial era which was that outsiders would rule the land, probably forever, because the people were unable to do it for themselves. While unscrupulous political leaders have decimated some parts of Africa (including the Zimbabwe Ian Smith was concerned about), one cannot justify what the outsiders (including some missionaries) were saying during the colonial period.

The Influence of Apartheid

One of the greatest tragedies of the twentieth century, and one of the most obvious forms of colonialism that our generation knew, was the apartheid system in South Africa. In the early years it was

---

[1] He was giving away land that was often unjustly taken from the African people who lived there for centuries before the westerners arrived. It is one part of the unresolved dilemma in places like Zimbabwe at the beginning of the 21st century.

[2] A *morgen* was approximately 2.1 acres in Southern Africa at the time.

[3] This is quoted in *Mission Education in a Changing Society: Brethren in Christ Mission Education in Southern Rhodesia, Africa 1899-1959.* (The original letter is in the archives of what was at one time the Government of Rhodesia in Salisbury, now Harare.) Missionaries often quoted this as "give the missionaries 3000 acres in the Matopo Hills because one missionary is equal to 300 policemen when taming the natives." Though the popular quoting is somewhat different from the official letter issued by Rhodes to his assistant, the part hardest to understand is that some missionaries considered it a compliment and quoted it in public in subsequent years to justify the acquisition of large land holdings

not very well defined, but by the middle of the twentieth century — about 1948 — it was formally accepted as the policy of the South African government. This was the attempt on the part of people of European descent to create a policy of "separateness." The tragedy of the apartheid system was that for many years it had the backing of the Dutch Reformed Church and other Christians in South Africa. Thankfully, it did not have the support of all churches, but it had the backing of many non-African Christians as well as some of the Western missionaries who went there from the outside. Many times when the South African government wanted to defend what it was doing, it turned to Christian theologians. Those theologians provided them with alleged Biblical justification for what they were doing. The government considered this a mandate, given to the white people by God, to subdue the world and bring it under His rule.

This was not altogether unlike the doctrine of Manifest Destiny in North America in which North Americans felt compelled to bring the Western Hemisphere, North and South America, under the rule of God and to bring the so-called "native peoples" under God's rule. Manifest Destiny, then, became to some a God-ordained plan for bringing people into submission.

This is part of the history of the development of colonialism. It is a legacy that has many ramifications lingering today. What is the result of apartheid?

From 1985 until about 2000 I conducted many seminars on self-reliance in East, Central and Southern Africa, many of them in the country of South Africa itself. One day I got a letter from a non-white South African pastor that said, "Glenn, you must add another point to your sermon." He was referring to something he felt I was leaving unsaid. "What you need to deal with is the long-term effects of apartheid on the mentality of those of us who are non-white and now living in South Africa. For three hundred years we were told *not* to think, that we *didn't need* to think, that *someone else would do the thinking for us*. We only needed to listen, obey, and work. Now that apartheid is being removed as an official policy, we are free to think. But we do not know HOW to think. I and a few of my friends have broken this pattern for ourselves and become successful, but many of our non-white brothers and sisters are still living with that mentality that they do not need to think.

That is one of the legacies of apartheid." The full force of what he was saying puts the policy of apartheid into perspective and points to a major reason behind the dependency syndrome.

The Christian Movement in Colonial Times

As colonialism was developing, the Church in Africa was also developing. The missionary movement was changing as well. There came into the missionary movement in Central Africa, a big push towards bigger and better ways of doing things. More money, more people, more institutions! It was not necessarily that way in the beginning of western missions in Central Africa. In the earliest days of the missionary movement in that part of Africa, many missionaries went about on foot or by bicycle. They would travel out from where they lived, spend a day visiting in a village and sleep at night in the homes of local people or in a school classroom. The next day they would move on to another village, spend the day and sleep there that night. At the end of the week they came back home. This allowed for close interaction with people in their villages. Of course it could not be done without mastering the local language.

But, by the middle of the twentieth century, which coincided with the coming of the motorcar, it became possible to go out, spend the day, and come back home at the end of the same day. One could go out the next day and come back home again for the night. As a result, a distance began to grow between those who were taking the Gospel and those who were receiving it. The people in the villages no longer saw the missionaries eating their food, staying overnight in their villages, or—as someone said – even using a toilet! Such things often happened out of sight – perhaps only in the missionary's home. The gap between the missionary and the people they were trying to reach began to widen. As the gap grew larger, the place where the missionary headquartered himself also grew in size. After a while, the people began to "come in" to where the missionary lived. This was the beginning of the *mission station*. This became the alternative for the missionary going out to the surrounding villages. People came to the mission station for church services, to buy things from the mission store or farm, for employment or to attend school. In this transition, the "mission station" became much more of a service center, rather than a place from which the missionary went out to evangelize.[4]

Following this transition, the *consolidation stage* began, and the work of missionaries became more and more tied to mission stations. This was the time of building "more and bigger" schools, boarding facilities, secondary schools, clinics, hospitals and guesthouses. The "box" I mentioned in Chapter 1 grew significantly during this period. Sadly, it became increasingly impossible to manage on local resources alone.

The Gradual Reduction of Outside Funds

In the 1950s and 60s, there came a growing consciousness that building "the box" bigger and bigger wasn't the solution. Hence, missionaries began to think about transferring the box and thereby trying to reduce the amount of money needed to support it. In short, they began a process which they hoped would turn over leadership and ownership to local people. In an attempt to move toward local ownership, sometimes unique financial schemes were devised to reduce outside subsidy. Some used a ten-year plan in which outside subsidy would be reduced 10% each year. The first year, 100% represented the amount of subsidy from the outside, but the next year only 90% would come from the outside while the local church was expected to put in 10% — then 80% and 20% — then 70% and 30% and so on. It was assumed that eventually ownership would transfer, and in ten years local people would be 100% in charge, carrying full responsibility for their financial affairs and leadership responsibilities.

Unfortunately, there seem to be few examples where this worked. I know, however, of one place where a plan was launched in 1962 and in 1990 funds were still coming in from the outside. So much for that ten-year plan.

Why does this kind gradualism so often fail to work? Why does the transfer not take place as expected? It is clear that gradualism alone is not the key to the transfer of psychological ownership. As I have

---

[4] For those interested in the place of the motorcar and other observations on missionary work in Central Africa see the book by Adrian Hastings entitled *Church and Mission in Modern Africa*. He wrote from his experience in Zaire.

said before, somewhat tongue in cheek, in such schemes where missionaries say they are going to cut off the support 10% at a time, they are honorable people and they will do it; they will keep their promise. But there is no guarantee that true ownership will transfer and that local support will rise 10% each year. Consequently, sometimes when outside support is cut off, church leaders are left with bank overdrafts, just trying to maintain "the box." Unless true psychological ownership transfers, there is little hope for such ten-year reducing schemes. However, when real ownership transfers, dramatic things can happen!

A pastor in Zambia told about his church which had been started by an American mission society. At one point the missionaries set up a ten-year reducing scheme, hoping that the plan would produce local ownership. Three years into the plan, however, the Zambian pastors looked at each other and said, "Why do we have to wait ten years to take full ownership of our church?" So they ended the plan and took full ownership immediately. When that happened, those pastors took psychological ownership saying, "This is ours; we can do it." The result was dramatic.

Several years later, I saw one of the pastors in that church and discovered that he was about to leave for a visit to North America. I asked him about the purpose of his trip, and he said he had been invited to attend a conference in the USA. So I asked him, "Who will pay for your air ticket?" "Well," he said, "we insist on paying AT LEAST half of every ticket when we are invited to go anywhere." That is a change from feeling that one cannot go anywhere unless the ticket is bought from overseas. By insisting on participating financially in this way, those African church leaders were determined to preserve some of their dignity.

We have learned that it is possible for Christian businessmen from Africa to travel widely overseas and not ask anyone else for assistance. If business people can afford to travel, then it is only natural to think that they can afford to send their pastors to conferences if they choose to do so.

The Rise of Independent Churches

Another part of the historical situation in East, Central and Southern Africa is the rise of independent churches. Where did these churches come from?

First of all, there are many of these churches. David Barrett in his book *Schism and Renewal in Africa*, published in 1968, said that by the time of that writing there were ten thousand *independent denominations* in Southern Africa. That is a major proliferation of independent churches. Barrett observed that independent churches were most prevalent in the parts of Africa where there was a land problem. He meant by that those places where outsiders had taken away the land and deprived local people of personal ownership. He maintains that where there were no severe land problems, as in some parts of West Africa, for example, there are not as many independent churches.

But where do African Independent Churches (AICs) come from? AICs were started by people—usually men, but sometimes women—who came to the Christian faith in mission-established churches, but found such churches an impossible place to live and carry out their ministry. In other words, mission-established churches were too often a place where they did not feel at home.

The Low-Ceiling Principle

A place where one does not feel at home may be characterized as having a "low-ceiling principle." Because of the way some mission churches were structured, anyone in them who had initiative and wanted to do things differently (perhaps in a more African way), would sooner or later bump his or her head against an artificially low ceiling. When they bumped their heads often enough, they would get the message that this was not a place to feel at home. So they would go out and start an independent church where, by comparison, the sky was the limit. In 1976 in Kenya there was one new independent church started every two weeks. Here again, these were often people who became Christians in mission-established institutions but who had to get out in order to preserve their dignity, self-respect and sense of integrity.

Are AICs perfect? No. Are they all evangelical? No. Are some of them into practices in which Christians should not be involved? Yes. However, their growth reflects the fact that the atmosphere within the mission-established churches in which many of them had been could no longer be tolerated so they went elsewhere to find fulfillment. Leaders simply needed a higher ceiling under which to function.

Second Generation African Independent Churches

A part of the historical development of the dependency syndrome is yet another phenomenon related to African Independent Churches. In the second generation, some leaders in the AICs began to look round at the development projects of other churches. They saw the Anglican or Presbyterian Church, for example, and asked, "How do they get those development projects or that block of flats which they use as an income-generating project? Perhaps we could do that", they concluded. Unfortunately, the second-generation leaders of some AICs forgot what they were delivered from, as they now look wistfully over the fence wondering whether they, too, could get money from Europe or North America.

The Time has come: Enough is Enough

In the early 1970's, as part of missions to East, Central and Southern Africa, there was a unilateral decision-making movement (particularly in East Africa) in which local church leaders said, "Enough is enough! We do not want to be dominated any more. We do not want outsiders to make decisions for us, and we do not want their money. We want to stand on our own two feet." I referred to this movement earlier on. It is sometimes called the Moratorium Movement. It has received a considerable amount of unfavorable attention, sometimes because missionaries felt threatened by this new attitude. However, looking back after more than thirty years, it is possible to see the progress that some churches made because of that. In some cases, the progress was dramatic, to say the least. One could spend a lot of time discussing the good and bad parts of that movement.

Interestingly, here again there are second-generation leaders who don't know about the dependency from which their forefathers were delivered. The result is that they, too, now wistfully look over the fence and say, "Maybe partnership is the way to go." It would be sad if the independence the older generation of church leaders fought hard to gain would be lost because of so-called partnership or interdependence.

The Call for Partnership

When looking at a history of the dependency syndrome, it is necessary to look at the current phenomenon of what is often called "partnership." This is a major challenge for those who seriously promote self-reliance among mission-established institutions. In October 1996 a conference was held in Wheaton, Illinois (USA) specifically to encourage westerners to give money directly to so called "indigenous ministries." (One might ask about how truly indigenous such ministries are if funding comes from the outside. After all, is "self-support" not a characteristic of an indigenous church?) Organizers of the conference reported having fifty-two organizations present at the conference representing $110 million a year with an emphasis on supporting so-called "indigenous ministries." Most missiologists who have had first-hand experience in cross-cultural church planting do not believe that the missiology behind this practice is defensible. By promoting the "paying of nationals" (their term) they are appealing to what they believe is the economic desire of westerners who want to see more "mileage" from their missions dollar. Little do the promoters — or the donors — realize that they could well be creating a problem of dependency which someone, sometime will need to overcome.

Reading the current promotional articles by those who promote this position one gets the impression that they are advocating something new — that we are entering "a new wave of missions." Using western money to pay non-western church leaders is a very old idea — not a new one. Most disconcerting is that it reinforces the idea that the non-western world can't propagate the Gospel without western money. We know by now how misleading that is. There are many testimonies, especially from church leaders in Africa and Asia today, that demonstrate that, given the opportunity, their continents can support the missionary vision God has given them. Some of them know instinctively that healthy Spirit-led self-reliance is the only way to restore the dignity which they feel has been so often been taken from them by remaining in a prolonged state of dependency.

Imagine this scenario: A missionary goes out to plant churches using valid principles of self-support. He or she works hard to encourage local people to pay their own leaders, build their own buildings and manage their own affairs. After some years, along come outsiders looking for "partnership." They offer to pay salaries with outside funds. This results in good leaders being attracted away from self-supporting churches by the outside funding. That is what one might call "shepherd stealing" — drawing away leaders by offering better salaries that can only be paid with outside funding.

Development organizations have frequently used this tactic. They attract church leaders into development projects with salaries that are sometimes twice or three times what the local church is able to pay. Then the drought ends, overseas funds dry up, and the development workers can no longer be paid by the aid agency. Will they really go back to working for one third the salary (or less) which is what their churches are able to pay? Probably not, so they look for another agency which pays with foreign funds. Little wonder that some churches lose their best leaders in this way.

This is a personal plea to those who use the term "partnership" to promote western funding for so-called indigenous ministries. Do not allow outside funding to create or perpetuate the problem of dependency. Do not give the impression that the Gospel is about the benefits that come with outside funding. Do not pay leaders or third-world missionaries and evangelists with outside funding in places where it is the privilege of local people to provide for their own members. And most importantly, have respect for the places where local believers are struggling to overcome a long history of dependency and are beginning to experience the benefits of healthy Spirit-led self-reliance. Such believers do not need anyone enticing their church leaders away with outside funding that will keep them in (or take them back into) the dependency which they knew for so long.

The problem with the term "partnership" has to do with how it is defined. (I personally do not use the term partnership because of the manner in which it is often used, or rather misused.) As I said before, partnership most often means "outside money and local labor." That is hardly an equal partnership. The responsibility on the part of those receiving the funds is "accurate reporting of how the funds are used." Read through the reports of the partnership promoters, and you will see that they frequently use the term "accountability." One such promoter of outside funding defined partnership this way: "We give the money, and you write the reports." What kind of partnership is that? A more watchful eye follows locally raised funds. Indeed, one of the reasons for the shortage of funds in local churches is that misuse or the undeclared use of local funds accounts for why people do not put money into the collection.

A final word on partnership is in order. By now it should be clear that I do not believe that the most effective spread of the Christian gospel is through the widespread use of outside funding. In the same way, petro-dollars from the Middle East are not the secret to the spread of Islam. Millions of Christians and millions of Muslims who are reached with outside funding are more likely to have a marginal religious experience than those who come to faith with a true spiritual experience. This means that the best defense against encroaching Islam across Africa is a strong indigenous, self-supporting church – one that cannot be bought with outside funding. Remember, when it is learned that people can be bought with money, the only thing left is to determine the price. Churches which take a stand against outside funding have the best opportunity to stand on their own two feet, especially when economic times become difficult all around.

QUESTIONS FOR DISCUSSION
Chapter 5

1. *Do you agree or disagree with the three-self principle? Why?*

2. *Do you agree with Roland Allen that too many missionaries can hinder the healthy formation of a mission-established church?*

3. *Discuss the role of colonialism and apartheid in relation to the problem of dependency.*

4. *When is a ten-year plan of reducing outside funding valid? When is it not valid?*

5. *Discuss the strengths and weaknesses of African Independent Churches in relationship to mission-established churches.*

6. *What are the advantages and pitfalls related to partnership in the development of non-western mission societies?*

SUGGESTED READING

Allen, Roland. *Spontaneous Expansion of the Church and the Causes Which Hinder It.* Grand Rapids: Wm. B. Eerdmans, 1962.

Barrett, David. *Schism and Renewal in Africa.* Nairobi: Oxford University Press, 1968.

Nevius, John L. *The Planting and Development of Missionary Churches.* Philadelphia: Presbyterian and Reformed Publishing Co, 1958.

Speer, Robert E. *Christianity and the Nations.* New York: Fleming H. Revell, 1910.

Taylor, Mrs. Howard. *Behind the Ranges. Fraser of Lisuland, South West China.* London: China Inland Mission, 1944.

Tucker, Ruth A. *From Jerusalem to Irian Jaya.* Grand Rapids: Zondervan Publishing House, 1983.

CHAPTER 6

What can Missionaries Do to
Avoid or Break the Dependency Syndrome?

Practical Suggestions for Missionaries

The next two lessons are designed to be practical suggestions for missionaries and church leaders on how to avoid or overcome the problem of dependency. We begin with what missionaries can do to deal with this problem.

Let's back up a bit and take a quote from Professor Alan Tippett. [1] He used to say, "If you ever face the problem of changing over from the mission to the church, you must have made a mistake somewhere. It should have been the church from the very beginning."

We are faced with a compelling question: What does one do when it is too late to start right? Many of us inherit situations we did not create, finding ourselves in the midst of an existing problem. Can anything be done about it?

The Impact of Large Mission Stations

For some who are facing this problem the roots can be found in large mission establishments. There is a curious phenomenon related to this which has to do with what we think of ourselves as western missionaries. We arrive on a mission station. We look at the size of the establishment - especially the substantial buildings—and eventually we are taken around to the most solemn place of all—the cemetery. There we are shown the graves of missionaries who died in previous generations. All of a sudden the full implication of the missionary enterprise hits us, and we say, "Wow! Look at this. These missionaries were here only two or three years, and they died of the dreaded fever or malaria at an early age."

---

[1] Dr. Tippett was an Australian missionary with the Methodist Church in Fiji for more than 20 years during the 1940s and 50s. He later became a professor of missiology at the Fuller Theological Seminary, School of World Mission in Pasadena, California.

I've stood by such graves. We tend to experience this with a sense of awe and say, "These people gave their lives, yet look what they built." All of a sudden history descends on us, and we feel that we are on holy ground—and in some ways we are. However, it soon becomes clear that it may be very difficult to change anything, given all that has occurred in this place in the past. Recognizing this history, yet being aware of the need for change, poses a great challenge that requires courage, wisdom and sensitivity. Yet without implementing the required change, the past may continue to be an unmanageable millstone around the neck of the church.

The Burden of Foreign-Built Church Structures

First of all, such millstones frequently prevent the church from becoming a growing, multiplying fellowship capable of sending out its own evangelists and missionaries. When that happens, someone or something needs to change. The sense of history that first fills us with awe must be put into proper perspective, because if change is ever going to take place, those things that hinder the growth of the church must be recognized and dealt with. One can't forever go off and start something new—though many have done so, and others wish they could. Even new institutions will one day need renewal. This is a good lesson to keep in mind when we think about re-structuring a church or other institution.

Restructuring needs to occur from time to time, because restructuring is how institutions stay alive and remain effective. Those who oppose change might be writing the prescription for ineffectiveness—or perhaps the very obituary for the institution they inherit. Hence, we must assume that an institution like the Christian church in Africa or anywhere else, especially if it has a massive "box", will one day need to be restructured.

Missionary Attitude and Motivation

In order to overcome the dependency syndrome, we need to give attention to missionary attitude and motivation. One of the challenges that must be faced during a time of change is the expectation level of the outsiders (such as missionaries) when they enter into the process. I referred earlier to the attitude of reverence for those who went before. Add this to the long history of colonialism, and the result can be a potential major stumbling block. In the past, unfortunately, missionaries were often viewed by local people as comfortable under the colonial system. Outsiders, often because their skin was white, had privileges in Central and Southern Africa that local people did not have. In Southern Africa generally, white people were allowed to travel in parts of the train where non-white people could not travel. They were allowed to go into restaurants where non-white people were not permitted to go. Given this history, missionaries who want to deal meaningfully with the past must face the fact that, whether they like it or not, they might be seen to be part of the colonial system, even though it is *assumed* to be dead and gone. It may take a serious conscious effort to show that one is no longer part of that mentality.

Many missionaries saw the advantages of the colonial system and benefited from it. Too often they did nothing to show that they separated themselves from the prevailing political system of the day. Unfortunately, as I said earlier on, in some places this was defended on Biblical grounds. Missionaries who are *willing to change their attitude and motivation* can adopt a different way of interpreting the Bible and a different way of living in today's society. This is of critical importance if missionaries are to make an impact in nations formerly under colonial rule.

Some years ago, I heard a story of a Nigerian churchman who met a young missionary in North America. Someone asked the Nigerian, "What would you say to a young missionary who is going out to your country in West Africa for the first time?" The Nigerian reflected for a moment and then said, "I would say, just remember you are *not* taking God to West Africa; God is taking *you* to West Africa." That remark speaks to the very heart of missionary motivation and attitude.

Let's look at the alternative to such an attitude. An attitude of superiority can be reflected in many ways. It is often reflected in Western preaching. For example, painting Africa as the "dark continent" indicates that one's attitude could well use adjustment. We absorb this spirit and forget that the place that God may be taking us to has had a Christian presence for several centuries – much longer than we have been alive. We may even discover mature local Christian leaders who could teach *us* something if we were willing to learn! But, for a long time, we and our African brothers and sisters, sat under preaching which assumed western superiority. Sometimes our own conversion experience makes us say, "Thank God I am not like that!" This attitude of superiority can be very subtle, yet those we seek to serve often readily recognize it. Sometimes even our call to ministry is based in some way on a kind of Western superiority.

The Important Difference between Being and Doing

I find it important to make a distinction between "being" and "doing." Consider the recruitment process or commissioning services when young western missionaries are preparing to go to their fields of service. How many times are young missionaries in a commissioning service, when someone proclaims: "These young people are going out to **do** this and that." This is heady stuff for young people because they are going out to **do** something; they are going to assume positions of power and responsibility.

There is something glamorous about going to help people in remote parts of the world whom we perceive to be less fortunate than we are. It is how we as westerners raise money to go and do what we do. Unless that spirit is challenged, however, the seeds of the dependency syndrome will continue to be sown before we even leave our own country. The challenge is to present the Gospel in such a way that people will not become dependent upon the good things that we go out to **do**.

The alternative to "doing" is a broken spirit and contrite heart which says, "God is taking me there, and even if I do not have a position of power, authority or responsibility, I will be God's person. I will **be** whatever He asks me to be."

PRACTICAL SUGGESTIONS

The following are a few suggestions for Western missionaries regarding how to break a pattern of dependency where it already exists.

Recognize that God is at work, and that we are to become part of what He is already doing. It is not for us to come up with a plan and then say, "Now, God, help me with my plan." Part of our need for attitude adjustment results from our saying, "Listen Lord, your servant speaks", twisting the advice Eli gave to Samuel in that Old Testament story. God is there; He is already at work. He is already speaking to the people we have come to serve, both leaders and laity. How can I become part of what He is already doing, rather than insisting that He become part of what I have in mind?

Consider the importance of cross-cultural training. I have referred to this issue before and will continue to do so. I maintain there is no excuse for Westerners to go anywhere without missionary training. In the middle of the 20th century there weren't very many missionary training institutions in North America and Europe that specifically prepared missionaries for cross-cultural ministry. But that is no longer the case. There are institutions all across North America, England, Germany, Korea, South Africa and throughout other parts of the world which are concentrating on preparing missionaries for cross-cultural ministry. I heartily encourage missionaries to get the kind of training that is available.

The triangle below is my attempt to show the importance of cross-cultural training. At the top of this triangle is the **spiritual** element. We wouldn't think of sending a person into missionary service who is not spiritually prepared. Then there is **professional** training. We wouldn't think of sending out a medical doctor or a teacher who was not properly trained in the area in which they will serve. But the third point of the triangle, **cross-cultural training,** is where we often fail missionary candidates. We assume that cross-cultural training is not necessary or that it is a waste of time.

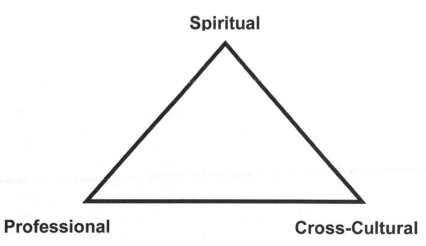

Spiritual

Professional   **Cross-Cultural**

I am somewhat skeptical of three-week training programs for missionaries. Training of that kind sometimes represents "immunization." People sometimes say, "Oh yes, I've been trained: I had three weeks of missionary orientation school." It normally takes longer than that for good cross-cultural training to be effective. Imagine, learning how to get inside someone else's worldview with only three weeks of cross-cultural training. True missionary training involves getting deeply enough involved in cross-cultural exposure so that we get a dent put into our own worldview. It is that dent that makes us question the assumptions on which our own life and spirituality are built. Indeed it is many of our own assumptions that need to be analyzed because they often have more to do with our culture than our Christianity. I will give more attention to this in chapters 13 through 15.

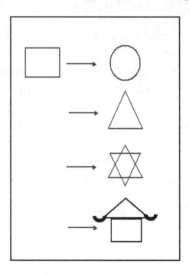

The accompanying diagram illustrates that if I come from a society in which I live in a square house, and my purpose is to minister to people who live in round houses, it is my obligation *to move into the round frame of reference* in order to think, feel and theologize. It is not "their" obligation to move into "my" frame of reference. It follows that if people live in triangular houses, my challenge is to learn to think just like they do. If I am called to minister among Jewish people, I need to think like the Star of the House of David. And my final illustration is that if I were called to China, I would need to think like people who live in houses with hooks on the roof!

Unfortunately, many of us assume that the people among whom we minister simply need to come into our frame of reference. Obviously they will need to learn English because that is the language we speak! Sadly, many missionaries do not take the time to learn enough language and culture to move into that other frame of reference for ministry.

This problem has become more and more critical in our day when a million short-termers each year are going out from North America. For those who stay only two or three weeks, in whose frame of reference will ministry most likely be conducted? Indeed, with the use of interpreters, little is done to get the giver to think in the frame of reference of the receiver.

All missionaries should take a serious look at the psychological frame of reference in which they live. To check on this, ask yourself some questions:

From where does my primary fellowship come? Does it come from the missionary community around me, or does it come from the local people among whom God called me to live and work? For example, a missionary living in culture shock will find that it affects many of the things one encounters on a daily basis. (For more information on this, see Appendix C for my treatment of what I call *Stages of Missionary Development: A Study in Cultural Adjustment.* It is my attempt to use a little humor to deal with what can otherwise be a difficult subject.)

It takes cultural adjustment to begin to understand all that is happening around us as missionaries. Unfortunately, many missionaries, instead of adjusting to the society in which they live, draw back from it and become isolated from day to day reality. The greatest tragedy occurs when a person in cultural disillusionment (what I refer to as Stage 2) leaves the field and says, "I'll never have anything to do with that place or those people again." Thankfully this does not need to be career-ending; missionaries **can** adjust culturally. They **can** make a wholesome contribution in the society to which they are called. Unfortunately, many in Stage Two fail to see how this could ever happen.

A second question to be asked is this: Is my identity tied to my position and responsibility, or is it tied to who I am in Christ?

Missionaries would do well to examine themselves in this regard because it is often in "doing" that an unhealthy attitude develops. That attitude says, "These people need me, and they can't get along without me and what I do for them."

I would suggest that missionaries should not seek or accept a position of responsibility that could be filled by a local person. Several years ago I was in West Africa and attended a meeting where they were discussing polygamy. I found it fascinating. But while the discussion was going on, a young missionary came to me, tapped me on the shoulder and said, "May I talk to you outside?" I followed him outside, assuming that this was a problem that could not wait. We went to the end of the classroom block and sat down on the verandah. He began by saying, "Glenn, I am very concerned. I have a problem, and maybe you can help me. Are you really interested in what is going on in there?"

I replied, "Well, it is a discussion on polygamy, and missiologists are always interested in that sort of thing. But what's your problem?"

"Well, I'm chairman of the Evangelism Committee in this district and . . ." I stopped him and said, "You're what?!"

He repeated, "I'm chairman of the Evangelism Committee."

"Wait a minute; how can you be chairman. You are a missionary!"

"No, no, no — they selected me."

"What do you mean they selected you?"

"Well, they couldn't get anyone else, so they asked me to do it."

"And you said yes?", I replied

"Well, yes, they asked me . . ."

At that point I interrupted him to say, "Now let me get this right. You were smart enough to take the position, but you were not smart enough **not** to."

He asked, "What did you say?"

I repeated, "You were smart enough to do the job, but you were not smart enough **not** to."

He sat there shaking his head with disbelief. Declining to be in a position of responsibility was apparently a new idea to him. I saw that missionary three days later, and he was still shaking his head and saying, "Smart enough to do it, but not smart enough not to; smart enough to do it, but not smart enough not to."

Decline the invitation to take charge of anything that could be done by a local person. Unfortunately, some missionaries haven't been good at learning how **not** to be in charge. Indeed, some seek positions of authority. They want to be present when local decisions are being made. They get a good feeling, not only from what they do, but also from influencing decisions that could and should be made by local people in church business meetings. When a missionary says "No, thank you" to a position of leadership, an important message is being sent.

Why do local people ask missionaries to lead in the first place? There is a long history behind that. Local leaders believe they must ask; they believe missionaries assume they are there to be used. When they are present, it is assumed that missionaries are to be appointed for some position or simply asked to preach. I have personally seen positive results from those occasions in which I have declined the offer to preach in favor of a local pastor preaching to his own congregation.

There is another very important reason why missionaries are favored for positions of leadership. If church leaders find they can get a missionary to do the job, *they probably won't have to pay the salary from local funds*! Missionaries ought to be able to say, "No, thank you, I believe it is your privilege to appoint one of your own people to fill this or that position."

Missionaries should excuse themselves from business meetings whenever possible. Many missionaries find this temptation hard to avoid. As I mentioned above, they want to be present at administrative meetings because they want to know what is going on, and perhaps influence the outcome. Some years ago a church leader from Central Africa said, "When there is a missionary present, we will vote the way he wants us to vote—even if he doesn't speak.

We will watch his eyes and know how to vote." That's why I suggest that people who represent the missionary system, with its colonial history and its financial resources, should absent themselves, whenever possible, from local business meetings. That provides a better opportunity for a decision to be made that is "of the people." As long as someone is present who represents power and money, the danger is that he or she will influence the outcome.

Such a decision does not mean that missionaries are disloyal or unwilling to serve. It sends a message when a missionary says, "Thank you very much for the invitation, but I believe it is the privilege of your own people to hold that position or to make that decision."

Dr. Alan Tippett told us as his students, "The mission must die before the Church can be born." I sometimes ask missionaries a potentially unsettling question: "How do you feel about having a funeral for the mission, to let the mission die?"

What Dr. Tippett was saying is that there comes a time when the mission should have finished its work and be prepared to move on. Dr. McGavran's word for this was to "move the scaffolding elsewhere."[2] He would say that the mission society is like scaffolding that is used to build a building, and that scaffolding is designed to be moved elsewhere eventually. As long as it is there, one cannot really see what the building looks like. Sadly, the kind of scaffolding that some mission societies erect and maintain is the kind that actually holds the building up. Removing it could jeopardize the structure!

Have you ever seen a building or bridge made with poured concrete? The builders put wooden or metal trusses under the bridge, and then pour concrete over the top to form the road over the bridge. Suppose for a moment that the engineers and the construction people built such a structure with concrete so weak that they couldn't take out the framework used to hold it up. That is sometimes why mission societies hold on the way they do, because the structure they built is tied to the mission. And if one were to "take down" the mission scaffolding, the fear is that the entire structure would collapse. It

---

[2] This is sometimes referred to as "euthanasia in mission activity."

may take a heap of Christian grace to acknowledge when this is the case and to do something about it.

Missionaries should avoid creating a personal agenda of things to be accomplished before leaving their assignment. Agendas created by outsiders — the things that missionaries want to see happen — are often at the root of the dependency problem. Such projects may be unsustainable without outside funding or administration, and the problem of prolonged dependency will be inevitable.

Some years ago I was conducting a seminar in which church leaders and missionaries told about the problems they were facing. During the seminar I began to deal with the issue of personal agendas, and I asked everyone present – missionaries and local leaders — to write down a list of things they wanted God to help them accomplish in the next six months. Especially for missionaries I said, "List everything that you want to see accomplished before you leave for home." Some of them very carefully wrote down their list. One missionary in particular wrote a long list of things he wanted to see done; he was only about six months from finishing his service of many years in that country and was soon to leave the field permanently.

I didn't ask to see those lists at that time. In fact, I never did collect them. I simply allowed them to think about their list for the next few days during the seminar. Several days later I said, "Do you remember the list I asked you to prepare several days ago? I have a suggestion for you. For those who are missionaries, tear up your list and throw it away. The things you feel pressured to accomplish before you leave this place will most likely become problems for someone else to solve one day." Little did I know the prophetic nature of what I was saying.

Following that experience I often thought about that one missionary who had done such a careful job of preparing his list. About a year later, after he had left the country, I returned to that area for another seminar. Local church leaders began telling me what happened. "You remember that time when you asked people to write up their lists? Well, that one missionary tried to accomplish everything on his list. Now we are bringing him back from overseas to resolve some of the problems he created during the last six months he was with us." It would have been better if that missionary had thrown his list away!

What, then, is a missionary supposed to do? He may have put in fifteen or twenty years of missionary service; and all of a sudden in the last six months, it looks like time is running out. "If I don't do this, what will happen? I have so much I want to accomplish. It is how I will save (or establish) my reputation."

I suggest that such missionaries run the risk of ruining their reputation in the last six months after they have served faithfully for fifteen or twenty years. *Throw the sacred list away!* It would be better to leave the field six months early, because, if one is not careful, the last six months can destroy many good years of faithful service.

A missionary may say, "But I can't go home six months early. People will ask why I came home early." My reply is, "That's fine, don't go home early. Just ask local church leaders to re-assign you to street, hospital or village evangelism where you won't be attending business meetings. Then spend your last six months 'being' instead of 'doing'." That might be your best way to finish well.

I alluded to this above, but it bears emphasizing. A missionary **may have been selected for a position because of the salary which comes from overseas.** There is a phenomenon in which missionaries are attractive because they don't need to be paid from local resources. Local church leaders sometimes reason, "If we elect one of our own people, we will have to raise the money ourselves to pay them." Missionaries often become the church treasurer for a reason such as this. So I suggest to any missionary, "Be careful. If you are suspicious that you are being chosen because of your salary, then, as gracefully as you know how, back away from that, and don't let it become an excuse to step in where an outsider should not be found."

Attitudes Which Affect Local Ownership

In the section that follows I will list those attitudes which I believe either help or hinder effective missionary work. Some of these are out of my own missionary service, and others came from meeting and listening to many other missionaries over the years.

Constructive Missionary Attitudes

1. I will give away all my rights — they belong to the Lord anyway.

2. I will resist the temptation to have an answer for everything on every subject.

3. I'll defer to local people whenever I can so that they will know both implicitly and explicitly that I do not want to become a source of power for them through money or any other influence.

4. I will not condemn anyone if the program I built is closed because it cannot be maintained.

5. I will not allow a spirit of dependency to develop around me.

6. I will not become bitter or even discouraged if any of my rights, privileges and responsibilities are taken away.

7. Having someone else take my job is why I came here in the first place.

8. I will not get angry when someone begins to talk about how the church I have been working with will one day be able to stand on its own two feet without the need for outsiders like me to prop it up.

Destructive Missionary Attitudes

1. "These people" don't appreciate what we have tried to do for them.

2. As a missionary, I am most productive when I am "doing" something. I don't think this idea of "being" is very important.

3. Of course we will give "these people" authority when they are ready for it . . . (Maybe in a hundred years).

4. If we turn this work over too soon, the work of the Lord might be destroyed.

5. When we are gone everything will be up to "these people." Then we'll see what happens.

As a missionary, what is your attitude toward the coming transition to local responsibility?

- Do you secretly hope that it will never come?

- If it comes, will it be against your better judgment as a missionary?

- OR — Will you seek the leading of the Holy Spirit for a peaceful and graceful transition to local ownership?

The Secret of a Peaceful Transition from Mission to Church

The secret to helping a local church make a peaceful transition, as a missionary, is not to take — or even feel — ownership of local projects. This applies especially to those projects that the missionary has been instrumental in launching. Everything needs to be laid at the foot of the cross, remembering, "This project is not mine; it belongs to the Lord. I realize it may be changed when I leave. It may even end when I leave; but it belongs to the Lord. It is not mine." The secret for a successful transfer is for the missionary to give up any "rights of ownership." I do not say this is *easy*, but I believe it is *necessary* if the churches we help to plant are ever to be truly locally owned and operated.

A Few Questions for Missionaries

1. What would you do if your present role as a missionary ended?

2. Could you move your part of the "scaffolding" to another location?

3. Could you joyfully help a local church to develop a sending ministry?

4. Could you serve in an existing church without a position of power or leadership?

5. Could you actively help to develop local resources and thereby break dependency which may have developed in the past?

6. Could you become a mobilizer for missions—looking for Great Commission Christians who have the potential to serve in the wider Christian movement?

Conclusion

There are many effective missionaries who have learned the joy of stepping back and allowing others to assume roles and positions of responsibility. In my own experience, this has been far more rewarding than holding on to positions that might give me fulfillment, but at the expense of others. I have concluded that *if a missionary thinks it feels good to be in charge of something, he or she should learn how good it feels not to be in charge and then watch others become successful.* For us as missionaries, to be given the impression that our help is not needed should be looked upon as a blessing, not rejection. Missionaries with the right attitude will recognize the difference and work toward the right end, of finishing well.

QUESTIONS FOR DISCUSSION
Chapter 6

1. *Do you agree with Professor Tippett that "the mission must die so the church can be born"? Discuss the implications.*

2. *What steps can a mission society take to move the scaffolding elsewhere?*

3. *How can a missionary gracefully decline a position when he or she knows that an overseas salary is behind the request to serve?*

4. *Discuss the relationship between "being" and "doing."*

5. *Discuss the importance of "mobilizing" as a key to world evangelization.*

6. *Discuss what it means to have one's psychological residence in the local frame of reference. What do mission compounds say about the psychological residence of missionaries?*

SUGGESTED READING

Allen, Roland. *Missionary Methods: St Paul's or Ours.* London: World Dominion Press, 1960.

Dekker, John. *Torches of Joy.* Westchester: Crossway Books, 1985.

Lingenfelter, Sherwood G. and Mayers, Marvin K. *Ministering Cross-Culturally.* Grand Rapids: Baker Book House, 1986.

McGavran, Donald A. *How Churches Grow: New Frontiers of Mission.* London: World Dominion Press, 1959.

Steffen, Tom A. *Passing the Baton: Church Planting that Empowers.* La Habra: Center for Organizational and Ministry Development, 1993.

Tippett, Alan R. *Church Growth and the Word of God.* Grand Rapids: Wm B Eerdmans, 1970.

Tippett, Alan R. *Introduction to Missiology.* Pasadena: Wm Carey Library, 1987.

Tippett, Alan R. *Verdict Theology in Missionary Theory.* Pasadena: Wm Carey Library (2nd Edition), 1973.

Chapter 7

What can Local Leaders do to Avoid or Break the Dependency Syndrome?

This is the second part in the series of practical suggestions regarding how to break the dependency syndrome. These suggestions are for local church leaders while the previous suggestions were for missionaries.

The observations that I make here are a result of my travels primarily in East, Central and Southern Africa. Many church leaders told me about their experiences in mission-established institutions. I tried to distill their thoughts and bring together suggestions that would represent encouragement for those still facing the challenge of promoting self-reliance within their churches.

The Question of Motivation

One of the first questions that must be asked of any church leader wanting to move away from dependency is this: "What is the motivation for wanting to become self-reliant?" As we consider our service in the Lord's work, we can all find things that have given us problems in the past. This would include such things as the problem of colonialism, apartheid and paternalism.[1]

Both motivation and attitude have a serious bearing on how well church leaders (or missionaries) will handle problems that arise in the process of change. That is of great importance. For example, we cannot let what happened in the past destroy us in the present. We cannot let the past control us to the point where we become embittered about the church or mission, and especially the Christian faith. If that is allowed to happen, it is a victory for Satan and healthy positive change will most likely not occur.

---

[1] It may be helpful to remember that it was not only local church leaders who suffered under the colonial system. Some missionaries also took a stand against what they saw happening and refused to do what some of their missionary colleagues were doing. They stood out against the practices of their times and suffered for doing so. Admittedly many of us as missionaries could have done much more to oppose or expose the evils of that system.

The second part of the motivation question relates to whether the process is meant to become self-serving. Church leaders must take care not to embark on a journey of self-aggrandizement. The purpose must always be to honor the Lord and not to build one's own personal kingdom.

How to Deal with Personal Hurt in One's Past

Local church leaders (a well as some missionaries) were sometimes hurt and alienated during Africa's colonial period. If they carry that baggage into the present and do nothing about resolving it, they will then carry it into the future, and it has the potential to affect everything they do. My suggestion is that all of those past hurts should be carried to the foot of the cross and left there. We do not remain in that prone position by the cross. After kneeling and leaving our burdens, we arise and move forward, empowered by the Holy Spirit for the remainder of the journey.

Church leaders often face criticism as they begin the journey on the path toward change. While spiritually sensitive church leaders will not thrive on criticism, it is to be expected that it will come. Some of it obviously must be heard. But sometimes, under the direction of the Holy Spirit, church leaders will simply need to say, "If I am going down this path, there will be people who may not approve or even understand, but we as a body of Christ will need to carefully evaluate the criticism and then move forward."

Criticism can be valid and helpful, but it does not mean that the vision should be abandoned. Neither does it mean that we should run roughshod over the feelings of others. It is helpful to remember that as a church leader you may have been one of those who accepted the old system for a period of time and then became aware of the need for change. There may be other church members, leaders, pastors (especially older pastors) who were comfortable under the old system. They found a measure of security in it. The money coming from overseas, for example, helped to care for their families. So when you or other church leaders begin to discuss the need for change you may be affecting those whose livelihood is being threatened. We should all be sympathetic to those in the system who feel trapped by history or current circumstances.

Once again, care must be exercised so that those who are simply afraid of change are not allowed to derail the process of change.

Suggestions Regarding the Move toward Organizational Self-Reliance

1. **Make a strong commitment to the process of change.** Knowing that difficulties will most likely arise, one must make a determination to go forward. Church leaders in East Africa who, back in the 1970's, made the decision to move toward a self-reliant church, say that they did not know where that path would lead. One of them said that when he asked the mission overseas to keep their money for five years, he began to realize that he didn't know how long the process would take. He didn't know whether they would accomplish the goal of becoming self-reliant in two years or five years; perhaps it would take even longer. There was a lot of uncertainty as they went through the process. The thing that kept them going was the will to see the process succeed. Some of them thirty-five or more years later are still being criticized for the changes they began long ago. Sadly, some overseas missionaries consider that move to self-reliance as anti-missionary. This emphasizes the need for Spirit-filled determination on the part of local leaders.

2. **Get your entire local leadership team and ministry colleagues on track for the transition process as much as possible**. It might not be possible for every single individual to accept what you as a church leader are trying to do. Some of the older members of the church might be thinking, "Our time is past, younger people are going to take over." But as much as possible, bring people together. This is not the time and place for someone to become what we call-in American English—a Lone Ranger. One person should not simply disregard what others are saying about the process of change. One must attempt to bring people along and keep them informed about the direction in which the new vision is heading.

3. If some of the older people feel that they can't become part of the process, **encourage them to move on to something less stressful and not be active at the heart of the process**. Perhaps some will have to take early retirement. If this is deemed necessary, it should take place in a way that older leaders do not feel they

are being rejected by the fellowship. Most of all, don't let Satan get a foothold in interpersonal relationships. Remember, the last thing Satan wants is a healthy church, standing on its own two feet, joyfully sending out its own missionaries. Nothing will do more to weaken the effort to move forward than a lack of spiritual unity.

4. **Give some attention to how outsiders (such as missionaries and mission executives) feel, BUT, do not become paralyzed by what they think and say**. Sometimes church leaders find that those overseas who have been providing funding and personnel are not happy about the move toward local self-support. One must listen to those concerns; but one must also be able to say, "Under the guidance of the Holy Spirit, we believe the time has come, and we are asking you who are overseas not to do anything that prevents us from moving in the direction that God is leading us." After all, the purpose of the process is for the local church to learn how to stand on its own two feet. If it becomes necessary, I encourage church leaders to tell outsiders who might wish to derail the process: "Don't give us money, don't make decisions for us; we want to do this for ourselves."[2] When done with the right attitude, this can receive the blessing of the Lord. Remember, this should all be viewed as a part of a spiritual battle.

5. **It is very important to begin the process with spiritual renewal**. Only spiritual weapons can be used in this process. In chapter 9 I will describe *Three Things of Importance* and how they relate to the process. The first of those three things is spiritual renewal. I mentioned earlier the priest in Zimbabwe who called his people together for two days of prayer and fasting and three days of teaching. He did not begin by re-structuring the church but with prayer and teaching; he began by reminding them of their spiritual obligations before the Lord. That brought spiritual renewal and prepared the people for restructuring. Without doubt, spiritual renewal is the place to begin.

---

[2] Some research done at the masters level in England found that the best sign that community development has occurred is when people say, "Don't help us any more." Some missionaries will rejoice at hearing this, but unfortunately some others will not want to hear such words lest their power and authority are taken away.

6. **Good planning is also part of the transition process.** Remember Nehemiah the prophet who rebuilt the walls around Jerusalem. God gave him a vision while still living in exile. He began by praying. He did serious planning ahead of time which is evident in Nehemiah chapters 1-4. He included in this process, negotiations with the King, seeking his approval and backing. It was all part of the preparation he went through as a good manager. By the time he was ready to start his journey to Israel, he had what he needed to begin the job he set out to do. The process of rebuilding was hard work, and Nehemiah suffered opposition. There were people who said, "What you are trying to do can't and shouldn't be done; it is wrong." But Nehemiah rose above all that, as he went on to fulfill the vision God had given him. Notice also that he spent time praying about how the project should be done, even walking around the walls alone and praying for God's guidance.

7. **Give some attention to restructuring the box**. A church leader faced with the weight of an enormous "box" may find that it is actually getting heavier and heavier. If the weight of such programs is crushing, then restructuring could well be the most important step. Remember, the Presbyterian Church in East Africa divided things in the box into two kinds of activities. They put congregations, synods, sacraments, discipling, evangelism, and theological education on one side and put churchmen in charge. The other things in the box such as guesthouses, bookstores, clinics, printing presses, schools, colleges, development and literacy projects were put into the hands of business people.

This kind of planning and serious decision-making freed the church to be the church. Business projects which thrive on profit and loss were given to business people to be managed according to their expertise.

A Few Practical Suggestions Regarding a Move Towards Financial Self-Reliance

1. **Let local imagination flow**. Along this line there is an interesting illustration from East Africa. One day a congregation of the

Presbyterian Church in East Africa (PCEA) decided to buy a new vehicle for one of their pastors. They told the pastor who was leaving, "Since you are going to a congregation where there is no vehicle, we suggest you take this present vehicle with you. We will buy a new vehicle for our new pastor." The congregation gave all of the money needed to buy the vehicle. On the day the presentation to the new pastor was to be made, the congregation gathered outside the church building in a big circle with the new car in the center. Someone made an announcement, "Brothers and sisters, we have bought this vehicle, and it is completely paid for. We don't need any money for that; you have already given enough. All of you know that it takes money for insurance, repairs and petrol. So today we are asking all of you to give something toward those expenses." Then they opened all the windows on the car and asked people to come forward and throw money inside. On that day they threw 30,000 Kenya shillings inside the vehicle. That was about 1500 US dollars at the time. They said that the treasurer had to get down under the seats and dig out every shilling and record how much had been given!

This is just one example of letting local imagination and creativity flow. It is the kind of creativity that inspires people to participate.

2. **Learn from the example of the Harambee.** Some years ago I had the privilege of attending a Kenyan *Harambee* to raise funds for a new church planting. Harambee is the East African custom of joining efforts to raise resources for a good cause. Sometimes they bring and sell produce; other times the women prepare a special meal for which people pay or give an offering. Of course, all proceeds go toward the cause. There can be plenty of good fun in the process. On this particular Sunday morning, following the morning worship service, they raised 490,000 Kenya shillings for the planting of a new congregation in a nearby community. According to the exchange rate at the time that was about 9,500 US dollars. It was truly a time of "hilarious" giving. (II Corinthians 9:7 in the King James Version says, "God loves a cheerful giver." The Greek translation of "cheerful" in that context is "hilarious.") What fun this event

turned out to be! There was nothing dull about being in church that Sunday morning.

It was obvious that the participating congregations that day had learned something of the joy of giving. They had unleashed their creativity and were doing something that had its roots in the local cultural tradition. I turned to my wife and said, "It doesn't look like these people are being forced to tithe." It was obvious they were not.

When the event was finished, I said to one of the church leaders: "I never saw so many people so happy and so broke (out of money) at the same time." He replied, "Don't be misled; they still had money left over, even after giving all of this." I learned an important lesson that day: I should not put in all my money the first time I was called upon to do so! They gave me three or four other opportunities to give, something that was expected of a visitor.

3. **Remember, there are two ways to balance a budget. One is to decrease expenses; the other is to increase income**. Sometimes one needs to do the first, and sometimes one needs to do the second. But there is something very important about decreasing expenses.

One of the things that carried over from the colonial period was the appearance that there is plenty of money if one just knows how to plead for it or wait for it. In fact, this points to one of the biggest problems in raising money among churches in Africa: the appearance of wealth. It **appears** that the church — through the mission — has so much that "my small amount" won't make any difference.

In the past, this happened because unseen sources of income provided things that the local people could not otherwise afford. Outside resources often provided vehicles, buildings, printing presses and even the pastor's salary. In order to convince local people that "this church is ours and can be supported with our income", some of those big expense items may have to be dispensed with – at least for a time. It may only be when expensive programs established by outsiders are cut back or discontinued that local people will get the message that "this church needs my tithes and offerings because we no longer receive funds from overseas."

When church leaders consciously cut out such expensive projects, they are sending a powerful message to their people: "We are only going to do what God will provide for us through our own resources." That message will eventually sink in — **if outsiders do not rush to the rescue!** And this is where outsiders will need wisdom and discernment.

Cutting expenses? Yes. But a second way to meet a budget is to increase income. There are creative ways to do that. I mentioned some of them in the section earlier on tithes and offerings. Remember also the negotiation between the treasurer and church members among Lutherans in Tanzania. Harambees, harvest offerings, offerings for the poor and thank offerings are all creative ways to increase income. [Unfortunately, there is the seemingly ever-present mentality that the easiest way to increase income is to ask for it from overseas.] When expenses have been brought into line, it is then reasonable to turn to those on the local scene and seek to increase local income. If the expenses are not first brought into line, securing increased income may be next to impossible.

I met a man in East Africa some time ago who told me that he believes it is possible to raise money in Africa. He believed this to such an extent that he said, "I am going to start a business of raising money for churches and other non profit NGO's in Africa." After doing this for a while, he came to this conclusion: "We have learned that money is available in Africa. We have proven that we can raise money here, but the problem we have is that 'other money' which is coming in from the outside. That money must stop if we are going to successfully raise money locally."

If what he says is true, then outside money is distorting reality. It makes people think that things are not as they really are. Large sums of outside money continue to make people think they are too poor to give anything meaningful to the Lord.

I heard a testimony a few weeks ago of a bishop in a diocese in East Africa who set about to secure overseas grants. For ten years he brought money into his diocese from the outside. Then one day he began to wonder what affect this might be having on his church. To learn the answer he set about to do some research. He surveyed the church members to see how much they were putting into the church collection NOW compared to what they had put in ten years before when the outside funding began to arrive. He came to the startling conclusion — which should not be surprising — that the grants coming in from the outside had lowered the level of local giving. The local church members simply came to depend on it. Where they had once been generous, they were now giving less. Conclusion? When seeking to increase income, do not let overseas funds distort reality.

What about church-run businesses?

In chapter one I showed the "box" being held up mainly by outside income with the smaller post of church offerings off to one side. One of the clever ways that money was brought into that big support post was through church-run businesses. Missionaries started literature projects, farms, community stores, schools, guesthouses, clinics and various other projects to get money to help hold up their box. In some cases, projects actually earned a substantial profit which was used for the work of the church. In many other cases, the projects lost money and needed subsidy from the church or mission.

Church-run businesses, whether they succeed or fail, can have the same effect. What do I mean by that? If church-run businesses succeed and earn a lot of money, local people may say, "This church doesn't need my money; let the church-run businesses provide it." And what happens when the businesses fail? Suppose a church-owned business runs a deficit and isn't able to balance its budget, then local people may rightly say, "Am I to give MY money to the church to cover the deficit of a poorly run church-owned business?" Therefore, I maintain that whether such businesses make money or lose money, there is a good possibility that church members will not be motivated to put money into the collection. What is the alternative? It is for the church to learn to exist on the income from tithes and offerings from dedicated believers, not from projects run by the church.

As I have said before, legitimate income for the church should be from the tithes and offerings of the members. It should come from the pockets, purses, bank accounts, cattle pens and fields of those who are blessed by God. That is legitimate income for God's work. Business income or overseas grants which take the place of tithes and offerings are illegitimate by comparison.

One church in Central Africa had a very profitable business. The business was putting hundreds of thousands of units of currency into the overall church budget each year. But then times changed, and profits began to dwindle. Unfortunately, by that time the church had come to depend on the income from their church-run business. Income kept on dropping, and soon the business began to run a deficit. Now the church found itself running a business which needed to be subsidized; so people were asked to put money in the church collection to pay the overdraft on a failing church-run business.

But there is more. Church-run businesses sometimes compete with private businesses owned by their own church members. Advantages enjoyed by the church or mission in transportation or overseas contacts for importing materials make it difficult for a small local businessperson to compete. Now the church-run business has become his biggest competitor. Now that the church-run business is losing money, is he as a church member expected to take tithes from HIS earnings to put into the church collection to cover losses of his competitor? It is not difficult to see how this can have a negative effect on business people who are members of the church. Churches simply should not find themselves in the position of competing with their own members. Also, bishops should not have to spend their time balancing budgets when they are called to do the work of ministry. Little wonder that such churches cannot reproduce themselves elsewhere!

Encouragement for Leaders facing Change

The following represent a few words of encouragement for leaders who are facing the change from dependency toward self-reliance.

1. **Remember that you are not the first one to face this need for change**. Others – in other places—have faced it and have been successful. Though it may seem like you are the only one

who has ever had to go through this, remember, it can be done under the leadership of the Holy Spirit. I suggest finding one or more church leaders from another denomination that has already broken its dependence on outside funding and seek to learn everything possible from them. Perhaps through such fellowship, the Lord will strengthen both you and them as together you face the process of change. Consider gathering a small group of church leaders from various denominations or agencies for group discussion and fellowship

2. **Pray for the guidance of the Holy Spirit in identifying the appropriate time for change.** Professor Tippett referred to this as the "appropriate psychological moment" for change. When that moment comes, be prepared to seize the opportunity and take advantage of it. "But," Dr. Tippett warned, "if that appropriate psychological moment is missed, then a long hard struggle may follow."

Some time ago I was asked to analyze the work of a certain mission society. The more I got into the project, the more I realized that there was something dynamic happening at that point among their people. Therefore, I went to their leadership and said, "You have some really interesting things happening here. You have several up and coming young leaders; they've got vision, they've got gifts and they are willing to work. I believe you have a window of opportunity in the next three to six months to do something unique in transferring your work to local ownership." I also said that if they missed that moment, there might be a long hard struggle in the future.

Unfortunately, they didn't take notice of what I was saying. I went back two years later and asked how things were going. The top leader in that mission said, "Glenn, we missed the appropriate moment for change, and now we are in the long hard struggle." Feelings of bitterness within the fellowship had replaced the youthful vigor and enthusiasm I had observed earlier. Pray that the Holy Spirit will reveal when that appropriate psychological moment arrives.

3. **Ask for divine guidance**. Through prayer, seek for a combination of humility, spiritual discernment and determination as you enter into the process. A leader promoting the transition to self-

reliance needs to walk humbly before the Lord. Find a healthy balance between humility and determination, both of which will be required. Seek for the leading of the Holy Spirit through concentrated prayer. This kind of venture is not to be done in human strength and wisdom alone.

Some time ago I read *Long Walk to Freedom*, the life story of Nelson Mandela. He led the anti-apartheid struggle in South Africa for many years. I was impressed with Mr. Mandela's ability to know when an issue was important enough to press forward—either with government officials or prison guards—and when an issue was <u>not</u> crucial and should not be pushed. He seemed to have an unusual sense of discernment in this regard. Sometimes I thought, as I read, why isn't he pushing **now** and on other occasions, why is he pushing **this time**? He somehow knew instinctively when to push and when to hold back. Knowing this difference is a unique gift. Ask the Holy Spirit for such discernment as you go through the process of change.

4. **Allow a reasonable time for change to take place**. Healthy change may take time to occur. Remember, however, that the time required for change is often shorter than many people may think. It doesn't need to take an extremely long time, especially if the appropriate psychological moment has come.

5. **Be sure to include both evangelism and missionary outreach in the new agenda.** Don't promote self-reliance in the work of the church just to maintain the status quo. Do it because of the importance of the Great Commission, remembering that is what the church is all about. Remember that just a better mode of survival is not enough.

Conclusion

These suggestions for church leaders facing the need for change are not exhaustive. This is partly because the situation is different in different places. However, I am convinced that the advantage belongs to those who humbly come before the Holy Spirit in concerted prayer. The price to be paid may include the **courage to change**. It may include asking for forgiveness. It will require bold new steps of faith into an unknown future. But remember, many new and fruitful ventures included that kind of stepping out into the unknown. I heartily encourage everyone to seek out like-minded people who can support each other in the process. Thankfully, in the Kingdom of God, it is not necessary to go it alone. That is what other brothers and sisters are for.

QUESTIONS FOR DISCUSSION
Chapter 7

1. *How important is the issue of motivation on the part of local church leaders when considering a move toward self-reliance?*

2. *How do you view the role of spiritual renewal in preparing for a transition toward self-reliance?*

3. *Discuss examples of how restructuring can or should take place.*

4. *How do you feel about closing down missionary-founded programs in order to cut expenses?*

5. *How do you feel about fetes, raffles, teas, etc., as a way to raise funds for the church?*

6. *"The initiative for change should be with the church, not the mission." Discuss the implications.*

7. *How big is the problem of a lack of integrity among church leaders today?*

8. *What would you say to church leaders or missionaries who fear the change that accompanies the move toward self-reliance?*

SUGGESTED READING

Jacobs, Donald R. *From Rubble to Rejoicing: A Study of Effective Christian Leadership Based on Nehemiah.* Pasadena: Wm. Carey Library, 1991.

Kaluzi, Jackson. *A Mission Strategy for Tanzania.* Unpublished thesis, Nantwich (England): Elim Bible College, 1995.

Mfwilwakanda, Nlongi. *Mandate for a Missionary Church in Africa.* Unpublished thesis. Ann Arbor: University Microfilms, 1982.

Schwartz, Glenn J. *Suggestions Regarding the Move from Dependence to Self-Reliance.* (Available on the worldwide web at www.wmausa. org.)

Nthamburi, Zablon. *From Mission to Church: A Handbook of Christianity in East Africa.* Nairobi: Uzima Press, 1991.

CHAPTER 8

MISCELLANEOUS ISSUES RELATED
TO DEPENDENCY AND SELF-RELIANCE

The following issues do not fit neatly into any of the previous chapters, but they are related to understanding issues of dependency.

Qualities of a Leader Committed to Change

What qualities should characterize a leader who is committed to change?

1. First of all, if we want to lead our churches through change, we must **be at peace with ourselves, and with God**. We must know that our personal past is totally under the blood of Christ and that things which happened to us before are not dominating us now. If one has been through disappointment, bereavement, heartache or a sinful episode in one's life, it is important to plead the blood of Christ and then let the past be the past. Thank God for the Gospel of Christ which includes the privilege of laying our past at the feet of Jesus. Unless one does that, so much of what happens in the present and the future will be affected by the unresolved past. Dealing with some of the things that happened in the past may be difficult, but being dominated by them is clearly not necessary. Thank God for the forgiveness that our Gospel represents. This provision of God's grace is for church leaders and all who seek to reach out in ministry to others.

2. **We must believe that our present calling of God is valid**. Our calling must be accepted as from the Lord. When that is settled, we can put the present and the future into God's hands. If we fear the future or do not recognize that it is in God's hands, then the challenge of promoting change is not for us. We must recognize that this job has come as an assignment from the Lord, and with God's help it can be carried out.

    This brings up the question of calling. Blessed is the person who knows that God has led them in the past and has called them to the task at hand. Unfortunately, not everyone has a clear word or calling from the Lord. But for those who do, they have something that will undergird them when the going gets difficult. What about those who have not had a dramatic "come over to Macedonia and help us" kind of experience? There are times when I have had to personally and literally take one step at a time in the fear of the Lord. How I longed for a visible sign from the Lord! But then I realized that my part is faithfulness before the Lord. His part is to lead; mine is to follow.

3. **We must be committed to "leading people", not just "fixing problems."** It is easy for all of us to fall into the trap of maintaining what already exists. When we do that we become a maintenance person simply trying to keep projects going. But when facing the need for change, real leadership has to do with deciding what things must be done and what things should be left undone. This requires a vision for the future. We cannot simply resign ourselves to maintaining what we have in the present.

4. **We must respect the need for change, but not fear it.** We all have different personality types. Some of us would naturally like to have everything "smooth and in a groove" all the time. The idea of calling for change is just not in our nature. Others of us look forward to new and different challenges. We thrive on things that are new and different. But, if we are called to lead our church through change, we cannot be satisfied with business as usual for the rest of our lives. Transition implies change; it brings new experiences. Yesterday's way of doing things will not be adequate for today and especially not for tomorrow. If a leader is afraid to think new thoughts, that is hardly a qualification for going through change.

5. **Those who are committed to change should be prepared to be criticized.** I have met church leaders who have made difficult decisions as they led their churches towards self-reliance. Some of them were misunderstood during the transition, and some are still misunderstood after many years, despite the many good things that have happened. It may be ten years or more before some leaders are appreciated for the courageous stand they took on some of the difficult issues. One church leader in East Africa is still being criticized thirty-five years later — in spite of

the fact that his church is healthy and growing and has taken many steps toward self-reliance. He knows that God gave him the vision, and he saw it come to pass. It takes a special portion of God's grace and no small amount of courage to lead people through change under such circumstances. But the need for change is as much a part of institutional growth and survival as the air we breathe.

6. **We may need to sacrifice personally.** It may be necessary to say "no thank you" to the outside money that has kept the system going and paid salaries in the past. When a church leader says "no thank you" to outside funding, and it is demonstrated that he is willing to sacrifice with his people, that has a powerful effect on the move toward self-reliance. Don't underestimate the power of a good example of personal sacrifice.

Some time ago a church leader in Central Africa told me his own story along this line. He said, "I needed income for my family and went to the chief and asked for some fields to plow. The chief gave me six acres, and I began plowing. While I was plowing, a villager came to me and said, 'Reverend, what are you doing? Why are you are working in this field? You are a man of God. You should be preaching the Gospel.'"

He told the villager, "I am working to supplement my income because the church offerings are not adequate, and I need school fees for the children. So the chief gave me this land."

"Pastor, you go and do God's work, and I will plow this field for you", the villager replied. So he did; and when harvest time came, he returned and helped the pastor with the harvest.

My pastor friend went on to say, "All of this happened because I was willing to go out and start plowing my own field." In this way he demonstrated a simple form of personal sacrifice. "I have a feeling", the pastor said, "that if those of us who are church leaders would be willing to do more of this kind of thing it would show that we don't have an unlimited amount of money from overseas. I believe our people would then be more willing to help us with the work at hand."

7. **A church leader committed to change should be humble when there is progress**. If God blesses a church with a genuine move toward independence or self-reliance, the glory belongs to the Lord. There will be times when failures, too, will need to be brought and laid at the foot of the cross. One will have to say to the Lord, "Lord, I didn't do well here; please cover for my failure. I wish I could have done better." If we are going to lay our failures at the foot of the cross, then we must be willing to also lay our successes there as well and give the glory to the Lord.

8. Leaders committed to change **must be people who can see the long-term picture.** As a leader, if I am greatly encouraged one day and then greatly discouraged the next day, that up and down existence will become emotionally draining. We must learn to focus on the long-term picture, accepting the fact that there will be good days, and there will be bad days. But the process of change is for the long term, and we must view it that way.

    Furthermore, short-term up's and down's should not be interpreted as long-term successes and failures. Serious problems of dependency were not created overnight, and they won't be solved overnight; but with God's help they CAN be solved.

9. Leaders committed to change **must have unquestioned personal integrity.** That means church and mission leaders must be honest, open people who live above a desire to commit sin in their daily lives. It is equally important that leaders surround themselves with people of integrity. Without that, our followers will judge us for the company we keep. Part of the responsibility of leaders with integrity is to be willing to confront those who work with us when their behavior is questionable. *The failure or inability to confront diminishes our ability to lead.*

10. **Leaders committed to change should be personally secure enough to employ others who are gifted.** It is a serious matter for a leader to sit on the top of an administrative pyramid and be so insecure that no one else can function, except to do only what they are told. In fact, a person committed to leading a church through change might need to do away with the pyramidal

structure itself. Unfortunately, missionaries often used the pyramidal system for their own benefit. Some of us sat on top of the pyramid and gave orders, expecting everyone to obey. Many who looked on saw it as a very arrogant thing to do. One alternative is to turn that pyramid over on its side and recruit people to work in a horizontal relationship. In such a system, leaders actively look for gifted people to come alongside them, to help accomplish the goals of the church or organization. If leaders can do this and not be threatened by gifted people, God can work through more than just the leader. He can work through many others in the Body of Christ.

11. **We must make sure that our agenda is God's agenda.** I have mentioned various times before that spiritual renewal needs to be at the heart of the process of change. This means making sure that personal gain does not take the highest priority in our lives. The kingdom of God is the goal, not building up "my" kingdom.

What are the long-term effects of foreign subsidy?

1. One of the ways foreign funding distorts reality is **that outsiders often set the agenda**. Outsiders who provide funding sometimes decide what can and can't be done because of what donors will think. Indeed, the donors and the outsiders may be one in the same. Therefore, one of the effects of long-term subsidy is that local people can't manage their own agenda.

   There is an English language proverb that says, "The one who pays the piper calls the tune." If someone is paying the musicians, he can decide what they sing; the same principle applies when outsiders attach conditions to the funding they provide.

2. **Progress is often determined by the availability of outside money.** Sometimes local church members conclude that those leaders funded by outsiders can do what they do because they get paid to do it. The agenda that God has for a group of local Christians should not be determined by whether someone overseas provides the resources for what is being done. Since overseas funding often comes with strings attached, **foreign-**

funded agendas are often **foreign-devised** agendas. Healthy churches do not let themselves be dominated in this way.

3. **Foreign-salaried local leaders are often not free to make decisions and to innovate.** Indeed, they may find themselves constantly looking over their shoulder at those who provide the funding. Out of respect for the donors — sometimes out of fear of losing their jobs — they have to do what the donors tell them to do. They can't innovate because many times innovation is considered to be suspicious activity.

It is sad to see local creativity diminished simply because outsiders are controlling the agenda. It was characteristic of the colonial period that many people lost the will or courage to be creative because outsiders were setting the agenda. How many good ideas were lost because there was no place for local ingenuity? One has only to look at churches like the Presbyterian Church in East Africa to see how creative local leaders can become when they are given the opportunity.

4. **Long-term subsidy affects both the *self-image* and *community image* of the church.** I once spoke with a woman from Uganda who told what it is like to be a church member in the part of Uganda from which she comes. She said, "Do you know what people think of us when we become church members? They say to us, 'Why do you join those Christians who are poor and beg for money from overseas? I don't want to do that.'" Comments like this give us an understanding of the *community image* of the church.

When people who are in the church don't feel good about themselves, that creates a *self-image* problem. A long-term effect of outside subsidy is that both the self-image and community image of the Church are affected.

5. **Local value systems may suffer from long-term subsidy.** Some time ago a man from Nigeria spoke about the problem of unhealthy dependency in his part of the world. Among other things, he said, "Someone needs to do research on the value systems of African people, to see what long-term damage has been created by the dependency syndrome." We would all benefit from analyzing how local value systems are affected by

long-term outside subsidy, especially when common Christian principles are not followed.

6.   Another problem with long-term subsidy is that **what looks like a short-term solution may turn into a long-term problem.** That is what happens when local people conclude, "If money is that easy to get overseas, why do we work so hard to get it locally?" When local people come to that conclusion, they are choosing a short-term solution with long-term consequences.

Why does Stewardship Teaching often Fail in Mission-Established Institutions?

1.   **The hearts of the church members may be cold.** This brings us back again to the matter of spiritual renewal. I once conducted a seminar in Lusaka, Zambia in which a pastor said, "What can I do in my church? I can't get the members to give. In fact, the people don't even know the Lord." My response was, "Are you expecting people who don't know the Lord to put money in the church collection?" It was clear that preaching the Gospel needed to precede stewardship teaching.

   What if they claim to be Christians but are not living a daily walk with the Lord? Again, if their hearts are cold, don't expect them to joyfully put money into the church collection. Sleeping Christians must be awakened first.

2.   **Outside funding creates the appearance of wealth.** I mentioned this point earlier. If it appears that church leaders have money coming from some unknown source – other than church offerings – church members might simply decide that the church does not need their meager gifts. They may be thinking, "What can my small offering do when you can get so much money elsewhere?" The remedy for such a situation is to prepare a budget in which the people are involved. They should know how much the budget is, and how all the money will be used. They should know that if they give, the budget can be reached and that outside money will not be an alternative. There is no way to estimate the amount of harm that comes from the simple fact that outside money is present and destroying local initiative.

3. **Stewardship teaching in mission-established churches often fails because of hidden income and hidden expenses.** This is often a direct carryover from the missionary period. During the missionary period, people often had no idea how much money was coming in or what it was being used for. They often saw new vehicles, new programs and buildings, buildings, buildings — all paid for with money from somewhere else. Assume for a moment that I am a local church member in Central Africa standing with my friend, and a big new mission lorry (truck) goes past. The dust is flying, and I turn to my friend and say, "What was that?" And he says, "That was the new mission truck."

I say, "Yes, but where is it going?"

"I don't know, but if you follow it you may get work."

"Who paid for it?"

"I don't know, but the mission always has money for things like that. None of us know where the money comes from; we just see the evidences of it. All we know is that church offerings could never pay for such a vehicle."

Hidden sources of income and hidden expenditures are a serious problem in mission-established churches. When so many things are done in secrecy, it affects the morale of local church members. No wonder stewardship teaching seems such a fruitless task.

4. **Stewardship teaching often fails because the project or the church is seen as belonging to someone else.** Why do some mission-established projects fall down in disrepair after missionaries leave? Could it be simply because local people don't believe those buildings belong to them? They may say, "Let the people who built them keep them going." This mentality prevails when people perceive the missionary or the pastor to be the real owner of a church: "Let him do it; it's HIS church." In some congregations members sit back and let a few wealthy members pay the expenses because the members perceive them to be the real owners of the church.

5. Unfortunately, **there is often inadequate training of treasurers.** It is clear that many churches could do with a combination of simple accounting procedures and genuine integrity. There is no excuse for poor accounting of what the Lord provides. Coupled with a lack of integrity, poor accountability will discourage giving. Those who receive and handle funds must be able to do it with integrity, efficiency and openness. If this is not done, the confidence of those who put money in the collection will be destroyed.

Why is there an urgency regarding the matter of dependency among mission-established churches?

1. An important reason to pay attention to the matter of dependency is that **churches and mission societies often experience broken relationships over money.** Sadly this sometimes results in Christians taking each other to court. It is not a good testimony before an unbelieving world when two parts of the Body of Christ are in court regarding money or other church and mission issues.

2. Another reason to pay attention to the problem of dependency is that **missionaries and mission executives sometimes do not know how to gracefully and effectively remove the scaffolding** used to build the building. This lack of knowledge or courage to deal with the problem means that someone must pay attention to the problem so that a healthy church will result. Otherwise, the crippled and dependent church will continue, and it will not be able to fulfill its role in society.

3. A third reason for urgency is that **paternalistic mission societies are an embarrassment in the Kingdom of God.** The world is watching, and the church or mission should not provide them with reasons to turn away from the Gospel. God wants his people to be fundamentally sound and attractive to a watching world, not continually putting unbelievers off through improper attitudes like paternalism.

4. A fourth reason to pay attention to dependency problems is that **discouraged church leaders go elsewhere for fellowship and employment** – perhaps for the wrong reasons. Maybe the ceiling is too low, as I mentioned earlier. Healthy churches have a better

opportunity to hold their leaders than unhealthy and dependent churches.

5. Another reason to deal with the problem of dependency is that **dependent churches often find they cannot reach their potential before the Lord.** First, members have not discovered the joy of supporting themselves and the work the Lord has given them. Second, they have not discovered the joy of reproducing themselves through cross-cultural evangelism and missionary outreach of their own.

6. A sixth reason to deal with dependency in the Christian movement especially in Africa is that **dependent churches run the risk of being tempted by funding from Muslim countries** (using petrodollars) — or others who are willing to support them. The best defense against encroaching Islam or other non-Christian movements is churches joyfully standing on their own two feet, not needing outside support. When it is discovered that those in dependent churches can be attracted with money or shipping containers, they may very well end up going to the highest bidder. It reflects what is wrong with our presentation of the Christian gospel when people go from one alliance to another in order to gain the outside support they are craving.

Why is the position of Treasurer often the last position to be filled by a local leader? The following are reasons often given.

1. "Local leaders do not trust each other."

2. "The system is too complex for local people to manage." (This is no credit to those who established it in the first place.)

3. "If a local treasurer is appointed, foreign funds will no longer be available to pay his or her salary."

4. "A foreign treasurer can best look out for the interest of overseas donors."

It should be clear that none of these reasons are valid in church-mission relationships, no matter how sincere the people are who create them.

It is not a sign of a mature church to hide behind the fact that leaders do not trust each other and that an outsider might just as well manage their financial affairs for them. It may take courage to break the pattern of foreign control through the use of funds, but the freedom that comes from standing on one's own two feet is worth the effort it takes.

Promoting Local Ownership

The following is a list of suggestions regarding how to promote that illusive thing I have been calling local psychological ownership. Everyone who has seen local ownership established will have ideas that could be added to the list. Hence, this is by no means complete. My list is in the form of a series of questions.

Why don't local people take responsibility for their church or other mission-established institution?

First, a feeling of ownership must precede responsibility. If there is no sense of ownership, don't expect people to excitedly make things happen. **Second**, programs could well be inappropriate and therefore local people do not have the desire or means to keep them going on local energy and resources. **Third**, sometimes programs begun by outsiders are simply too expensive for a local budget to carry. Outsiders would do well to remember from the beginning that locally sustainable projects will have a different financial structure from those which need a significant flow of outside funds when they are started.

What process leads to a transfer toward local ownership?

First, there must be a **conscious decision** to move toward local ownership. It doesn't work well simply to **slide** in this direction. Sliding might actually happen in the wrong direction. Indeed, there are examples of churches, previously independent, sliding in the direction of foreign support and losing the ground they had once gained — hence, the importance of making a conscious decision to move toward self-support and self-governance.

Second, allow a reasonable amount of time to make the transition toward self-reliance. Remember that the problems related to dependency were not created overnight, and they will most likely not be resolved. Having said that, *one should remember that the time* *required for the transfer to local ownership is often less then we think.* When psychological ownership changes, many other things can follow quickly. Without the change of psychological ownership, the process can be long, drawn out and may even fail. This points to the importance of the appropriate psychological moment for change to which I referred earlier.

Third, it is important to both **anticipate** change and also to **precipitate** it. Anticipating change means looking forward to the good things that will follow if change is pursued. Precipitating change means doing things to help make it happen. I have given a number of illustrations along this line earlier. Precipitating change means working for it and not against it. This requires people of vision who are not insecure. Being grounded in the Holy Spirit and confident in one's own future are two of the best ways for both church leaders and missionaries to prepare for change.

What dangers are to be avoided in the transfer to local ownership? **One** of the first dangers to be aware of is that all the positions might be filled with local people, but true local psychological ownership does not transfer. *One way to test this is to ask if leaders need to check with any outside person before a significant decision is made.* When such a situation prevails, local people may fill the positions, but the old paradigm is still in place.

A **second** danger is that control may be maintained by outside finances. Some people, missionaries among them, are born manipulators. They have learned many ways to get their agenda accomplished. They may even be such smooth operators that local leaders do not realize how much they are being controlled.

A **third** danger is that the freedom to make genuine local decisions will not pass to the new owners. People need to be free to decide and, sometimes, to fail. But giving them freedom means that they will also have the potential for great strides forward. We should all agree that there is risk involved; but without risk, there is little opportunity for true progress to be made.

Where is the money to do what God is asking us to do?

The question about where to find the money brings to mind something Professor Arthur Glasser used to say. When someone had a great idea he would respond with, "Don't forget that famous quote from Shakespeare's *Merchant of Venice*: 'But, where is the money?'" I believe the money to do what God is asking African and other Christians to do is in three places.

1. First, there is money **in the pockets of sleeping Christians.** Sleeping Christians are those who live below their privileges in the Lord. Perhaps they are Christians in name only. Some are following the Lord afar off. To be useful in God's kingdom, they must experience a spiritual awakening. Do not expect them to joyfully put tithes and offerings into the collection if they are not spiritually in tune with the Lord.

2. A second place to find resources is **in the pockets of non-believers.** Some time ago a pastor in the city of Lusaka asked me, "Do you remember a certain businessman?" When he mentioned his name, I said that I did remember him.

    The pastor went on to say, "For the past twenty years he was a businessman here in the city, but he wasn't following the Lord. He recently came to know the Lord through our congregation. After he accepted the Lord, in thanksgiving to God, he gave 100,000 Zambian kwacha to the church." (At that time, that was equal to about 2,500 US dollars.)

    I began to think about that event and asked myself: "Where did that 100,000 kwacha come from?" It was earned by a non-believer who confessed Christ as Savior and, in thanksgiving to God, gave that money to the church. Then I began to wonder how much more money is out there for the church if appropriate evangelism were done and people, in thanksgiving to God, were to turn resources over to the church. Please remember, no one should do evangelism to get money; that would be an improper motivation. But one of the results of effective evangelism **can be** mobilizing resources for the church from those who are recently converted.

3. **The money the church needs may be with the unemployed.** I've had pastors say to me, "Glenn, you don't know what it is like around here. In my church I have to help people. They can't pay MY salary; I have to give money to THEM because

they are so poor." My reply is rather startling: "Don't you realize that unemployed people can pay the pastor's salary?"

In chapters 1 and 2, I spoke about the Assemblies of God in South Africa. Remember the message God gave to Rev. Bhengu? "Teach them to make something with their hands, then teach them to give some of it back to God in thanksgiving?" *If the concept of Christian stewardship is built into the earning process, then the unemployed* **can** *learn how to help pay the pastor's salary.*

How does this process work? First, sit down and pray with someone who is unemployed. Begin by saying, "Let's pray that God will help you find employment; and when you are successful in finding a job, we must remember to say 'thank you' to God by giving something back to Him in thanks-giving." Could God be pleased if we ask and ask and then never show gratitude when He makes provision for us? Could a lack of gratitude be behind His slowness to provide for those who are in need? Obviously ingratitude is not the only reason, but God honors those who acknowledge Him and His provision for them.

A word of caution is in order. Development projects that help people become employed should also include a spiritual emphasis on Christian stewardship. If that does not happen, people might end up with more of this world's goods, but not be spiritually transformed. Our goal is not to make wealthier non-believers; it is to produce believers who acknowledge the role of Jehovah Jireh – their provider—in their lives.

A Successful Trust in East Africa

There is a story of a trust in East Africa that helped people become employed. Their slogan was "Don't be a beggar for employment. Be a creator of employment." At first thought that sounds impossible. How can I create employment for someone when I don't have a job myself? But their philosophy was simple: Create a job first for yourself and, when possible, create a job for someone else. Here is how it worked.

An unemployed person would approach the trust and ask to borrow money to begin a business. He or she would be told to prepare a business plan to show how the funds would be used. Someone could borrow enough money to buy a bicycle in order to deliver cut flowers to people in their homes. He borrowed the funds and then repaid his loan. If things were working well he could find a friend who needed employment and borrow enough to get the second bicycle for his friend. He soon paid off that loan and returned with a more ambitious idea. He asked if he could borrow enough to build a kiosk along the street in order to sell flowers to passing motorists. It was not long until he had created employment, not just for himself but also for someone else. During the early days of the trust they experienced a 90% loan repayment rate. Some schemes had repayment rates of 100%.

One interesting factor related to this particular trust is that local businessmen provided the funds being lent out. The funds were carefully managed because of the "ownership" which the local businessmen had in their project. After all, they were watching **their** money at work. The repayment rate of loans can be much lower when the bulk of the funding comes from outside. There are disaster stories of places where that has happened. One way to deal with this is: *Keep it small. Keep it local. And keep a watchful eye.* Revolving loan funds such as this are not guaranteed to succeed; but when properly managed, they have an enormous potential to do good.

Another Illustration from West Africa.

A church in Nigeria coupled stewardship teaching with the attempt to raise the local standard of living. Because it was done successfully, the church was the beneficiary. They referred to it as the "faith and farm principle." Improve the standard of living in a community, couple it with sound stewardship teaching, and church income increases.

How does the church gain access to local funding?

The following are intended to be practical suggestions for raising funds among mission-established churches. The list could easily be lengthened by the many successful experiences that church leaders have had far and wide. If you have something to share, find another church leader and let him or her know what you have learned. Now for a few suggestions from my experience:

1. Promote the concept of "ownership" before "stewardship"

2. Promote the full heart experience before teaching stewardship.

3. Emphasize the joy of giving, not just the law of tithing.

4. Emphasize "thanks" giving.

5. Don't underestimate local creativity.

    a. Remember the story of throwing money inside a vehicle that I told in chapter 7.

    b. In Tanzania a young man brought two chickens to church and dedicated them and their offspring to the Lord.

    c. In Kenya a congregation sold several heads of cabbage several times during a Harambee to raise funds for the church.

    d. In the city of Nairobi in an unfinished church building, each family took responsibility for a door or a window. Soon the entire church building was complete, while it had been sitting unfinished for several years prior to that time.

6. When teaching stewardship, remember the importance of training treasurers in issues of integrity.

7. In raising funds for the church, be careful to avoid the use of gimmicks which more often reflect the way the world operates. Don't rely on raffles, teas, games, fetes, etc. There is nothing wrong with church members enjoying themselves, but such things should never take the place of serious tithes and offerings.

8. Remind everyone that *everything we have comes from the Lord.* (1 Chronicles 29).

9. Remember that giving "in kind" (non-monetary gifts) is as important as giving money. Unfortunately many people

have the impression that money is all that can be put into a collection.

What sources of income hinder giving to the church?[1]

There are some practices which actually hinder giving to the church. Frequently these things represent a substitute for tithes and offerings.

1. Income from church-run businesses such as rental properties can have a negative effect on local giving. Think of it this way. If the church just had enough rental properties, no one would need to give their tithes and offerings. What kind of church would that end up being?

2. Avoid money gained from illegal sources – even in times of crisis. This would include using a church-owned vehicle as an illegal taxi, a common practice in some places. This violates God's laws and is a poor testimony to government officials and others. When that is done, church leaders should not expect to receive God's blessing.

3. Avoid private gifts to church leaders which are unknown to the members of the church.

4. Be wary of relief supplies that have the potential to ruin the value of locally grown products in the local market place.

5. Avoid securing a vehicle for church leaders through a development agency working in the area. The support of the church should be through tithes and offerings from the members.

What are the advantages of privately owned businesses and community-based projects?

What follows are a few suggestions regarding the benefits of individual, family or community ownership rather than ownership by the church.

---

[1] Further information on this and related issues will come up later in chapter 14.

1. Improved community income benefits all people, not just members of the church. With community-wide improvement in income it is less likely that people will join the church for the wrong motivation. A good example would be to make a clinic a community project rather than a church-owned project.

2. An advantage of a community-based project is that it can draw on the resources of wealthy non-believers to which the church does not have access. The project can still have a witness in the community if believers are involved. But it is possible to avoid the criticism that the church is in the project for the money.

3. The church thrives on giving from its members rather than church-run businesses. This frees the church to be the church and not to be consumed with profit and loss. Church leaders are free to concentrate on the spiritual ministry of the church.

4. The church avoids competing with business people, including their own members, who are expected to pay tithes and offerings to the church.

A Few Suggestions for Local Church Leaders Regarding the Transition Toward Local Ownership

1. Determine the need for the transfer under the direction of the Lord. Make sure the process is Holy Spirit-directed.

2. Meet with others to determine the seriousness of the desire for local ownership.

    •   For this you won't need expatriate permission. It may be your first sign of becoming independent.

    •   Be sure that mature leaders are present for the initial discussions.

    •   Remember that not all older church leaders will feel comfortable with the uncertainty that accompanies a move toward independence.

3. Strive for near total agreement.

- This is to ensure that the Body of Christ is not divided in the process.

- If general agreement is not evident, than "the appropriate psychological moment" may not have arrived.

- Remember that "timing" is more important than "time." I mean by that taking advantage of the right time, not taking a lot of time for the transition. In other words, strike when the iron is hot, as every blacksmith knows.

4. If general agreement is evident, then a timetable can be set up for the foreseeable future.

- This should mean that outside decision-making will no longer be the basis on which decisions are made.

- It is important not to be derailed by **indecision**.

5. Expect that difficulties will arise and that Satan will oppose the process.

- Satan is not keen on healthy churches standing on their own two feet, joyfully serving the Lord with all their hearts.

- Allow for the fact that local support may take some time. The old pattern of dependency may have been in place for a long time, and people might be comfortable with it.

- Pray earnestly for the Lord to remove any difficulties that may arise.

6. Avoid fearing too much what others will think — especially outsiders who were previously providing the funding.

- Expect that outside funding may be arbitrarily cut off. When outside funding is arbitrarily cut off, it is another example of an outside-imposed decision.

- It is better for local leaders to take the initiative and say "no thank you" to the funding from the outside that has kept the church dependent.

7. Encourage local creativity.

- Search for local solutions to local problems.

- Introduce new music from the hearts of the people.

- Find local ways of raising funds by looking at churches which are successfully funded with local income. (Independent churches can provide an inspiration here. Ask how they do it.)

8. Expect some feelings of insecurity.

- Remember, while the old system offered some security, our security should not be in earthly systems. It should be in the Lord.

Conclusion

This lesson is an attempt to introduce more practical suggestions about how to avoid or overcome the dependency syndrome. Those of us who work on these issues are sometimes accused of only pointing out the problems with unhealthy dependency. I trust by now that the reader will see that these last several chapters contain many positive suggestions that are useful in day-to-day ministry. Share what you have learned so that others will be encouraged and better able to do the work of the Lord.

QUESTIONS FOR DISCUSSION
Chapter 8

1. *How much control should Western donors exercise over the funds they send to mission-established churches?*

2. *"Ownership must precede stewardship?" Discuss the implications.*

3. *How serious is the problem of hidden sources of income?*

4. *"Local people don't trust each other." Is this a valid reason for having an outsider manage their money?*

5. *What steps will help to ensure that complete psychological ownership transfers?*

6. *What can missionaries do to show that they personally trust the Lord when it appears that they have unlimited access to funds?*

7. *"Sleeping Christians, non-believers and the unemployed all represent potential for giving to the church." Discuss the implications.*

8. *How important is "thanks" giving in your church?*

SUGGESTED READINGS

See suggested readings for Chapter 7.

CHAPTER 9

THREE THINGS OF IMPORTANCE
FOR MISSION-ESTABLISHED INSTITUTIONS

There are three things of importance for mission-established institutions: **1) spiritual renewal, 2) restructuring,** and **3) vision (or imagination).**

Spiritual Renewal

I begin with spiritual renewal because of its importance to the subject at hand. This is not a Biblical study on spiritual renewal. Biblical theologians will do a better job than I at explaining the truths of God's Word. But I will raise a few issues that show the importance of spiritual renewal *as it affects mission-established institutions.*

Two Ways that God's Work Gets Done

First, there are two ways in which God's work prospers. **One is by hard work,** diligent human effort, where we labor faithfully, doing the best we can—praying, working, and expecting God to bless our efforts. This represents the human effort we all put into serving the Lord. **The second way God's work prospers is by a widespread spiritual awakening** in which God's spirit moves among the people. This is the divine element which can make our human effort look small by comparison.

I once heard a pastor describe two different ways he prepares his sermons. He said, "There are times when I prepare a sermon and work very hard to get it all together. To get it just right may take all the time I have available for study without a moment to spare. But there are other times when it is like going to a waterfall and simply holding my bucket under the falling water. The water pours down, my bucket fills very quickly, and my sermon is soon ready." This describes the difference between the hard work approach—which for many of us is most of the time—and those special times when God's Spirit is released in an unusual way.

Dr. J. Edwin Orr, in his many books on revivals and awakenings, makes a distinction between two kinds of spiritual awakening. He writes about <u>revival</u> among "believers", and <u>spiritual awakening</u> among "non-believers." I will describe what he means by that distinction.

Those who have not known the Lord cannot be revived. Therefore, revival is for nominal believers, believers who know something of Christianity but may be living well below their privileges in the Lord. Spiritual awakening—which Dr. Orr sometimes refers to as " an awakening among the masses"—occurs when God's spirit moves among non-believers. During this time many become aware of their need for the Lord for the first time. We should pray earnestly for both of these to occur so that the Church will be revived, and the masses awakened.

The East African Revival

One of those times when God's spirit was released in Africa was during the East African Revival. About 1930 a missionary medical doctor by the name of Dr. Joe Church and an African colleague came together to pray for God's blessing and to ask forgiveness of one another. That was the beginning of a revival that has continued in one form or another until this day—more than seventy years later. Obviously this happened among believers, but it touched many unbelievers as well. This movement did much to strengthen the Church in East Africa. The East African Revival emphasized that brothers and sisters in the church were a family, just like the extended family in African society. They began to recognize each other by warmly greeting one another in the fellowship as brothers and sisters. They emphasized confession and repentance. Public repentance is how one prepared to come into the Revival fellowship. Without confession and repentance one would not feel at home in the "revival fellowship."

The Revival Brethren (as they are called in many places) spoke quite a lot about "walking in the light." Brothers and sisters would confront each other if they thought that someone was not walking in the light. They would say, "Now, brother, are you sincere about this? Are you sure that what you are doing is walking in the light of the Gospel? If not, let's sit down, talk and pray about this." They also spoke about the "warm heart" experience—taking the term from John Wesley's experience in which he said his heart was strangely warmed. The warm heart experience not only touched the lives of East African believers but also transformed the lives of missionaries as well. One missionary said that he went to East Africa, encountered the Revival Brethren, and found his own cold heart warmed by an encounter with the Holy Spirit.

One interesting aspect of this revival is the impact it had on believers in North America, England and Switzerland, among other places. For example, this movement particularly blessed the Mennonite Church in the USA. One of the benefits for the Mennonites was the recognition that the legalism in which some of them were involved could be given up in favor of freedom through the spirit of God. For further reading on this see A *Gentle Wind of God: The Influence of the East Africa Revival.* Details are in the bibliography.

The East African Revival also helped to prepare the way for restructuring the church — which I will describe later in this lesson. The testimony of some East African church leaders is, "Thank God for the revival, because it made the restructuring possible. We sat down to make decisions about the future of our church, and inevitably we would come to a difficult point. Some members or leaders would be resisting change, and others would be promoting it. We would look at each other and say, 'Brothers and sisters, we believe these steps are ordained of the Lord. Let's pray. The Holy Spirit will lead us through this process.'" In that way the process of restructuring the church was helped by the revival, and church leaders thanked God for it.

When the Impossible Becomes Possible

Spiritual renewal makes possible some things that were previously thought to be impossible. Sometimes there are enormous challenges to be overcome in the move toward self-reliance. Serious change will be needed, and perhaps humanly speaking it does not look like it can be done. But when God's Spirit goes before, and His Spirit takes up residence among the people, hearts are rightly aligned with Him and the rough places made plain. Things previously thought to be impossible suddenly become possible. Dead churches become living organisms. A church that has just been plodding along simply trying to maintain itself, suddenly finds God's spirit coming upon the people with a new spirit of excitement. Sermons take on a deeper meaning. People are transformed in their service to others. There is an increased flow of giving into the church, and there is a renewed concern for those who are unreached. This spirit of revival is characterized by the Scripture which says, "Not by might nor by power but by my Spirit, says the Lord" (Zechariah 4:6).

In conclusion, without spiritual renewal, restructuring and imagination may not be worth very much. Without spiritual renewal, restructuring and imagination become human efforts that may reorganize the church but leave it spiritually impoverished.

The Importance of Re-Structuring

Restructuring is the second important factor in this process of transitioning from dependency toward self-reliance.

Those familiar with the business world will realize that restructuring takes place constantly. Business people are continually evaluating where they are and what they are doing. Those that do not engage in regular restructuring often pass off the scene because they didn't keep abreast of the times. Business people make sure that the products they are creating are what people need and want. They continually try to find the most efficient and inexpensive way of making their products. Otherwise they will lose money and eventually go out of business, unable to compete in the marketplace.

Change also happens in the political world—sometimes violently, and not always easily. But those who work in the political world, and do it well, realize that they, too, must make adjustments from time to time. They cannot hold on to a political party with rules that were appropriate in the nineteenth century when we are now living in the twenty-first century. Sometimes plans are launched for a major reconstruction of a whole country. That is what happened in South Africa following the apartheid era. At other times there are just simple changes that need to be made in order for the country to keep abreast of what is going on around it.

When it comes to the church, leaders must also be prepared to make changes if they want to be here to serve in the future. Too often the church has had a tendency to lag behind the times and turn to tradition even when it is no longer a useful way of doing God's work in our day. For the church to remain abreast of the times, some of the leaders will need to become trailblazers, rather than drag their feet.

One thing that affects the relevance of the church is what is called *countervailing power*. This is the kind of power that ordinary people have who are not in any position of authority. It is the kind of power a young person has to embarrass his or her family by engaging in immoral activity. It is the kind of power which says, "I'll teach you a lesson my way."

Customers have *countervailing power* when it comes to which products they buy. Airlines know that people have a choice when it comes to flying. Therefore, they take seriously the countervailing power of their customers.

How does *countervailing power* affect the church? Since the church is a voluntary organization, those who attend can exercise their choice about where they want to be involved. Church leaders who find themselves losing members might need to deal with what is behind the countervailing power being exercised. In other words, keeping the structure and atmosphere up to date in the church is one of the ways to retain the attention of those who attend. A church can ignore how the people feel, but leaders must remember that their members have the power to go elsewhere. All of this adds to the importance of restructuring when the time is right for it.

Restructuring May Not be Easy

We should not assume that restructuring will be easy or cheap. In fact, restructuring might not be the cheapest way to go forward, and it might not be a guarantee of success. But everyone should be *prepared to pay the price* for restructuring so that their church remains on the cutting edge of what God wants done in the world.

Restructuring should, in terms of dependency and self-reliance, include a new way of decision-making. Churches that attempt to come into today's world and hold on to the old way of decision-making most likely will not make a healthy transition. Without a new way of making decisions they might even fall back into old patterns. Some may even allow outsiders to continue to make decisions for them because it is the path of least resistance. After all, if someone else makes the decisions, they must also bear the responsibility. If outsiders continue to make decisions — particularly decisions related to funding – that may need to be openly confronted if true restructuring is to take place. If it is not acknowledged and dealt with, church leaders will be constantly looking over their shoulders to see whether they have the approval of those providing the funding. That's why I suggest, as I have in a previous lesson, that those who represent outside resources should absent themselves from local business meetings when decisions are being made.

Restructuring is necessary because old structures may be not only inappropriate for today but too expensive to maintain. Finding the **courage** to deal with expensive structures may be one of the most important steps to take in the restructuring process.

The **freedom** to restructure is a sign that independence is on its way. If church leaders are still bound to those who provide funding and who continue to make decisions for them, it is a sign that the dependency syndrome still has a strong foothold. True ownership occurs when local churches are free to make decisions on their own.

Without restructuring, well-meaning church leaders with spiritual integrity find themselves trying to manage unmanageable organizations. However, **with** restructuring, unmanageable elements can be dealt with; and, under the Holy Spirit's direction, progress can be made. If restructuring does not happen, things can go from bad to worse. Those with the money from the outside may then feel they need to step back in and take control.

What Happens when Restructuring Fails or is Delayed?

1. **There is an enormous waste of human and financial resources — as well as spiritual resources**. The time and effort of church leaders will be given to solving problems that the church shouldn't even have – such as poorly run businesses which I mentioned previously. Such businesses can become a burden which ought to be set aside, given to someone else, or closed down, in order to stop the enormous waste of human and financial resources.

2. A second thing that happens when restructuring fails is **that good leaders sometimes go elsewhere.** Earlier I mentioned African Independent Churches which were established by leaders from mission-established churches who left in frustration. Sometimes those were the very people that mission-established churches needed. Sometimes good people became so frustrated by an un-restructured church that they went into civil service or government positions. Their attitude toward the church may not have been positive because they became victims of an inappropriate structure that leaders were holding on to far too long.

Sometimes an unrestructured church causes a schism or division. Recently I was in Central Africa where I began to hear noises of dissatisfaction among the believers in one of the churches. When I was asked what was happening, I was told, "People can't tolerate the present structure of the church and the way things are being done, so they are taking signatures for a new church." Within a few days they had collected many signatures for the formation of a new independent church, and two denominations resulted. This did not signify church growth as one church became smaller as another gained members.

3. Another thing that happens when restructuring is delayed is that **church and mission goals are not met.** I come back to this theme again and again. If Christians in Africa and elsewhere are going to become a missionary-sending church and fulfill their role in world evangelization, restructuring **must** be done. How else will the church in Africa join the globally expanding movement of getting the Gospel to those still unreached and living in the 10/40 window? If restructuring isn't done, the goal of mission, as set forth by our Lord in the Great Commission, will not be accomplished. If that happens, many African believers will never discover the joy of being part of a globally expanding non-western missionary movement.

4. **Both the self-image and community image of the church will suffer if restructuring does not take place.** I have dealt with the importance of these two concepts previously. But it bears repeating — healthy churches have a good feeling about themselves and the community looks upon them favorably. Without restructuring, the millstones to which churches are

tied distort how they feel about themselves and how others view them.

5. Another thing that happens when restructuring is delayed is that **the church consumes all of its resources on itself.** When that happens, there is nothing left over to give toward others in need. In fact, because of the enormous burden and the weight of the structure of the church, it not only means that the church does not have anything to give away; it often does not even have enough to keep itself going! If restructuring does not take place, dependency for mere survival continues. The result is that local church leaders continue to ask for outside assistance.

Sometime ago I met a church leader who confided in me, "Our church is in trouble. We are running deficits. Can you go overseas and find money to help our church?" As I began to think about the weight of "the box" that his church was trying to carry, I became convinced that it was not God's plan that mission churches should always be dependent on assistance from overseas. In this particular church, if restructuring were to take place, the things that are such a heavy burden could be set aside, and the church would be able to be the church. Unfortunately, that church leader is in a church in Central Africa that has a very large un-restructured "box." Needless to say, they are still getting help from overseas after being in existence for more than a hundred years.

The Importance of Vision and Imagination

In Proverbs 29:18 we read: "Without vision, people perish." The kind of vision about which I am speaking says, "God has given us a burden for the future. God has given us a burden for our own unreached people as well as for people in other parts of the world." This is the kind of vision the Lord gave the church in China to carry the Gospel back to Jerusalem.[1]

---

[1] If you haven't done so, get hold of the book entitled Back to Jerusalem. It is the testimony and vision of church leaders in China as told to author Paul Hattaway. They have a burden for carrying the Gospel all the way back to Jerusalem. Details are in the Bibliography.

But there is also another kind of vision and imagination, and that is the kind which makes change possible. This kind makes it possible to think new thoughts and create new ideas.

1. One of the tragedies of the colonial period was that **local imagination was not encouraged, appreciated or rewarded.** Local people who had good ideas were often told, "Now you be careful; we don't do it that way. You sit back and listen." In this way, God-given initiative was often destroyed. As a result local people began to believe that their ideas were of little value. Imagine outsiders giving the impression that they had so many good ideas, while local people were given the feeling that they had none! Little wonder that unhealthy dependency developed.

2. **Where churches have been turned around, local creativity exists in abundance.** Creative people do not wait for someone else to think for them. Their own ingenuity may get them into trouble from time to time, but they do not wait for someone else to do their thinking for them. They put into practice what God tells them, using their own vision and imagination. Some creativity leads to apostasy while others grow strong and large. Take, for example, the Kimbanguist Church with several million believers in Central Africa. It is an independent church in which people set aside the outside constraints and let their imagination flow. Is this a perfect church? No. Does it have problems? Yes. But, has it made progress toward independence and standing on its own two feet? It certainly has. For most of us living and working with mission-established churches the question is whether we encourage or deny local creativity. Local imagination is the key element in discovering and promoting indigenous practices such as local forms of music and fresh new ways of increasing tithes and offerings, etc.

    Sadly, during the colonial period, there wasn't a felt need for local creativity because so many ideas kept coming from the outside that local people simply tried to keep up with all that was going on. They didn't need to have ideas. Their music came from the outside, church structure was often "imported", and vehicles and many other things flooded onto the scene. People were in awe of everything that happened, and there was little or no need to be creative regarding local ideas or resources. A local expression we often heard among the Amandebele people was *Amakiwe! Amakiwe!* This was the word for a white person, used when local people were amazed at some new innovation white people brought from the outside.

Sometimes missionaries would do well to sit back and do nothing—not even hinting that there is an alternate solution to a problem. The purpose would be to allow local creativity to flow.

One church in Central Africa had a hymnbook with two hundred hymns and gospel songs. A hundred and eighty-four were clearly western hymn tunes. The other sixteen were marginally western. There was not one song in the book written by a local person about which one could say, "This is an indigenous text with indigenous music." Indigenous music appears when there is a spirit of freedom —coupled with local creativity.

3. **Not every new local idea will work, but imagination is the fuel which keeps the process going.** There will be trial and error; some things will work, and some will not. But without the freedom to try new things, local church leaders and their members will never know what contribution they have to make to the wider Christian movement.

4. **Imagination and inspiration help to make restructuring possible.** When people are free to think of new ways of doing the work of the church, restructuring becomes possible. If local inspiration and imagination are quashed every time a good idea comes up, the trial and error period may never come about—and restructuring may never happen. But when these two—imagination and inspiration—are coupled with spiritual renewal, the potential for change is enormous! Things can happen which were assumed in the past to be impossible.

5. **Courage is an important part of developing vision.** Add courage to inspiration and vision, and the church's prophetic role can become effective in society. Finding the vision and imagination to devise a message which not just the **community** but, in some societies, the **government** should also hear, takes courage. It takes courage for someone to stand up and say, "This is the word of the Lord." If that word is from the Lord,

God will bless it. So coupling courage with imagination and vision is the process that leads churches to healthy change. Sometimes courage will need to be coupled with a willingness to be misunderstood.

The Church's Prophetic Role in Society

A few comments are in order regarding why church leaders sometimes find it difficult to have a prophetic role in their communities or to the government where they live. I offer a few observations.

1. **Church leaders may suffer from a sense of inferiority that takes the cutting edge off of their public witness.** This happens especially when they are embarrassed about their church. Perhaps they don't have a healthy self-image. Their feelings of inferiority prevent them from speaking out with boldness to their society.

2. **They may lack imagination regarding how to present a prophetic message to those who need it.** Perhaps they don't know how to get into government circles. Perhaps during the missionary period, there was no demonstration of how to prophetically speak to government. Perhaps someone should convene a "school of the prophets" in which we can learn from each other how to conduct an effective prophetic ministry.

3. Because of the need for spiritual renewal, **church leaders may have no spiritual base from which to speak to the larger community of which they are part.** This is a spiritual battle, and both spiritual weapons and spiritual strength are required for it. If we are to minister to the wider world, including government and community leaders, we will need to do so from a strong spiritual foundation.

4. **Sometimes church leaders have compromised their principles and — because that is known — they are not in position to prophetically instruct others.** When this happens, the cutting edge of prophetic ministry is gone. For example, ministry can be compromised by getting money illegally, and those to whom they try to minister know that church leaders are living below God's standard. The same is true of missionaries who

compromise God's principles. We should all pray that church leaders and missionaries will see the importance of integrity in all they do, so that the cutting edge is not taken off of their prophetic ministry.

Conclusion

Spiritual renewal, restructuring and spirit-filled imagination are a powerful combination. These three will bring healthy change to churches that have too long been paralyzed by dependency, carnality or apathy.

QUESTIONS FOR DISCUSSION
Chapter 9

1. *Is your church in need of spiritual renewal? What would be necessary for this to happen?*

2. *What are the strengths and weaknesses of revival movements such as the East African Revival?*

3. *Give some examples of local vision, imagination or creativity with which you are familiar.*

4. *How can your church have an effective prophetic ministry to society? To government?*

5. *Give examples of how compromising principles hinders the witness of church leaders.*

SUGGESTED READING

Allen, Roland. *Missionary Principles*. Grand Rapids: Wm B. Eerdmans, 1964.

Hattaway, Paul. *Back to Jerusalem: Three Chinese House Church Leaders Share their Vision to Complete the Great Commission*. Waynesboro: Gabriel Publishing, 2003

Sanders, J. Oswald. *Spiritual Leadership*. Chicago: Moody Press, 1967.

CHAPTER 10

ISSUES OF DEPENDENCY
AMONG THE POOR AND UNEMPLOYED

I am frequently asked two important questions regarding dependency and self-reliance in Africa. One comes from people who have excess spendable income and want to know how to give it away responsibly. I dealt with that in chapter 4. The second question often asked is this: "But what about the poor? Are we not supposed to help the poor?" In this lesson I will seek to deal with issues of dependency among the poor and unemployed.

A Personal Statement about Helping those in Need

I have a personal involvement in this issue because over the years I have been sympathetic to the poor and have tried to help when God brought them to my attention. I acknowledge that it is not always easy to decide which requests I should respond to. To illustrate my dilemma, while in the process of preparing these lessons, I received a letter from a church in the southern part of Africa that was suffering from a natural disaster. They had suffered drought for three years in a row; then when the rains finally came – in downpours – houses made of poles and dried mud began to disintegrate. Some lived in houses made of sun burnt bricks rather than kiln dried bricks. In either case they were vulnerable to heavy rain.

I agonized over what I should do with this request for help. After thinking it over for some time, I needed to come to a decision. I actually got to the point where I could not continue preparing these lessons until I resolved in my mind whether I should help and, if so, *how* I should help. God led me through this process, and I actually sent a contribution for those who were suffering under those circumstances. But, I sent it to the church rather than to the individual who was making the request.

Just because I promote local sustainability for churches in Africa does not mean that I am unmindful of the needs of the poor. We must not be without compassion. Jesus spoke some of His harshest criticism against those who offended the poor, and I do not want to give the impression that I am opposed to helping the poor. As I will show later on, what we are talking about here are dependent churches in a part of Africa which aren't necessarily poor. We must find ways to help that do not leave people less motivated to help themselves than before the assistance was given.

A Brief Look at Scripture

What does the Bible have to say about helping the poor? Both the Old and New Testaments have a lot to say about helping those who are in need. It was a theme in Jesus' teaching. In the Old Testament, there were carefully prescribed laws given to the people of Israel regarding the poor. Under Old Testament law there were several levels of tithing involving such things as first fruits and percentages of income. We are familiar with the first tithe, normally considered to be 10% of one's income. However, there were actually several more levels of tithing.[1]

The Old Testament system included not only supporting the priests (Levites) but also caring for the poor. In other words, those disadvantaged in society were cared for by a system of giving money to God—through the priests—which was then made available to those in need. There were other rules built into the system, such as leaving food for those who gleaned in the fields following a harvest. A farmer was not supposed to take every last thing out of his field but was to leave some for the poor.

The concept of jubilee, as commanded by Yahweh, was also built into the Law. This brought about a "leveling" in society every fifty years. It was a mandatory redistribution of wealth. Over the years, an economic pyramid would grow up in society, with the wealthiest people at the top. Jubilee meant that the pyramid was regularly brought down and leveled out. In this process, servants were freed, land was returned to its owners, and debts were forgiven.

Someone has said that the bankruptcy law in our current society is one of the most humane laws we have because it gives a chance for

---

[1] The Old Testament records two tithes in addition to the main tithe mentioned in Leviticus 27:20. One tithe came to Jerusalem three times a year during a time of fellowship. Another was almsgiving for the poor and needy. Deuteronomy 12:6 shows the number of ways that gifts were given: "... bring your burnt offerings and sacrifices, your tithes and special gifts, what you have vowed to give and your freewill offerings, and the firstborn of your herds and flocks."

a person to start over. Of course, there are people who abuse the bankruptcy law and sometimes additional safeguards need to be put into place as was done in the USA recently. But the original purpose of bankruptcy was similar to the jubilee concept of forgiving debts and giving people a second chance. Obviously, not everyone will agree with what I am saying about bankruptcy laws. But this is one way some communities seek to deal with those in financial difficulty.

An interesting proposal began circulating around the time of the new millennium regarding third world debt. The idea was that perhaps by the year 2000 there should be a general forgiveness of third world debt. And since then some debts *have* been forgiven. We should all pray that there will be some resolution of this massive problem because many people in various parts of the world are poor because of their country's external debt. Governments spend what money they have on repaying loans and interest rather than on re-building their economies and infrastructure.

So what about forgiving international debt? If done appropriately, it could help those who are poor. However, my concern is that unless appropriate steps are taken—following the forgiveness of such debt—the problem may re-occur. Unless old patterns of paternalism, dependency, mismanagement and corruption are dealt with, the cycle of debt will simply be repeated.

The Concept of the Poor in the New Testament

The term "the poor" or "poor people" is used about 40 times throughout the New Testament. Jesus commanded us to help the poor. He said in Matt. 19:11, "to be perfect" or to "have treasure in Heaven" (Mark 10:21 & Luke 18:22), sell all that you have and give to the poor. In some parts of the New Testament the term "poor" is used in relation to "poor in spirit." This is not a place to go into the different ways the term is used. For those who are interested, I suggest the recent work done by Dr. Christopher Little entitled *Mission in the Way of Paul*.[2]

"Selling all we have and giving it to the poor" may not sound like an appropriate emphasis for lessons on self-reliance unless you

---

[2] This was produced as a dissertation at the Fuller School of World Mission and has been published by Peter Lang Publishers. Details are in the bibliography.

make the distinction which I made earlier: that many churches in Africa are not poor but simply **dependent**. In the churches that I am primarily concerned about, there are often wealthy members. Some own two homes—one in town and one in the rural village. Some of the members own motorcars, have good jobs with government or business. Some own televisions and satellite dishes and an increasing number have cell-phones. Yet people in such churches sometimes allow outsiders to pay their pastor or build their church buildings for them. Clearly such people are living below their privileges in the Lord regarding how much they have to give to the Church.

It happens in Africa when people "confess poverty"—a term one hears when traveling throughout the area. Confessing poverty simply means that people are saying, "We are poor, that's the way we are, and we will probably always be that way." Those who confess poverty but have resources which they could be giving back to God are part of the dependency syndrome.

What about the Widow's Mite?

The biblical story of the widow's mite is one of the justifications some have used for not putting much money into the collection. They say, "That woman was justified, and she put in only two coins." However, we should remember that she was actually the heroine of the story because **out of her poverty** she gave something – from the last that she had. The villains in that story were the people who had much more to give but didn't put it into the collection. The widow, out of her poverty, gave sacrificially. In other words, God honors the person who is poor and still remembers to give something back to Him.

A Handful of Rice

There is a story about the missionary outreach of the church in Myanmar (Burma) in which each family set aside a handful of rice at mealtime. That rice was collected, sold and the proceeds used to send the Gospel elsewhere. That was how they financed missionary outreach! Though it was not a wealthy church, they discovered something about setting aside a portion of what God had given to them. This story comes from those with very few possessions by western standards, yet they found that they could set aside something for the Lord's work.

So we must conclude that, in this matter of self-reliance, even the poor often have something they can give back to God. And we should not underestimate how God can use, bless and multiply the little that the poor give back to Him. One church leader in East Africa said, "If you give nothing to God, He can multiply it, but it will still be nothing."

So then, how does one help the poor? Especially, how does one help without creating the problem of dependency?

What about those who live in Absolute Poverty[3]

The first and most important thing to remember is this: **if people will not survive without outside assistance, then someone must help.** Someone must show godly compassion toward them. Who are those who need that kind of help? They are refugees from war and political upheaval and victims of natural disasters such as hurricanes, floods, famines and epidemics. They must all be helped. But great care — I must add — should be exercised regarding **how** to help. Even in devastating situations it is possible to destroy the initiative of the people that we are trying to help.

As I mentioned earlier, following the war in Indo-China in which pastors' homes were destroyed, well-meaning missionaries wanted to help then rebuild. However, the people said, "No, let us rebuild our own pastors' houses; it is our privilege to rebuild them ourselves." It would have been possible, through compassion, to enter into that situation and do for them what they really wanted to do for themselves. In the process outsiders would have had a negative impact on their self-respect.

There is a book written about the concept of compassion in North America. It's called *The Tragedy of American Compassion*. According to the author, Marvin Olaski, the tragedy of American compassion is that we assume too much regarding how to help the poor. He makes the point that our desire to give sometimes overshadows

---

[3] For a more in-depth treatment of this subject turn to Chapter 20. I have titled it *Searching for Meaningful Ways to Help the Poor*

legitimate concerns about the best way to help people stand on their own two feet and move out of what he calls pauperism. His conclusion is that an overemphasis on giving to people who should stand on their own two feet moves them from a state of minor dependency to major pauperism. Various instances are cited in this book.

There are two important questions to be asked when helping the poor.

- What is the best way to help?

- Where should that help come from?

Any practice that robs the dignity of those already humiliated by need should be avoided. Any gifts that adversely affect local commodity pricing or do damage to the local infrastructure should be avoided.

Sometime ago I learned about those who were ministering among Rwandan refugees in Zaire. Because of the large number of people fleeing into Zaire, aid organizations arrived on the scene one after another. As those organizations were trying to do their work, they went out to buy firewood, and found themselves paying eight times as much for a bundle of firewood as the local market would normally bear. When they paid eight times as much for the firewood they were buying, imagine what was happening to local people who also needed firewood. Local people suddenly had to pay eight times as much, which put the price of firewood out of reach for many.

Aid organizations ought to look seriously at any practice which distorts reality and makes it impossible for those who live on the scene to cope. When this happens, one could use Marvin Olasky's term "the tragedy of compassion."

There is an interesting concept in development circles that, even among the poor, it is appropriate in some circumstances to set a "social price" (a token amount) for what people need. In other words, giving things to refugees absolutely free, requiring nothing in return—unless they have absolutely nothing —can rob them of their dignity and self-respect. They might be able to exchange work for food, for example, though some of these programs do not build long-term stability and growth into the community. We should not underestimate what refugees might be able to do for themselves.

A few years ago, efforts were made to help Mozambican refugees pouring across the border into southeastern Zimbabwe. I discovered, in listening to stories about that situation, that there were some very enterprising refugees among them who were not only able to survive, but were able to begin businesses in the refugee camps for the benefit of themselves and others. It would be a tragedy to replace that kind of creative enthusiasm with outside resources that made their business impossible. It is another reminder that we should not underestimate what some refugees are capable of doing for themselves.

The Principle of Geographical Proximity

What is the best source of help for those in need? I will now describe what I refer to as the principle of "geographical proximity." I use the following diagram to illustrate what I mean.

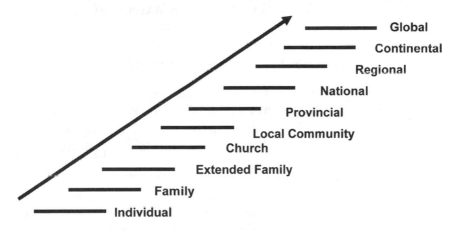

How does my diagram work? If I as an individual have a minor problem, I can usually handle it myself. I should not expect others to put on my shoes if I can do it for myself. However, if I break my ankle, then I will need the help of my immediate family. If my problem is more serious, we may need to ask the extended family to assist. When the extended family is unable to cope, we may turn to the church and they will provide meals or some other assistance needed. Sometimes in the wake of a disaster the entire community might show up to help us get back on our feet. This happens when there is a tornado or hurricane. If our whole province or state needs help, the region might come to help us. When the region is in distress other parts of the nation might be called upon. So it goes with the region of a continent, the continent itself and eventually the global community, as a last resort.

What sometimes happens is that global resources are mobilized to assist with needs far down this scale. For example, child sponsorship programs are global resources helping with an individual need. Going back to my earlier statement that in situations of real need where someone must provide assistance, care must be taken that other resources in between are not bypassed in favor of the global resources that westerners often provide. As one aid worker in South Africa said, child sponsorship from overseas is taking the place of what families are supposed to be doing for their children. For further information on this, see chapter 24 which I have entitled *AIDS and Orphanages in Africa*.

Let's look at an example of how my scale of geographical proximity works. A few years ago a church in Zambia collected a planeload of relief supplies for those who were suffering in Southern Sudan. When the Rwandan refugee crisis occurred in the 1990s a church in South Africa collected goods to be sent to Rwandan refugees.

These illustrations represent *regional* solutions to *regional* problems. I suggest that the ideal is for local needs to be met with resources that are closest at hand. The problem occurs when *global* resources are used to meet needs that could or should be met with *local* resources. When we do that, we risk destroying local initiative.

When local resources are used to meet local needs, the blessing derived from helping others stays in the local community. When one part of a nation helps other parts of their nation, the blessing stays within that nation. Likewise, when one part of a continent helps another part of the continent, the blessing stays within the continent. But consider what happens when global resources are used to meet local needs. The blessing goes to those on the global scene who may get a very good feeling from giving—but it just may be at the expense of those who could meet the need from resources closer by. Unfortunately, sometimes the global sources are used because of excesses in western countries that farmers want to get rid of.

In 1984, the country of Zambia experienced the worst drought in its history up to that date. A member of cabinet in the Zambian government told me that, during that year, the country as a whole still produced more food than it needed. The Southern Province had a severe drought resulting in a food shortage. The Northern and Eastern Provinces had more grain than they could use or sell. The problem was distribution and storage; but the nation **did** have the resources. Anyone who wanted to help in that situation would not seek to import maize into the country, but rather to do something to store and distribute what the rest of the country already produced.

Unfortunately, it is sometimes easier simply to obtain outside food-aid. That is a short-term solution that might prove counterproductive in the long run. Think of the blessing that could have gone to another province if Zambian resources had been used. Sadly, sometimes the rationale for providing outside food aid includes helping the farmers in the west who have produced an abundance they cannot otherwise sell. Think about that as a motivation!

A Sad Story from an Aid Worker

Sometime ago I met a man who was working in an aid agency in Southern Africa. As we sat and talked he told me the following story. "I am a pastor in a local church, and I took this position with an aid organization to help meet the needs of those who are suffering in the villages. [The aid agency was helping villagers with contributions of food because of shortages due to drought.] When I joined this organization", he said, "the first question I asked was, 'How much do you expect me and my people here in this city to give toward meeting the needs of the people who are suffering because of the drought in the villages?'"

In response to his question, those in the aid organization replied, "We are not really expecting you to do anything because we have ten thousand US dollars a month coming in from overseas which we **must** give away. If we don't give it away, we won't get our allotment next month. So we have this quota that is given to us, and we must distribute it." (This is a good example of global resources being used to meet a local need.)

The pastor went on to say, "You realize that those living in the villages are our relatives. They are our fathers, mothers, aunts and uncles and so on. It is the responsibility of those of us in the urban area to meet the needs of those who live in the villages if we are able to do so. We should be the first who are asked to help. If we don't have enough, then someone else can help; but as long as we **can** give toward those needs, we are the first who **should** be asked."

Consider for a moment the two different sources of help that were available. One is the local response that says, "We can do it, and we should do it. We should be the first to be asked because the people in need are our relatives." The other is an outside quota that must be given away or "we won't get it next month."

Sadly, the pastor went on to say, "I have given up. I have decided to look at this simply as a job to get money, because they did not accept my offer to help. Since I am not being listened to, I have decided to go on for further studies, so I am looking at this simply as a way to earn money for my studies." He gave up trying to compete with the quota system.

Consider for a moment what happened in the heart of that pastor when he ran headlong into the quota system. He lost the argument and decided just to consider his work as "a job." Think it through, and you will begin to gain some appreciation of why the dependency problem is so severe and so widespread in many parts of the world. *I maintain that the initiative that died within that pastor on that occasion is what Africa desperately needs in so many places today.*

Grants versus Loans

The following is a quote from a development officer in India who had this to say about grants versus loans:

> *The moment that you tell someone you are giving money to them free because they are a failure in life and you don't think they can repay it, you affect their motivation to return it.*[4]

---

[4] From an interview in TEAR Fund magazine *Footsteps* Issue 26, March 1996, page 16 by authors Rajan Samuel and Mathew Titus.

In other words, what is communicated through the grant is this: "You are poor, you can't help yourself. Here, have this handout." And what is communicated when someone is given a loan is: "We realize you have a temporary problem. But we would like to help you get on your feet; and when you are, if you could return this, two things will happen. First, your self-respect will be retained, and, second, what is repaid will be available for someone else to use."

On the more cynical side, consider this quote from TIME Magazine:

> *Developing countries which develop spoil the mission of the self-appointed First World shepherds who look upon the Third World as their flock. For them to play savior there must be someone to be saved . . .* [5]

Consider the following statement by an Indian development worker describing the value of loans versus grants:

> *Because of my previous experiences as a development practitioner, I felt that the donor agency was being foolish when it insisted on making a grant rather than a loan, to the project. Since the potato project was about adding value to the crop, it had the obvious potential for making money. Therefore, the farmer-beneficiaries could be asked to repay the initial investment. The primary beneficiaries were not starving paupers but landowners (the landless laborers were only the secondary beneficiaries). They did not need handouts. Also, they would work much more diligently if they knew that they would be well rewarded if the project succeeded, but would go into debt if the project failed. Because of this, the money to finance the drying units should come as a loan, and not as a grant. For one thing, a grant would make the beneficiary careless, since their own money would not be at stake. It would not matter to them if the project failed. Another factor was that working with the local (nationalized) banks would provide the structure and the authority to ensure repayment of*

---

[5] See TIME Magazine, December 4, 1995, page 108.

the loans. This was something a [donor] . . . agency could
not do.[6]

Conclusion

This is a very quick treatment of how to help the poor, and nothing
has been said about how to help the unemployed. For a more
in-depth treatment, especially illustrations about helping the
unemployed, see Chapter 20, *Searching for Meaningful Ways to Help
the Poor.*

QUESTIONS FOR DISCUSSION
Chapter 10

1. *How do Biblical principles help the poor move toward self-*
   reliance?

2. *What are the lessons to be learned from the story of the widow and*
   two coins in Luke 21?

3. *How can dignity be preserved when helping the poor?*

4. *Do you agree that local resources when available are more beneficial*
   than global resources? Discuss the impact of global resources on
   local economies.

5. *To what extent do you feel westerners "need" an outlet for their*
   compassion?

6. *Discuss the difference in impact between grants and loans.*

7. *Discuss the relation between church-owned, community-owned*
   and privately owned businesses or projects.

SUGGESTED READING

Befus, David R. *Where There are No Jobs: Enterprise Solutions for
Employment and 'Public Goods' for the Poor.* Miami: LAM, 2005.

---

[6] See Grants vs Loans by Vishal Mangalwadi, *Stewardship Journal*, Winter 1994,
page 18.

Bolling, Landrum. *Private Foreign Aid*. Boulder: Westview Press, Colorado, 1982.

Desoto, Hernando. *The Mystery of Capital: Why Capitalism Triumphs in the West and Fails Everywhere Else*. New York: Basic Books, 2000.

Madeley, John. *Trade and the Poor: The Impact of International Trade on Developing Countries*. London: Intermediate Technology Publications, 1992.

Olasky, Marvin. *The Tragedy of American Compassion*. Washington: Regnery Publishing, 1992.

Prahalad, C. K. *The Fortune at the Bottom of the Pyramid*. Upper Saddle River: Wharton School of Publishing, 2005.

Sachs, Jeffrey D. *The End of Poverty: Economic Possibilities for Our Time*. New York: Penguin Press, 2005.

(There are many other good books available today on this subject.)

CHAPTER 11

THE JOY OF GIVING AND
THE LAW OF TITHING IN BIBLICAL PERSPECTIVE

Another Look at Scripture

We begin by looking at the Bible and asking ourselves this question: What is this Bible all about that so many of us have come to know, love and use on a daily basis? Dr. Arthur Glasser referred to the Bible "as one long complicated sentence – like a case study – revealing God's attempt to gain the undivided attention of men and women throughout history. It details God's interaction with the human race across the ages." While God is bidding for our attention, there are many "gods" that are doing the same. And one of these "gods" is money.

However, the Bible reminds us that it is not money, but the *love of money* which is the root of all evil. It is only when God gets our undivided attention that money finds its rightful place in our lives. The Bible teaches us that all we own comes from God, and that it is our privilege to give some of it back to Him in thanksgiving (I Chronicles 29).

The Willingness of African People to Give

I quote here from Emmanuel Olidapo who at one time served as International Secretary of Scripture Union. He had this to say about generosity in Africa:

> *It isn't that African people don't know how to give. There are hardly more generous people on earth. They give for festivals and many other special occasions. They give to relatives needing education or to unemployed or orphaned people in their community. However, many simply don't give generously to the church.*[1]

---

[1] This quotation comes from an oral presentation that Mr. Olidapo made at a gathering of missiologists in England in 1996.

So what then is the missing element? Why is it that many African Christians don't give generously to the Church? The same question could be asked of nominal Christians in other places – in North America, Europe and elsewhere. I maintain that the missing element is often the *joy of giving*. While I believe in the benefits and importance of tithing, **it is no substitute for the joy of giving**.

Consider for example, the people giving "hilariously" in that harambee which I described in an earlier chapter. They were not being forced to tithe but had discovered something of the joy of giving back to God.

The Building of the Tabernacle at the Time of Moses

Several illustrations from Scripture come to mind regarding the joy of giving. In Exodus chapter 35 we read about the building of the Tabernacle. The people of Israel had come out of Egypt carrying many things with them – things given to them by the Egyptians before they fled. They were on their way through the wilderness when God told Moses to create a moveable House of the Lord – a place to worship during their journey toward the Promised Land. This is commonly called the Tabernacle. A permanent structure – the Temple – would come later.

Moses made a call for materials to build this movable house of the Lord. In verse four he said to the people, "*From what you have*, take an offering for the Lord. Everyone who is willing is to bring to the Lord an offering of gold, silver, bronze . . ." Notice that the call is made to everyone who was **willing**. Then he issued a call for labor, "And all who are skilled among you are to come and make everything that the Lord has commanded." In verses 21 and 29 we read how the people **willingly** gave what they had (materials, skills or labor) to accomplish this great work. In Exodus chapters 35 and 36 the term "willing" occurs no less than six times in relation to giving toward the building of the tabernacle. Not a word is spoken about people being forced to contribute.

Notice the unusual response of the people to Moses' message. According to Exodus 36:4-7, the builders in charge of the work were inundated with the things that people brought. The builders finally had to go to Moses and say, "The people are bringing more than enough for doing the work the Lord commanded to be done."

In other words, "Tell the people to stop bringing their offerings; we have too much."

Again, not a word was said about being forced to give or to tithe. Clearly there was some other motivation for giving. When was the last time you heard a pastor tell a congregation, "Stop giving; we have more than enough for the work of the Lord?"

It is also interesting to note that this building project was followed by a mighty visitation of God's presence (40:34-35). A cloud covered the Tent of Meeting, and the glory of the Lord filled the tabernacle. Moses himself could not enter because the cloud settled upon it, and the Glory of the Lord filled the place. The story began with a call for giving and ended with a sanctuary so filled with the presence of the Lord that no one could go in!

The Building of the Temple Initiated by King David

In I Chronicles 29, we find the story of building of the Temple which was the permanent House of the Lord. While King David began the process for the building of the Temple, God did not allow him to actually build it because of his career as a military leader. However, his son Solomon was permitted to build it. In this story David provides the inspiration and motivation to get the fundraising process underway. He began by saying, "The task is great, because this structure is not for man, but for God . . . With all my resources I have provided for the Temple of my God — gold for the gold works, silver for the silver . . . all of these in large quantities." The first lesson here is that the project was for the Lord, not for man.

Later David prayed to the Lord in the presence of the whole assembly, saying, "Praise be to you, Oh Lord, God of our father Israel, from everlasting to everlasting. Yours, Oh Lord, is the greatness and the power and the glory and the majesty and the splendor, for everything in Heaven and earth is Yours" (29:10-11).

Verse 24 of this chapter has an interesting combination of thoughts. After the public prayer, King David says, "But who am I, and who are my people, that we should be able to give as generously as this; everything comes from You — and we have given You only what comes from Your hand" (I Chronicles 29:14).

David's words put three things into perspective:

- First, he puts into perspective who the Lord is – "Yours is the greatness and power."

- Second, he puts mankind into perspective — "But who are we that we should be allowed to give like this."

- Third, he puts in perspective our possessions – "All that we have comes from the Lord. We are only giving back what you have already given to us."

Verse 15 of this same passage indicates once again that "willingness" was involved in this successful fundraising project: "And now I have seen with joy how **willingly** your people, who are here, have given to you." The willingness of the people to participate in this project led to a period of praise (v. 20) – another indication that there is an important connection between the heart, the spirit and the things God has given us.

Notice how this story ended. In chapter 29:20 "They all praised the Lord . . . bowed low and fell prostrate before the Lord and the king." This project began with an appeal for resources to build the house of the Lord and ended with people on their faces before the Lord. By the way, the word **willing** or **willingly** is mentioned at least five times in this chapter.

The conclusion of this story is very fundamental to our treatment of the issue of dependency: We are simply giving back to God some of what He has given to us. Our proper response to God is to give from a heart of love and gratitude. In the end, God blesses us with His presence.

In neither of these stories in the Old Testament is it indicated that people were forced to give. Whether they offered God their goods, talents or labor, they gave willingly from hearts of love.

The Inspiring Story of the Macedonians as told to the Corinthians

In 2 Corinthians chapter 8 the Apostle Paul records one of the more remarkable stories of giving in all of scripture. Paul was holding up to the Corinthians the example of the believers in Macedonia.

He used the technique of "comparison" in his effort to get the Corinthians to give generously toward the poor in Jerusalem. I once heard a humorous story about a cockerel (rooster) that found a large ostrich egg which he rolled up to the hen house. He called the hens over to the fence, pointed to the egg and said, "I just want you to see what they are doing in other places." Paul was doing something similar when he said he wanted the Corinthians to know what the Macedonians were doing.

What were the Macedonians doing? Paul said that out of severe trial and extreme poverty they "begged for the privilege of giving" (verse 2). "They did not do as we expected, but gave themselves first to the Lord [spiritual renewal] and then to us" (verse 5). All of this was sacrificial giving for the benefit of the poor in Jerusalem.[2]

Paul goes on to say other things about giving in verses 13 and following. His point is that through giving, one's need is supplied from another's plenty. At first reading, one might conclude that is why those in western countries should give generously to those whom they consider to be poor. While there is merit in that conclusion, we must take into consideration whether the giving done by those with plenty is hindering the spirit of giving among those who are being helped. This gets at the heart of how and why a spirit of dependency develops. I must not let my giving destroy some else's initiative for giving.

For our purposes, there are several observations worth noting from this Corinthian passage:

1. The people in Macedonia (who were begging to give) were not wealthy. They gave out of severe trial and extreme poverty. They could be called "beggars", but beggars for the privilege of giving – not receiving (v 4).

2. They gave themselves first to the Lord. This emphasizes the importance of beginning with spiritual renewal.

---

[2] For an in-depth treatment of this subject see Christopher Little, *Mission in the Way of Paul*. He uncovered interesting facts about the motivation of Paul for taking the collection for the poor in Jerusalem. (See the general bibliography for details.)

3. In verses 20 and 21 Paul emphasizes the importance of accountability — so that the offering is well cared for, not only in the eyes of God, **but also the eyes of men**. Honest, open handling of church offerings will do more than anything else to instill confidence in the hearts and minds of those being asked to give.

4. Notice that Paul was encouraging the Corinthians to excel in "the grace of giving", in addition to excelling in faith, speech, knowledge, earnestness and love (v. 7).

5. Paul avoids legalism about giving by reminding the Corinthians that he is not commanding them to give, but rather testing the sincerity of their love by comparing it to others (v. 8).

Considering what the Apostle Paul said about the Macedonians in 2 Corinthians 8, even the poor should not be excused from giving something back to God. Stories abound of those who gave out of poverty only to see God bless and honor them for it. It does not mean that anyone should give to God **so that** He will reward them for doing so. In Romans 11:35 the writer asks the question, "Who has ever given to God, that God should repay him?" (These are very similar to words in Job 41:11.) I believe that those who demand health and wealth in return for giving to God have misinterpreted what scripture has to say about the motivation for giving. As in the story of King David and the building of the Temple, our motivation for giving is out of loyalty and devotion to God, not for what we might get in return.

Tithing in the African Context

Where then does the matter of tithing fit into all of this? Many years ago I met a missionary whose entire gospel message centered on tithing. I once asked him whether one should tithe on net income or gross income. His reply was swift: "That one is simple", he said. "Do you want a blessing on the net or on the gross?" Of course, giving to God cannot be made quite that simple.

Tithing has an important place in the giving of many African churches. I shared stories of how tithing is being done among Lutherans in Tanzania, Assemblies of God in South Africa, and the Seventh Day Adventists in Zambia. Tithing is central to each of these churches. In other words, churches in which members are giving generously to the Lord stress the importance of the concept of tithing. And many who tithe do so out of their love for the Lord.

Sometimes tithing is a law laid down by church leaders. Remember the story of the Lutherans, in which the treasurer went to each individual and talked to them about their giving. That is a practice put into place by the leaders, and it is expected that tithing will be carried out. Remember, in addition to tithing in several of the stories I told, there was also a system of giving offerings beyond the tithe. These included giving to the poor as well as contributing toward building funds and thank offerings.

One church leader in East Africa said, "In our church, **tithing is simply the place where our people begin to do their giving."** Think about that for a moment. Tithing is assumed, and then other giving is done through harambees and similar events. When you ask the question as to whether tithing is valid, you discover that in healthy churches the tithe just may be assumed. When God has the undivided attention of his people, they give joyfully "above and beyond" because they love the Lord! Where tithing is unlikely to work is where it is set as a standard for those who have only a marginal commitment to the Lord.

The Concept of Perpetual Jubilee

When considering the Biblical concept of giving, several other things come to mind. Under Old Testament law, debts were to be systematically forgiven during the year of Jubilee. Also, servants were to be set free. Land was to be returned to previous owners. In short, there was a "built-in" re-distribution of wealth. In the New Testament we find these words: "Don't lay up for yourself treasure on earth." "If you have two coats give one away." "Seek first God's Kingdom." "It is more blessed to give than to receive." Sometimes the pattern of giving that Jesus called for is referred to as the concept of "perpetual jubilee."

The concept of **perpetual jubilee** means that I do not accumulate a constantly increasing amount of wealth at the expense of others. Instead, we are to accumulate spiritual riches. When that mode of operation is adopted and built into our daily lives, then everything we have belongs to the Lord, as we saw in the story of King David and the building of the temple.

Recently someone said he didn't see any place in the New Testament where a person is to limit the increase in personal net worth. However, consider this: Jesus reminded one man that building bigger and bigger barns to store his wealth had consequences. According to Luke 12:13-21, his soul would be required of him that very night.

Unfortunately, we live in a day when some Christians, evangelicals among them, defend the right to accumulate as much as they can. They may give a portion of it back to God, but they often end up having far more than they need to live on. And there are some who feel that this is their privilege as children of God. Among these are those who espouse the "health and wealth" theology that I mentioned above. When I emphasize self-reliance for churches and breaking the dependency syndrome—I am *not* endorsing the concept of "health and wealth." I am *not* defending those who want to *get* as much as they can and *keep* as much as they want. I am talking about those who seek to make the Kingdom of God the highest priority in their lives. That means releasing control of what they have and saying, "It all belongs to God, and He is simply allowing me to use it for His glory."

Andrew Carnegie, a very wealthy man in American history, made a statement something to this effect: "Everything a person earns, beyond what he needs to sustain himself, should be for the good of the larger community." Andrew Carnegie is not normally quoted as an evangelical Christian to whom we look for inspiration regarding God's Kingdom. But he did advocate dedicating to the wider community everything that one receives beyond what he or she needs to exist. Christians might take a lesson from that. In the end, it comes down to this: How much do we really need to live on? How much is our fair portion? Depending on our aspirations, it may take more and more to sustain our lifestyle and the significance for the Kingdom of God is lost in the process.

Great Commission-minded people should know instinctively that when they have set themselves the goal of doing God's will, all their resources should be dedicated toward that end.

Who is the Real Owner of my Possessions

I may have a car, a house, an education and money in the bank. But, can I honestly say that these things belong to me? I have to say that God gave these things for me to use, and I will dedicate all of them for His purposes. The idea of hiding something away that is "mine", to be used on myself and not dedicated to the Kingdom, is simply not for Great Commission-minded Christians.

Dr. David Barrett is a missiologist and researcher who provides information for the Christian movement. He has made the statement that if Christians in Africa gave just 2% of their income they would be able to pay all of their bills. He says they would be able to support their leadership training, pay their pastors, build their own church buildings, fund their development projects, *and buy computers if they want them* — all on 2% of the income of Christians in Africa!

From time to time I try to check this out. Some time ago I asked a church leader in East Africa whether he agreed with Dr. Barrett's observation. His response was as follows: "It's interesting that you say that. We recently calculated that if the members of our church gave only *one percent* of their income we could pay all the bills at our church." Imagine what would happen in a church like that if the members gave *ten percent!* They would have far more than they need for local ministry. In fact, if they gave that much, they could give to missions and send their own people elsewhere with the Gospel.

In Tanzania I once conducted a seminar in which several different denominations were represented. At one point, one of the men from Central Tanzania said, "It is interesting that you quote Dr. Barrett. I am the administrator for a diocese of our church, and I just calculated that if everyone in our diocese tithed, at the end of the year we would have 100 million Tanzanian shillings left over." I am not sure of the exchange rate at that time, but "100 million" is a lot of money in many currencies. The important thing was that in the mind of this administrator it was a large amount of money, which could have been given to the church if tithing were being done.

Conclusion

Great Commission-minded people put God's Kingdom first. They do what He wants them to do. Remember King David's words: "Who are we that we should be able to give as generously as this?" And remember that word in Romans, "Who has given to God that he should repay him? " (Romans 11:35). This brings us right back to the importance of spiritual renewal. Giving in African churches — like everywhere else — is based upon a heart filled with thanksgiving toward God. It is from this overflow that God gets back some of what He has given to us.

QUESTIONS FOR DISCUSSION
Chapter 11

1. *Does God have the "undivided" attention of most people in your church?*

2. *Do you agree with Mr. Olidapo that African people are generous givers but not toward the church? Discuss the implications.*

3. *Discuss the relationship between the "joy of giving" and the "law of tithing."*

4. *Do you agree that Jesus encouraged people to live in a "state of perpetual jubilee"? What does that mean to you?*

5. *To what extent is the Kingdom of God the highest priority in the lives of believers in your church?*

6. *Do you agree that missionary outreach is dependent upon a general overflow of a spiritually energized church? What if a church is not spiritually energized?*

SUGGESTED READINGS

Exodus 35
Leviticus 25
Numbers 36
1 Chronicles 29
Malachi 3
Matthew 6
2 Corinthians 8

CHAPTER 12

EXPLORING THE CONCEPT OF THE
INDIGENOUS CHURCH AND MISSIONARY SENDING

Introduction

In this chapter I will explore two different concepts: 1) the nature of an indigenous church and 2) how an indigenous church can become a "sending" church. This chapter is not an in-depth treatment of indigenous churches and mission societies known for their missionary sending in areas *outside* of East, Central and Southern Africa. Also, some of these issues are touched upon in earlier chapters, but I re-emphasize and expand them here.

What is the Concept of the Indigenous Church?

Earlier on I mentioned the three-self principle as it relates to indigenous churches. This principle states that indigenous churches should be **self-supporting, self-governing, and self-propagating**. This principle came out of the 19th century in which missiologists agreed that without these three characteristics, a church could hardly be thought of as being indigenous. My own description of an indigenous church is one that is *locally owned and operated*.

For those who are interested in a critique of the three-self principle and additional information on this subject, I suggest a book called *Readings in Dynamic Indigeneity* edited by Dr. Charles Kraft. The part of this book that deals with a critique of the three-self principle is the first several chapters, one of which was written by Dr. Hans Kasdorf. He gives an excellent description of how missiologists look at this principle and the reasons why some of them have reservations about it as a valid definition of an indigenous church.

The primary objection to the three-self principle among missiologists is that it doesn't go far enough. For example, missiologists will say that a church could support, govern and propagate itself and still not have an indigenous theology or hymnology. From my perspective, I prefer to think of the three-self principle as a beginning point. For example, if any of the three are missing, then one could hardly consider a church to be truly indigenous. I agree that in addition to this minimum, an indigenous theology and hymnology are part of what makes a church truly indigenous.

Consider this analogy from medicine. The germ theory of sickness has taught medical people the importance of cleanliness. They simply must wash their hands when going from one ill person to another. However, today we know a lot more about sickness than the germ theory. We know about antibiotics and nuclear medicine, etc. Just because we know a lot more now, does not mean that the fundamentals are not valid. That is how I see the three-self principle. We should not let missiological sophistication replace the need for the fundamentals.

In spite of the reservations some have about the indigenous principle, many mission executives would say that their goal is to establish indigenous churches by whatever definition they use. In fact, it would be highly unusual to hear a mission executive deny this. The question we are dealing with here, however, is why so many churches are so far from being self-supporting, self-governing and self-propagating.

An Indigenous Church in China

In China there is a church called the Three-Self Patriotic Movement. This church was formed as a result of missionaries introducing the three-self principle during the days prior to the communist take-over of China. Such churches are self-governing, and in that way insist on carrying on the work that God has given them to do without outside interference. This is not the best example of an indigenous church, however, since many Christians would say that they are government-controlled and cannot, then, be faithful to the whole Word of God.

However, in China there are also millions of believers in house churches not affiliated with the Three-Self Patriotic Movement. The house churches generally follow the same principles of being self-supporting, self-governing and self-propagating. They do not carry the name of Three-Self, but they are characterized by the principle.

At the time of the Communist take-over in the early 1950s there were an estimated one million believers (some estimates are less) in the country. During the next thirty or so years, the one million believers multiplied to many millions. By 1980, estimates were that they had become between fifty and eighty million believers. By the turn of the millennium, estimates ranged as high as one hundred and twenty million believers. Because of the nature of an underground church, it is not possible to get accurate figures.

This enormous growth of the church in China signifies several things:

1) The self-supporting and self-propagating principles introduced by some of the missionaries prior to their leaving made the growth of the church possible. Had the church in China only learned to be dependent on outsiders for church buildings or pastors' salaries, it is doubtful that such dramatic growth would have occurred. There simply was no way to get resources to the church from the outside, so self-support was the only recourse. And what a dramatic result!

2) During the time of being cut off from the outside world, the Church gained its own identity as an indigenous movement. Hence, there is no need today to have someone else define who they are.

3) It was also during this time that the Church learned how to exist in a hostile political environment. Like believers in New Testament times, they learned discipline and how to cope (including suffering) when basically in a state of hostile occupation. They saw their primary battle as spiritual and not against a political system.

4) It was during this thirty to forty-year period under hostile conditions that the church in China decided that its mission would be to take the Gospel further to the west – all the way to Jerusalem. Knowing that they would encounter persecution under Hindu, Buddhist and Islamic conditions, they felt that their time under communism was training for what they would encounter on the way to Jerusalem.[1]

---

[1] For a thorough introduction to the Back to Jerusalem Movement see a book by the same title available through Gabriel Resources, Waynesboro, GA. It is the testimony of three Chinese house church leaders who share their vision to complete the Great Commission. It is written with Paul Hattaway whose website is www.asiaharvest.org.

There is no better endorsement for the importance of the indigenous principle than the church in China. Dependent churches simply do not grow like that. It may have been the forced removal of the missionaries that precipitated the move toward its indigenous identity, but thankfully those same missionaries introduced the concept of self-support, before they left. The church in China is the beneficiary. One might think of the church in other places today and what would happen if all outside resources and missionaries were removed. Would such a church die or thrive? I maintain that this points to the importance of local sustainability.

Indigenous Churches in Africa

The concept of the indigenous church has a visible demonstration in Africa called African Independent Churches (AICs). There are many interesting aspects of this phenomenon.

In East, Central and Southern Africa there are tens of thousands of AICs. Many of them are concentrated in areas where land was taken away from the people during the colonial period.[2] The term "independent" is often used to describe those churches led by leaders who left mission-established churches to start their own congregation or denomination. Some of them have very unusual names such as The Church of the New Jerusalem — Apostolic and many words signifying their Pentecostal nature. The name says something about their identity and desire to be different and independent. Dr. David Barrett in his book, *Schism and Renewal in Africa* said that in Southern Africa in the early 1970s there were ten thousand African Independent Churches. A survey in 1976 found that in Kenya alone there were twenty-six new independent denominations started that year alone. That represents one new denomination every two weeks during one year.

The following are some characteristics of African Independent Churches.

1. **They were often started by leaders from mission-established churches** where the "low ceiling principle" was in practice.

---

[2] See *Schism and Renewal in Africa*, page 94 in which Dr. Barrett says "protest movements [are] directed against exploitation of tribal lands or other riches by colonial powers."

This meant that there was not enough "psychological space" for leaders to be themselves. In other words, they often did not feel at home where they were. Sometimes it was because outsiders were in positions of leadership, and that did not leave room for others with leadership gifts and abilities to rise.

2. When AICs were formed, the **leaders often rejected foreign elements such as outside funding and, especially, outside control.** They were determined not to be controlled or managed by anyone other than themselves. This was particularly true of AICs in the early stages of their development in East, Central and Southern Africa. Later on I will mention how that is changing.

3. **They were usually led by a gifted or charismatic individual** who felt that he had a prophetic leadership role. He often called himself a "prophet" or "apostle" as he led the new followers.

4. **Not all of these churches would be called "evangelical."** Some of them engage in practices that, unfortunately, should not be known among those who call themselves Christians. But some of them *are* evangelical, and some of them have grown very large and are doing good work in society.

5. **The second generation of some African Independent Churches is re-thinking some of the isolationist stance of the first generation.** For example, some leaders of AICs are now beginning to realize that there are benefits that come with money from overseas. Some have started to look wistfully over the fence at so-called mainline churches that get money from the World Council of Churches, TEAR Fund, Bread for the World, Oxfam and other sources. They are asking, "Why can't we get some of that kind of funding?" Second generation leaders may not be aware of why their first generation leaders rejected such outside funding. For some second-generation leaders, it's safer for them to think in terms of getting outside support because they are not seeking to establish their identity in the way their forefathers were forced to do.

6. **African Independent Churches are a living example of the fact that churches can exist on their own resources – in Africa.** One of the ways that AICs found they could exist without

outside funding is through rejecting the enormous overhead that characterized the mission stations of mission-established churches. They did not establish hospitals, schools, clinics, guesthouses, etc. in the way that others did. Churches that had only their own church building were much easier to support than those which had a "box" such as I described in chapter one. With the lower overhead, some AICs found they could tap into the resources of villagers in ways mission-established churches never could.

In the days when the Zambian Kwacha was of significant value (in the 1980s) I heard a bishop of a mission-established church lament that his church was destitute while one of the AICs in his area was taking in a million Zambian kwacha for their annual support.[3] He simply wondered how they did it. Among other things, that AIC did not own a vehicle. Their bishop walked everywhere he went or took public transport. When it was learned that he was coming into town from his rural village, three elders of the church went to the edge of the town to meet and greet him as he came to be their guest. Bishops in mission-established churches had many other benefits; but sometimes they, too, looked longingly over the fence at some of the benefits enjoyed by leaders in the AICs.

7. **Many AICs have not engaged in E3 evangelism.** In other words they did not get involved in cross-cultural evangelism which takes the Gospel beyond their own borders. In fact, many of them grow only within the ethnic group in which they were started. In this respect they are not even practicing E2 evangelism which would mean going to ethnic groups with some similarity to their own.

To conclude this part, Dr. Donald McGavran used to say that being indigenous is no guarantee that churches will be effective at reproducing themselves. He said one had only to look at the decline of mainline denominations in North America to confirm that fact. Many of them are indigenous to North American culture, but they are declining in members.

---

[3] This happened in a day when the strength of the Zambian kwacha was about equivalent to the US dollar. In more recent years the exchange rate changed significantly.

The Place of Indigenous Churches in Society

An indigenous Church should look and sound like the society of which it is a part. In other words, it should not stand out as something culturally different or foreign. It *should* stand out in other ways.[4] It ought to be seen as a group of people concerned to carry out God's priorities in their communities. Believers should stand apart from the average person in the neighborhood because of their obedience to God's Word. But the church should *not* look like a culturally foreign institution. Unfortunately, many mission-established churches simply look and sound foreign to the eyes and ears of local people around them.

Some mission-established churches are very much like the church that started them. They are very loyal to that theology, church structure and doctrine. Some would not think of doing things any other way. If the church that started them uses sacramental wine for communion services, then the new church will use sacramental wine. These churches are in many ways duplicates or replicas of the church that started them. Such replicas can hardly be thought of as indigenous in the new society.

At the same time, some mission-established churches have greater freedom than others. They have freedom to operate differently from the church that planted them. This involves the mission society exercising some risk. But it is the only way that the new church has a chance of becoming indigenous in the society of which it is a part. I deal more in-depth with this issue in Chapter 15 where I explore the issue of ethnicity and also in chapter 19 under the title *Avoiding or Overcoming Dependency in Cross-Cultural Church Planting*. I make the point there that a church cannot be indigenous in its own society if it has the identity of the church from another society.

Indigenous Churches are a Mixed Bag

Some mission-established churches have local leadership, but a very expensive foreign structure that cannot be supported by local leadership. Local leaders may be convinced that they need help from the outside so they continually ask for it. In other words,

---

[4] On the WMA website I have an article expanding on this subject. I titled it *I Believe in the Local Church*

they may have indigenous leadership, but they do not have an indigenous support structure.

Truly independent mission-established churches do exist, but they seem to be rare because many of them are tied closely to the church that started them. Think about the fact that many **western** denominations were started as independent churches. Those who split off from the original church did so in an attempt to start an independent congregation. This small group grew larger and soon there were several congregations. Those who tend to be critical of African Independent Churches would do well to take a look at western church history and remember how many times our churches split off from other larger denominations. This should help us to see that the independent church movement is a part of history and a factor to be given consideration.

Foundation of an Indigenous Missionary Outreach Movement

What characterizes an indigenous outreach movement? The following are a few factors:

1. A healthy movement is born out of the full-heart experience. Don't expect people who do not know the Lord to be excited about establishing a missionary outreach program.

2. Missionary outreach is the result of widespread spiritual renewal. In other words, it is not based on only a few who are spiritually energized. A true missionary movement is built on the overflow from a congregation or denomination already filled with the Holy Spirit and with spiritual energy left over for others.

3. A sound missionary movement requires special emphasis and training. Pastoral training alone will not answer the questions that cross-cultural missionaries face.

4. It develops a caring sending base—a missionary society or department. This includes healthy financial support for those members willing to serve as missionaries at a distance. The precedent for this is the Apostolic Bands of the New Testament which were different from the structure of the local congregation.

5. It requires faithful reporting back to the prayer and financial supporters who are behind the missionaries.

6. It keeps before its members the vision of the unreached (as in the 10/40 Window). Those who pray and give need to have their own vision kept alive by regular reports of what God is doing on the front lines.

7. A healthy missionary movement is not dependent on foreign funding to get it started or to keep it going.

8. A truly indigenous missionary movement is suspicious of "partners" who want to help make "your" vision possible. There are some western agencies whose sole purpose is to provide funding for what they consider to be indigenous movements. Obviously they do not believe in the importance of local "self-support" if they justify providing outside funding.

9. An indigenous missionary movement is a source of inspiration for other churches that may not have their own missionary outreach. Imagine the benefit if such churches not only learned from each other, but cooperated in outreach efforts.

As you know by now, one of the people who influenced my thinking considerably was Professor Alan Tippett. He wrote a little book that I highly recommend to anyone interested in studying issues related to the indigenous church. It is called *Verdict Theology in Missionary Theory.* It is a series of lectures, given many years ago at a Christian college in the United States. I have used this book many times because it has very practical suggestions about what missionaries and church leaders can and should do when planting churches cross-culturally. At one point Dr. Tippett expands on the three-self principle using six "self's" to more fully describe an indigenous church.

Alan Tippett's Six Marks of an Indigenous Church

1. **Does the church have a healthy self-image?** Does it view itself as the Body of Christ in its own community?

2. **Is the church self-functioning?** Does it contain all of the parts necessary for caring for itself and its own outreach?

3. **Is it self-determining?** Is this church autonomous — capable of making its own decisions? Or is this church on a life support system which, if it were cut off, would leave the body unable to function? If that foreign life support system is critical to the existence of the church then it could hardly be called an indigenous, self-supporting, self-governing church.

4. **Is it self-supporting?** Does it carry its own financial responsibility? Does it finance its own service projects? Or is it dependent on a mission society, World Vision, TEAR Fund or some other organization to support it?

5. **Is it self-propagating?** Does the church have its own missionary outreach program? Dr. Tippett was part of a church in Melanesia, that area of the Pacific that includes the Fiji Islands where he served as a missionary. The church of which he was a part sent missionaries to New Guinea, so he knew first hand that the Melanesian church was self-propagating.

6. **Is it self-giving?** Does it manage its own service programs such as hospitals, seminaries, relief projects and so on?

I heartily recommend reading *Verdict Theology in Missionary Theory* by Dr. Tippett. It is now out of print, but it can be found in any good missionary library. It contains good suggestions regarding how to deal with the challenge of transitioning from mission to church and is particularly helpful in the area of financial matters.

Three Important parts of Indigeneity

Three other ideals come to mind when thinking about the concept of an indigenous church: 1) an indigenous theology; 2) an indigenous form of worship; and 3) an indigenous church structure. Let's look at these individually.[5]

What is Indigenous Theology?

The first ideal to search for is an **indigenous theology.** Unfortunately many westerners believe that there is only one kind of theology; and for them, that is western theology. If you go back to our earlier

---

[5] I am indebted to Dr. Arthur Glasser for these insights.

diagram of the excluded middle in chapter one, many who hold to a form of western theology exclude that middle because they don't know what to do with it. As a result they do not have a well-formulated demonology or even a good doctrine of the Holy Spirit, which is called "pneumatology." Western systematic theology tends to eliminate many of those things that are difficult to deal with, particularly where the primary worldview is spiritism. **But an indigenous theology is one that deals with all the elements that affect the lives of people on a daily basis.** If demon possession is one of those things, then an indigenous theology must speak to demon possession. If polygamy is one of those issues, a good indigenous theology will speak to that. A non-indigenous theology might simply recommend divorce as an alternative to polygamy.

An indigenous theology has to do with how a church **thinks**.

What is an Indigenous Form of Worship?

Worship has more to do with the emotional side of the church. For example, is this church a place to feel at home? Politicians sometimes speak about the "feel good factor." Do people feel good about their government? If so, their vote will show it. We can ask a similar question about a church. Is it a place to feel at home? The style of worship often dictates the atmosphere within the church. Is the music style culturally appropriate? Does it make one feel that he or she is truly worshipping God? Or is it something borrowed from the outside and so different that it doesn't even sound good to the ears?

What about the language used in the church? Does it speak to the needs of individuals at their heart level, or is it something borrowed from the outside? Many people in my generation went through a period of time when we began to realize that the English used in the King James Version of the Bible was no longer part of our daily vocabulary. So our generation began to accept more recent Bible translations. Why? Because there was something about King James English that seemed as though it belonged to another time and place. It was as if we were borrowing language and were trying to pour special meaning into words that were no longer in our daily use. While many of us came to know Christ through the King James Bible, many parts of it include outdated language. It felt good to move to a language nearer to what we spoke in everyday language.

An indigenous form of worship has to do with how the church **feels**.

What is an Indigenous Church Structure?

A good church structure will have something to say about where decisions are made. What are the sources of power that influence decision-making in the church? Does this structure fit the society of which it is part?

Dr. Tippett gave an illustration about the American Board of Missions which established churches in the Pacific Islands. Since they were congregational in structure, when they went to Hawaii they established churches that had a congregational format. He said that was culturally appropriate for the Pacific Islands. However, churches which went to East Africa – such as the Anglicans – had a hierarchical church structure, including priests, bishops and archbishops. Dr. Tippett pointed out that the Anglicans found themselves in a society structured similar to their churches. East African society had headmen, chiefs and a paramount chief reflecting that it was hierarchical in structure. He made the point that it was fortunate that the Congregationalists went to Hawaii, and the Anglicans went to East Africa where the receiving societies were similar to the structure to the sending churches. He was reminding us that the church structure should fit the society of which it is a part.

One question to keep in mind is this: Can a mission-established church afford the structure which it inherited? Can it be supported from local resources? Unfortunately, foreign structures often need foreign funds to sustain them.

Another serious question that should be asked is this: Can this structure be reproduced elsewhere? Or is it so complex, heavy, expensive and foreign that it cannot be reproduced in missionary outreach anywhere else?

An indigenous church structure has to do with how the church **works**.

The Relevance of Self-Image and Community-Image

One of the important issues that a church needs to examine is how it sees itself and how outsiders see it. I am referring to the concept of the *self-image* and *community image* of the church. I have mentioned this before, but I want to say something very specific about it now because it has a great deal to do with whether people feel good about their church or not. If, for example, people see themselves as belonging to someone else or being a "foreign mission church", it will affect how they feel about bringing other people into it.

We must ask ourselves whether the community thinks of the church as the place to turn in times of crisis. Or do community people see the church as something irrelevant? Perhaps the church is considered to be a good place if children need an education, but adults may think it has nothing to offer them in the realities of life. Is the church seen as a place for weak people, for poor people who need to beg for assistance from overseas? If it is, it may not be a place where one wants to have an association.

Another question needs to be raised: Does this church have a healthy reproductive system? Does it have a shared leadership system and a discipleship mode of ministry which brings people to leadership positions, making them want to be leaders? Does it have a concern for people outside of itself so that members feel they are there for a purpose, doing what God wants them to do?

Indigenous Churches and Missionary Sending

Up to this point I have concentrated on describing an indigenous church. Now let's shift to the issue of missionary sending. Why are so many churches without a missionary sending department? Why don't they have a society or agency that sends out their own missionaries? Why don't they have a training institute which raises up people who are prepared to serve in cross-cultural evangelism? I will suggest several reasons.

1. **There may be no vision for the unreached.** Perhaps the Gospel has not met the deepest needs inside individuals in their own society. If that is the case, then people may not be convinced that the Gospel is "the best news in the world." If so, they will most likely not be willing to cross language and geographical

barriers to carry this Gospel elsewhere. If there is no vision or evidence of the presence of the Holy Spirit in the church, spiritual renewal is the first step to take.

2. **Perhaps a poverty mentality exists.** I mentioned earlier those who "confess poverty." This is a term used in Central Africa which means that people simply plead, "We are poor, that's the way we are, and we can't do anything about it." If people feel they are too poor to support themselves, then they are probably not going to reach out to support others. They have probably resigned themselves to live with a poverty mentality.

3. **They may have inherited an expensive structure which takes all their resources to maintain,** so it can't be reproduced. I have referred to this several times before. Some missionaries cannot face the fact that the expensive things they created are now a burden preventing missionary outreach in the churches they established.

4. **Perhaps the church has adopted a maintenance mentality.** Unfortunately this is characteristic not only of mission-established churches. Many western churches have adopted a maintenance mentality. They feel that their responsibility is to maintain what they already have. And so the pastor *maintains* the fellowship, and the trustees *maintain* the building. Others *maintain* the various programs of the church. Such a church becomes a nice place to go each weekend for services, but it will probably not be concerned about reaching people beyond its borders. It might not be concerned about the globally expanding movement that seeks to take the Gospel to unreached peoples. All of this is a result of being in a maintenance mode of ministry.

5. **Perhaps there are no training institutes to prepare people for missionary training.** There may be schools for evangelism but not schools for missionary training. Schools for missionary training not only prepare members to do cross-cultural work; they bring inspiration to the churches for missionary outreach.

6. **The church may have no sending agency.** We learn from church history that special sending agencies are the key to cross-cultural evangelism. Local congregations should have a vision for

missions. But it usually takes a special department or society to function effectively cross-culturally. Some local congregations have tried to become their own sending agency, but they generally do not have the expertise to function internationally or cross-culturally. Indeed, congregations that serve as their own mission agency may just be duplicating themselves and not planting truly indigenous churches. Incidentally, replica churches can be very expensive to develop, especially if they do not have roots in the local community.

7. **There may be no prayer movement**—no spiritual basis within the Church for sending out missionaries. Dr J. Edwin Orr often reminded us that every major revival was preceded by a period of concentrated prayer. One might add that a genuine *missionary movement* in the church needs to be supported by a wide emphasis of prayer throughout the body of Christ.

The Importance of Living Testimonies of Faith

Testimonies of people who have gone out to share the Gospel, who then return to report on what God is doing, give vital impetus to the mission cause. Nothing will do more to motivate continued missionary outreach than having people testify to what God is doing in other places. There is Biblical precedent for this in Acts 14:27 when Paul and Barnabas shared with their sending church in Antioch what God had done in the course of their missionary journeys.

Conclusion

Paul Hattaway in his book *Back to Jerusalem* has a fascinating statement about what it meant to the church in China to be indigenous. It is worth quoting as I conclude this chapter on the indigenous church:

> In an ethnocentric and proud nation like China, an effective indigenous strategy was essential. The Chinese masses would never embrace a "foreigner's religion." The appearance and structure of Christianity had to change before the Chinese would accept it. One Chinese onlooker in the 1890s listened to a powerful sermon from a local evangelist. He made the following insightful comment:

Once a forest was told that a load of axe-heads had come to cut it down. "It doesn't matter in the least," said the forest, "they will never succeed by themselves." When, however, it heard that some of its own branches had become handles to the axe-heads, it said, "Now we have no chance."

So long as we only had foreigners to deal with, we were safe, but now that everywhere our own countrymen are enlisted on that side, certainly Christianity will flourish and conquer us.

Alas, many missionary organizations did not share Hudson Taylor's insights and continued to act like parents to the emerging Chinese church. Not surprisingly, China continued to view Christianity as a Western religion and its Chinese adherents as traitors and slaves of their Western masters. A common Chinese saying at the time was "One more Chinese Christian equals one less Chinese."[6]

In spite of that graphic description of Christianity, the church in China did overcome much of its "foreignness" and added millions of believers to the Kingdom of God.

QUESTIONS FOR DISCUSSION
Chapter 12

1. *Does your church or mission society believe in the three-self principle? To what extent do they practice what they believe?*

2. *Can you think of any examples of truly indigenous mission-established churches?*

3. *What is the self-image of the people in your congregation or denomination?*

---

[6] This is quoted from Paul Hattaway's Back to Jerusalem page 7. The original quote is from *Christianity in China: a Scholar's Guide to Resources in the Libraries and Archives of the United States* by Archie R. Crouch, Steven Agoratus, Arthur Emerson, and Debra E. Soled (eds). Published in New York by M. E. Sharpe, 1989 (page xxxi)

4. *How does the non-Christian community feel about your church?*

5. *To what extent are western denominations the result of movements toward independence? What can be done to improve relationships between denominations that were started in that way?*

6. *To what extent is music in your church truly indigenous? Can 16th century music be considered indigenous in today's society?*

7. *Does your church have a healthy reproductive system? How well are you producing leaders? And what is happening in missionary outreach?*

SUGGESTED READING

Allen, Roland. *The Spontaneous Expansion of the Church.* Grand Rapids: Wm B. Eerdmans, 1962.

Barrett, David. *Schism and Renewal in Africa.* Nairobi: Oxford University Press, 1968.

Hodges, Melvin L. *On the Mission Field — The Indigenous Church.* Chicago: Moody Press, 1953.

Kraft, Charles H., ed. *Readings in Dynamic Indigeneity.* Pasadena: Wm Carey Library, 1979.

Tippett, Alan R. *Verdict Theology in Missionary Theory.* Pasadena: Wm Carey Library, 1973.

CHAPTER 13

ASPECTS OF
CONVERSION IN AN AFRICAN CONTEXT

Introduction

In the next three lessons, I will take a deeper look at some of the issues I touched on in earlier chapters. In this lesson I deal with the first of these: **the nature of Christian conversion**.

A Description of Marginal Christian Conversion

In chapter 1, I gave a rather extensive quotation from a missiologist who worked in East Africa for some years, Dr. Aylward Shorter. While some may feel it is unfair criticism of Christianity in Africa, many African church leaders to whom I have spoken would not disagree with what Dr. Shorter says.

> ... At baptism the African Christian repudiates remarkably little of his former non-Christian outlook. He may be obliged to turn his back on certain traditional practices which the church rightly or wrongly, has condemned in his area. But he is not asked to recant a religious philosophy. Consequently he returns to the forbidden practices as occasion arises with remarkable ease.[1]

Concentric Circles and Christian Conversion[2]

Why is Dr. Shorter's observation so important?

I will now return to our example of the concentric circles which I mentioned in Chapter 1. There are various levels at which conversion can take place. On the outer levels there may be *evidence* of change. But there is much more happening than one sees on the surface.

---

[1] Aylward Shorter, *African Christian Theology: Adaptation or Incarnation.* (1977:10). A longer version of this quote was given in Chapter 1, but the issue will be given more in-depth treatment here.

[2] I am indebted to Dr. Donald R. Jacobs, a Mennonite anthropologist, for these observations.

182

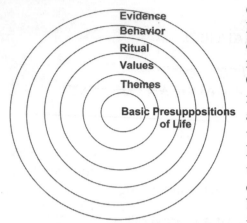

Evidence
Behavior
Ritual
Values
Themes
Basic Presuppositions of Life

Consider the issue of polygamy. In an African village one sees many children running and playing (*evidence*). One may ask why there are so many children in this society, and discover — upon investigation — that a man may have several wives. Each of these wives may have several children. And so the *behavior* behind the number of children is polygamy. Go one step further, and one finds that in that society fertility *rituals* are used to "enable" women to have children – especially designed to help barren women who want to bear children.

Going still deeper into this cultural practice, one discovers *a value system,* sometimes called humanism[3], in which everyone in society is cared for. That includes widows, orphans, the unemployed, the elderly, and those who are ill. The value of caring for everyone reflects the concern for everyone in society.

Continuing to analyze this society, one notices that at the center, there are *basic presuppositions* that drive the entire worldview. It is this series of assumptions that is behind the practice of polygamy. The idea is as basic as this: for a man to "live forever" (or at least to live a long time in the memory of the people) he must have many children who will remember him after he dies. This may be thought of as an animistic version of "eternal life" though the person who holds that view is unlikely to ever describe it that way. It is the nature of such deeply held assumptions that we rarely can verbalize them. Believe me, I have deep assumptions that I find it difficult to verbalize. Indeed, I learned that my African brothers and sisters could more easily recognize some of mine than I could.

For purposes of understanding Christian conversion, what Dr. Shorter says in the passage quoted above is that many African Christians have not had the kind of deep spiritual transformation

---

[3] I am referring to the kind of humanism described by Dr. Kenneth Kaunda in his book *A Humanist in Africa*.

that affects the presuppositions at the center of their worldview. Many African Christians (as well as many western Christians) have the kind of Christianity which overlays a traditional worldview, allowing them to hold two religious systems simultaneously. The traditional worldview (in this case, animistic) continues to be held as the primary (or ultimate) source of power in the face of demon possession or the threat of being cursed, for example. It may be used when one faces a terminal illness, the death of a child or another life crisis. The Christian worldview in this scenario, then, becomes another option (one offered by the church) which can be exercised when looking for employment, getting an education, or perhaps making an overseas visit sponsored by the church.

I should quickly add here that this sort of marginal conversion can be seen in many societies. Many westerners also exercise their Christian faith only at a superficial level. The reason I am describing it here is to show how it relates to the dependency syndrome.

I must quickly acknowledge that there are many African Christians who have been changed at the very deepest level. We thank God for each one of them. Many of them put western Christians to shame with their devotion to Christ. *However, developing a missionary sending movement is not built on individuals here and there who are soundly converted.* A strong missionary movement flows out of a congregation or denomination widely energized by the Holy Spirit. A missionary sending church is one in which an entire group feels like "this outreach movement belongs to us." They are already giving to the church, and out of the overflow, they support the mission of the church to the wider world.

Marginal Christian Conversion

What are the implications of *marginal Christian conversion*? One is that those values or beliefs which are held lightly can be easily laid aside – sometimes because of political or social pressure – and sometimes simply with the passage of time. This would be true of westerners who allow nationalism to take priority over their Christian commitment. Dr. Arthur Glasser said that nationalism is the unconfessed sin of our generation.

In the oriental world, Confucianism virtually passed off the scene in the last century. Since the Communists came to power in China one scarcely hears anything of Confucianism. Perhaps it's fair, then, to say that Confucianism was not held as a belief deep down at the center of a Chinese worldview. When the Communists came along with a new philosophy and adopted a new language for all (Mandarin), Confucianism was set aside in favor of something new.

Between 1968 and 1978 in Indonesia two million Muslims became Christians. We haven't heard anything like that in North Africa. In North Africa conversions to Christianity have not been in the thousands, perhaps only in the hundreds. With all the resistance to Christianity in North Africa, how do you account for the fact that in Indonesia two million Muslims became Christians in a ten-year period?

Obviously there are many factors in Indonesian society such as the communist revolution, bloodshed and the other disillusionment of that ten-year period from 1968-1978. But in actual fact, Islam in Indonesia *in those days* was, by comparison, on the surface; it was not held tenaciously by people who faithfully prayed five times a day and made the annual pilgrimage to Mecca. It was a more popular form of Islam, somewhat like nominal Christianity. And when something better came along, like genuine Christianity – Christianity with power – they gave up Islam. (I must add that in some parts of Indonesia, Islam was deeply entrenched as has become evident in more recent years.)

Catholicism is experiencing similar changes in Latin America where many Roman Catholics have given up a nominal form of religion for evangelical Christianity. That is why evangelicals are growing so rapidly in South and Central America. Later on I will come to some of the problems related to this, but suffice it to say that when religion is held only marginally, something else can come along and replace it. This is a current danger for Christianity in Africa and elsewhere.

What are Some of the Obstacles to Genuine Christianity?

1. First, we hear frequently in Africa about **the problem of "easy believism"**. Sometimes it is relatively easy for people to come into the Kingdom of God. New believers do not have to give up things from their spiritist past that are displeasing to God

because "conversion" has been made too easy. Many who come into Christianity were not asked to count the cost and, therefore, they are not likely to joyfully serve the Lord with their whole hearts — including putting money into the church collection. In this respect one can see how easy believism is part of the cause of dependency among marginally converted believers.

2. Second, there is **the problem of motivation.** Why do people decide to become Christians in the first place? Perhaps the motivation for becoming a Christian is **unrelated** to accepting Jesus as Lord and Savior — for life. Unfortunately, the motivation sometimes relates to those "extras" such as employment, learning English, a place in school, foreign travel, etc. Such shallow motivation for coming into the Christian faith is another way the seeds of the dependency syndrome are sown.

The attraction to Christianity is sometimes what Dr. McGavran referred to as "cultural lift." He was referring to such things as an increased standard of living that sometimes comes through associating with Christian missionaries. Religious conversion deep down inside may not take place at all when the motivation is as simple as acquiring a school, clinic, well or dam for the community!

3. Third is **the problem of conflicting worldviews.** This is the dualism I mentioned before. Later, I will deal more in-depth with the problem of disparate worldviews. Suffice it to say that there is dissonance that results from the clash between two worldviews when a person holds the western Christianity simultaneously with a spiritist paradigm from a previous religion.

What are the Implications of Marginal Christian Conversion?

1. The significant **rise of independent churches** has its roots in the nature of Christian conversion. Consider the 10,000 African Independent Churches (AIC's) mentioned by Dr. David Barrett. Many (but not all) who left mission-established churches and went to AIC's did not hold Christ firmly at the center of their concentric circles. They left searching for something "real." They were looking for something *culturally appropriate* and

perhaps something *filled with power*. If they didn't find that where they were, they went looking for it—and sometimes created it if they needed to. Sometimes what they created did not have a Biblical foundation, but it met a *felt need* – if not a *real need*.

2. Another implication is that **the old paradigm may still be the final authority in their lives**. It may not matter how many other good things happen in the church if believers are only marginally converted. In the final instance, the old paradigm may be the one that rules. Among marginally converted peoples, nominal Christians may have little to say about how decisions are made; it may simply be easier to "go along" with existing non-Christian practices. After all, where is the power needed to stand in a time of crisis?

    The Good News of the Gospel is that there can be a new way of solving problems, establishing relationships or resolving conflicts. While our Bible tells us how these things should be done, marginally converted people may not be able to take advantage of the benefits of the Christian faith.

3. Another implication of marginal conversion is that **the idea of unhealthy fatalism is never effectively dealt with.** I previously mentioned two kinds of fatalism. One is the western form that maintains, "Those people are poor, and they will always be that way. We may as well help them – forever." The other form is the kind of fatalism that says, "We are poor. We will always be that way, so you may as well help us." Among marginally converted people, this second form of fatalism renders local decision-making difficult and makes many other things virtually impossible. That is because marginally converted people cannot say *with firm conviction* that "God has called us, and we know that He will provide for us." They may hold to the notion that they are *victims* rather than *overcomers*, concluding that they will be victims forever. This all points to the need for sound Christian conversion.

4. Another implication is that **those who hold two religious paradigms are unlikely to become enthusiastic missionaries of the Gospel,** carrying it elsewhere. People who are only marginally converted cannot go out and say to those in the rest

of the world, "This we know to be true, and we have found that you can count on it just as we have. If you learn to know Jesus as Lord and Savior, as we did, He'll give you power over demons or other problems that you face." If that *hasn't* been one's experience, they aren't unlikely to carry the Gospel to others.

5. The fifth implication of marginal conversion is **that people are unlikely to feel that the church deserves very much of their income.** In other words, marginally converted people are not likely to be generous givers to the work of the Lord. But when people have been soundly converted, they give to the church in gratitude for what God has done for them.

I told the story in an earlier chapter about a businessman in Lusaka, Zambia who brought 100,000 kwacha (US$2,500 at that time)[4] to the church following his conversion. He probably didn't do that lightly. I know that it is possible for a person to give a large sum of money to the church with the wrong motivation. But I suggest that a person who comes to say "thank you" to God for his experience of salvation has probably been soundly converted.

Examples of Individuals who Exhibit Marginal Christian Conversion

After serving the church for many years, a church leader in Central Africa became terminally ill and was told by the medical doctors that nothing could be done for him. Though he served the church for thirty-five years as an ordained minister, upon learning of his terminal illness he decided to go to the village of a local practitioner of religion. It turned out that his treatment was not from only a herbalist, but from one who practiced "manipulation of the spirits", to quote others in his church. There he lived out the last few months of his life.

Some time later I came across that church leader's testimony. About ten years before his death he attended a seminar in which an

---

[4] It must be remembered that exchange rates fluctuate significantly over time. Hence, one cannot compare today's rate to what prevailed at the time of this incident

anthropologist was conducting a session on, among other things, the nature of Christian conversion. The anthropologist described what authentic Christian conversion should be. In the process this ordained minister, who had served the church for so many years, made the following statement:

> *"What you say about genuine Christian conversion deeply moves me, because I must confess that I have not been converted that way. My deeper African values have not been changed. I have merely become an imitation European on the outside. I have not learned to listen to the Holy Spirit, but I have been trained to listen very carefully to what the missionary wants."*[5]

This statement reflects the dualism with which this church leader lived. I find it very sad that he did not see the Christian faith as having the final power and authority in times of crisis. Unfortunately, there are many "Christians" who feel that way about their spiritual experience.

Remember, that if a church is to have a dynamic missionary movement, it will need to reconcile in its own mind whether it is the **Holy Spirit** or the **spirits** that have the final authority.

The Alternative to Marginal Christian Conversion: People Movements and Power Encounter

Professor Tippett describes for us what needs to happen for the problem of marginal Christian conversion to be dealt with. He shows that sound conversion in the islands of the South Pacific was often through a "power encounter" which resulted in a "people movement." He refers to the story of Elijah on Mt. Carmel, as found in 1 Kings 18.

All of this confirms that the alternative to marginal conversion is the enthronement of Christ at the center of the concentric circles, something that happens in an authentic power encounter and people movement.

---

[5] From *Let the Earth Hear His Voice*, by J.D. Douglas, page 250

How does that happen? Dr. Tippett says it happens when there is a serious encounter with "the powers" that exist, rendering them powerless while acknowledging Christ as the center of their lives. This is a true **power encounter,** resulting in a **people movement**. For those not familiar with these terms, I suggest looking at the Glossary of Terms in Appendix B.

A *power encounter* has to do with a people group saying, "We are finished with the old way of decision-making; we are making our relationship with Christ **the** primary paradigm upon which we will function." This sometimes follows a public confrontation with the old sources of power.[6]

A *people movement* occurs when many people turn to Christ at one time – whole villages, for instances. One of the tragedies of the Christian movement in various parts of Africa is that westerners often promoted individual conversion. In our preaching we often encouraged people to "stand up for Christ as an individual regardless what anyone else says or does." Sometimes we have encouraged them to live on a mission station because it was a safe place to live their new-found Christian lives. The assumption was that one could not live the Christian life in a village where the old paradigm was unchanged and where demons were still roaming about.

Dr. Tippett reminds us that the alternative is to take the Christian Gospel into the midst of the village where the old paradigm is still functioning. It is there that one needs to get the consensus of the people that the time has come for change. The Christian Gospel needs to be thoroughly explained before anyone is invited to become a Christian. In a people movement people are invited to make a decision together—to extend the Kingdom of God over their village. In this way, the village – not just the mission station—becomes a safe place for a Christian to live. Instead of traditionally promoting the *individual* coming to Christ as the ultimate experience, Dr. Tippett reminds us that it is more wholesome for the *entire family* to come to Christ together—father, mother, and children and others in the

---

[6] For a longer description of how a power encounter works, see *Christian Conversion in an African Context* an article by the author on the WMA website www.wmausa.org. For Dr. Tippett's description, see *People Movements in Southern Polynesia*, chapter 7.

extended family. That way the entire family can stand together against the powers of Satan.

More Dangers of Marginal Christian Conversion and a Partially Transferred Paradigm

1. There is a danger that people who are only marginally converted **will not destroy the sacred objects which they used in their previous way of life.** This is particularly important if people keep idols on their shelves or under their beds, or in some safe place that can be used in times of great need.

    A man in South Africa told about the experience of a family recently converted from Hinduism.[7] He said upon conversion, the family simply took their idols, wrapped them in papers, and put them in boxes under the bed in case they might need them some day. He warned them about the danger of such a practice. Once the old paradigm is dealt with, those once-useful sacred objects must be destroyed. Burning the old fetishes is often the sign that the old system is no longer going to be used. This includes destroying any objects of power, such as stones, sticks, feathers or rabbits' feet. Luke records such a "happening" in Acts 19:18-20 when Christians in Ephesus burned their sacred books.

2. There is a danger that **the former way of solving problems will not be replaced.** For marginally converted Christians this can be a serious problem. If the old way of problem solving is brought into the church there may be resentment when leaders are chosen – and the old ways (such as witchcraft) may be employed to silence someone with whom there is disagreement! If such things are not put away, then the church might not be a peaceful place to live one's Christian life.

3. Finally, where there is marginal Christian conversion it is unlikely that **Christianity will be seen as a way of life worth living or dying for.** And that kind of Gospel is not likely to be reproduced elsewhere.

---

[7] Demon possession can be a serious problem in Hinduism, every bit as serious as in African animism.

Conclusion

In Lesson One I said that without genuine Christian conversion or spiritual renewal it is unlikely that mission churches will develop a healthy cross-cultural missionary movement. Neither will they joyfully give tithes and offerings adequate to sustain themselves. Hence, the problem of dependency should be seen as a spiritual problem, with roots in marginal or inadequate Christian conversion. When that is the case, there is no alternative but to go back to the basics and do serious evangelism and discipleship. The remedy is either evangelism, spiritual renewal or both.

QUESTIONS FOR DISCUSSION
Chapter 13

1. *Reflect on your own personal conversion experience. At what level did it originally take place? Did any change take place later at the center of the circles?*

2. *How serious is the problem of "easy believism" in churches today?*

3. *To what extent should Christian medical doctors become involved in the spiritual problems behind some illnesses?*

4. *What place do people movements and power encounters have in missionary evangelism today?*

5. *Are "born again" Christians more or less likely to give generously to their church?*

SUGGESTED READING

Adeyemo, Tokunboh. *Salvation in African Tradition.* Nairobi: Evangel Publishing House, 1979.

Mbiti, John S. *African Religions and Philosophy.* London: Heinemann, 1969.

Tippett, Alan. *People Movements in Southern Polynesia.* Chicago: Moody Press, 1971.

There are many other books that will help a serious missionary understand Christian conversion. One good book will have a bibliography of others in the same category. Avail yourself of them.

CHAPTER 14

CONFLICTING WORLD VIEWS
AND THE PROBLEM OF DEPENDENCY

Introduction

In this chapter I will describe the difference between the differing worldviews as it relates to the problem of dependency. One of the reasons churches sometimes find they are unable to govern themselves is that the clash has not been resolved between their own local worldview and that of the worldview represented by a foreign Gospel.

How are Decisions Made?

Westerners are very fond of making individual decisions, and they often are prepared to take responsibility, as an individual, for those decisions. The assumptions behind that can be rather a foreign concept to those who live in group-oriented societies.

Decision-making in traditional African society is most likely to be group-oriented. I learned long ago in my missionary experience that if I want to discuss some important issue with a village leader or church leader, whenever possible I should have at least one other set of ears present. Many times I was grateful for the presence of that other person. Among other things, it helped to keep both parties accountable, knowing that someone else was listening to what was discussed.

In the context of decision-making itself, westerners are fond of voting and saying that "51% of the people voted for something to happen, therefore it will be done regardless of what the other 49% think or want." To westerners this is called "the will of the majority" and considered to be victory. Sometimes significant changes are brought about on the basis of a very thin majority like that.

That sort of decision-making is frowned upon in a society that operates by *consensus*. When decisions are made by consensus, a majority of 51% would not be sufficient to carry an issue. Instead, discussion will continue until consensus is reached. Westerners find that kind of decision-making time consuming and indecisive.

As I mentioned several times before, part of the problem has to do with how we view the world we live in. Many non-Westerners see the world as *family* in contrast to the world of the *individual*. One of the ways of expressing this difference is to say that "Man is an Individual" or that "Man is a Family." In John V. Taylor's book, *Primal Vision,* he describes "man as family."

The Role of Technology

Another issue one needs to address is the western preoccupation with technology in western life and work. Westerners are convinced of the importance of technology in helping us do a better and more efficient job, whatever our occupation. We tend to be **project-oriented**. This preoccupation with efficiency often clashes with people who believe that a new way of doing things is not nearly as important as preserving the relationships of those involved in the old way of doing things. The alternative is to become **people-oriented**. In one worldview there may be the introduction of technology at all costs, regardless of who may be offended. In the other, one carefully seeks to preserve relationships so that no one feels alienated. If the two approaches are not reconciled, clashes of the competing worldviews will result in broken relationships and a possibly fractured future.

The Western understanding of technology has many ramifications. We are trained in universities which are scientifically oriented. We then feel this to be the superior way of dealing with life. Because of this, missionaries have gone out from North America, to a place like Central Africa, arriving on location to begin their teaching assignment the very next day, not realizing they were walking into a completely different world (or worldview). Little wonder that tensions arise!

The Importance of Cross-Cultural Training

Consider the following scenario. A young western man who has never held a position of responsibility in his own country has recently graduated from university. Suddenly, he finds himself in the middle of Africa, being given a weighty assignment almost immediately – perhaps as a classroom teacher or head of a project. He has never had cross-cultural training and may know nothing about an animistic worldview or many of the other issues I have been discussing. What can he share with local people upon his immediate arrival? Unless unusually gifted of the Lord with cultural sensitivity, he is capable of telling them the only thing he knows – i.e., his understanding of the Bible, technology, or how decisions are made in a democracy where he comes from. He will probably go on to promote his own understanding of the world with little regard for how others think and feel. He may even introduce an idea and ask for a vote, not realizing how out of character that might be.

Consider the arrogance when outsiders move into such a different world and automatically become leaders. Think about how this is related to the dependency syndrome. When a person moves easily from one world into the other and is automatically assumed to be an "expert", something happens to the people in the receiving culture. Suddenly local people begin to feel, "This person is from the outside; this person's ideas must be important and, furthermore, he or she represents money and we should listen to what they have to say." When that happens, initiative dies within the local people. Yet their gifts are so much needed to build a strong indigenous church.

In the part of Africa that I have been talking about, it is not unusual to find people who feel that they have been repeatedly bombarded with the concept of "foreign superiority." Too many local people have concluded that they do not have the gifts, education, decision-making ability, or the resources to do God's work without help from the outside. What is the alternative to such a sad conclusion?

The alternative is for those of us who are outsiders to say with humility, "Brothers and sisters, I would like to learn from you. I would like to see how you do things or how you make decisions. I would like you to tell me what Christ means to you. Then I would like to encourage you to be all that God wants you to be."

God's Providence

The organization with which I have been working for the past twenty or more years, World Mission Associates, has the following philosophy of ministry:

> *God in His providence placed ordinary people, like you and me, all over the world in order to accomplish His purpose. Our Christian responsibility is to find each other and encourage each other to become all that He wants us to be.*

How does this relate to the subject at hand? It means that when God takes me to Zambia or to Malawi or some other place, I will find that He already has people there whom I am simply to encourage "to be all He wants them to be." He has placed them there for a purpose.

Some years ago I took an overnight train to western Tanzania. As the sun came up the next morning we were traveling through the countryside, and I saw a man walking on a path high on the hillside. I thought to myself that God in His providence placed that man there. He was probably walking from one village to another. God wanted that man to be all that he could be. I thought how nice it would be if I could just go up there on the hillside and say, "Brother, how are you doing? Do you know the Lord Jesus and how He wants to use you in this area where you live? Are you aware that God wants you to be all you can possibly be?"

I know that I can't take his place. I can't do what God may be asking him to do. I can't **be** and **do** what everyone else is called of God to **be** and **do**.[1]

To Control or be Controlled

Another potential conflict over the differing worldviews is the matter of **whether** or **how** the world can be controlled. The westerner often approaches this question with the assumption that the world **can** be controlled. Scientific discoveries, for example, convinced us that

[1] To reflect further on why many people in the world dislike the western display of superiority see *Why the Rest Hates the West: Understanding the Roots of Global Rage* by Meic Pearce. Details are in the general bibliography

that we can control disease. In the 1950's Dr. Jonas Salk discovered a vaccine for polio. At that time westerners became convinced that if we just had enough knowledge we would be able to control all the diseases in the world. And although we didn't have a solution for cancer at that point in time, we became hopeful when Dr. Salk made his discovery. At that time westerners were on the verge of putting people into outer space. The assumption was that we were controlling the world around us more and more, or so we thought.

But when we as westerners encountered Central Africa, we found a worldview that considered people to be victims. Many things in life were beyond their control and they could do nothing about it. One feels like a victim of evil spirits, demon possession or poverty. And that's "just the way life is." It is easy to see how this leads to the problem of dependency. Contrast that to the person who says, "I will rise up to change my situation in life. I can do it and I will." You can see how these two very different worldviews collide. One says, "I am in control." The other laments, "I have no control over life because things just happen." The good news of the Christian Gospel is that God allows some things to happen and then uses them for His purposes in our lives.

Assumptions about Integrity and other Moral Values

Some assumptions which outsiders carry with them can adversely affect local value systems. Let's look at an example relating to one important issue – personal integrity.

A church leader may feel obligated to hold up the heavy box I referred to in Chapter 1. Perhaps he does this out of fear that his reputation will be damaged in the eyes of those who built the box in the first place. In so doing, he may find himself making ethical compromises because he cannot afford to admit that this "box" cannot be sustained. In the process he compromises his personal integrity to accomplish the goal.

I was traveling in Central Africa with some church leaders several years ago. There were three of us in the vehicle and my place was in the middle seat in the front of a vanette, or pick-up truck. We were to drive quite a long distance with a bishop on my left and his assistant on the right serving as driver. Before we left for this journey we went around behind some buildings in the town center and found about a dozen people who were waiting for the transport bus. We learned that they were going to the same place we were, so they were invited to get into the back of our vanette. We started off on our three-hour drive to the capital city.

About an hour into the journey we came upon a police checkpoint which are quite common in that area. We stopped, and the police asked their usual question, "Where are you going?" The Bishop responded by saying, "We are going to the capital city."

"What are you going to do there?"

The bishop replied, "We are going to attend a meeting."

Then the policeman asked, "And who are these people in the back?" – to which the bishop replied, "They are our members, and we are going together to the meeting."

The policeman said, "Right, go ahead." After we drove away, I said to the bishop, "By the way, Bishop, are these people our members?" He admitted they were not. "But that is what you told that policeman," I said. He admitted that he had been untruthful and said he would not do that again.

Sadly this is not uncommon when cash flow forces leaders to do the unethical. What we were doing was a violation of the law in that country. We were carrying passengers without a bus or taxi license. Why had the bishop knowingly broken this law? Because (in his words), "If we don't carry passengers, we won't have money for petrol to get back home."

What happens to one's value system when this sort of thing occurs? What happens to one's Christian testimony and character? This is an example of how an inappropriate and expensive church structure and administration can lead to making moral choices that are not in keeping with Biblical principles. What happens to the police when they see this kind of thing happening by leaders in the church?

On one occasion I spoke with a pastor in South Africa who told me his story. "I cannot make ends meet in my church. I simply don't get enough money. My wife works, but we are not earning enough to maintain our family; and I refuse to do what some of my other friends have done. I have fellow pastors who don't get enough money from their churches, so they employ women to brew and sell beer to get money to increase the pastor's income." This is another of the ramifications of how the dependency mentality plays itself out in the local church, sometimes causing pastors to choose between illegal and unethical activities or leaving the ministry. All of these represent reasons to take seriously the mentality of dependency.

Worldview and the Concept of Western Science

To get an in-depth look at differing assumptions consider the following illustration provided for us by Dr. Donald Jacobs, a Mennonite missionary anthropologist. He uses the following diagram.

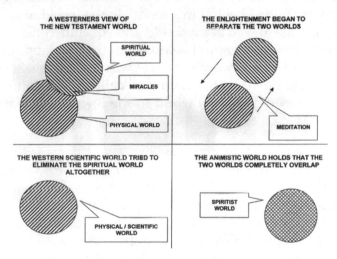

In the top left-hand box, the lines in the top circle going one way represent <u>spiritual</u> cause and effect. The lines going the other way in the second circle represent <u>physical</u> cause and effect. Where these two worlds overlap, Dr. Jacobs says we as westerners get our understanding of the New Testament. When we look at the New Testament, we observe physical and spiritual events going on. Where they overlap, miracles take place. We were taught that in this realm of miracles, Jesus healed people and cast out demons.

But then westerners went through the so-called *Enlightenment* and found science coming into its own; here the two worlds began to separate one from the other (see the upper right section of my diagram). While the *spiritual world* and the *physical world* were two distinctly different realms, it was believed that one could *go back and forth* between the two by having a devotional experience. In other words, by meditation one could enter into the spiritual world and stay there for a while, then come back to the physical world. Hence, the two worlds existed side by side, but they didn't necessarily touch each other. The scientific world of natural cause and effect was beginning to stand on its own.

The next world (shown in the lower left) represents the world in which I grew up in the 1950's. This increasingly became a scientific world. I went to high school when the Salk vaccine was discovered, and when there was a big push in science to catch up to the Russians. After all, the Russians had just put a satellite (Sputnik) that actually stayed in orbit. Americans were embarrassed because it looked like they were falling behind in science. In the world of religion in those days, some looked at the world and concluded that God was dead. When I went to *church* I heard about the overlapping worlds (upper left), but when I went to *school* I was taught to believe in the scientific world (lower left). **Then** God called me as a missionary to Africa represented by the world in the lower right part of my diagram!

The African world was a complete overlay of the spiritual on top of the physical. African traditional religion knew nothing of two worlds. Their world had physical characteristics, but their spiritual world affected all aspects of that physical world. For example, stones, rivers, trees could all have a spirit. In that worldview, ancestors have spirits. One did not simply cut down a tree because wood was needed. One looked at that tree and asked, "Is there some spiritual reason why this tree is standing here and perhaps should not be cut down?"[2] Everything in life brought the two worlds together. There was no secular/spiritual divide as I had been trained to believe. No wonder I was sometimes confused and mystified as a missionary in Africa!

Observations on Differing World Views

1. **As westerners we often look at these worlds as either/or.** We have trouble understanding a worldview that is a total cosmology, holding everything as sacred and secular at the

---

[2] Consider, for example, the sacred groves of Asherah trees in the Old Testament

same time. To us, one is right and the other wrong. That's why an American science teacher can leave a western university and begin teaching immediately in a non-western society because he or she doesn't have to take into consideration what's in that other world. The objective might simply be to invite other people to leave their complicated and mystifying world and join ours.

2. Second, **non-westerners** who hold an animistic worldview **often look at Christianity as a supplement to what they already believe.** They may function primarily on their own paradigm and use Christianity when it's convenient, doing their *primary* decision-making in the original worldview. This is often frustrating to missionaries not familiar with how the other worldview functions.

3. One observation that's critical for the subject of dependency is that **when one holds that unified worldview, it means that some things can be done and some things cannot.** For example, one doesn't have the freedom to run roughshod over tradition, history, and relationships without taking into consideration the implications of what might happen. For example, dealing with the "spirits" means that before we make decisions about this or that, we take into consideration the larger worldview and what might happen if the rules are not followed. A missionary who doesn't understand the importance may simply try to ignore the fundamentals and be unaware of who or what is being trampled in the process. He will not realize the relationships that he may be breaking simply because of his lack of humility or cultural sensitivity.

There is probably no place where this is more important than in the world of medicine. Western medicine is usually concerned with the scientific approach to solving the problem of illness. Westerners firmly believe in the germ theory of sickness. Westerners just need to find out what brought about the problem: "**What** caused it, and **how** did it happen?" At the same time, someone with the unified worldview may well be asking **why** it happened and **who** caused it, **not what** or **how**. Even if the problem is apparent, such as an automobile accident where the injuries are obvious, perhaps leading to death, the person holding the non-scientific worldview will want to know

who caused the accident and **why** it happened. Did someone curse this person? A westerner, on the other hand, would highlight the fact that the brakes failed, and that is **what** caused the accident and **how** it happened.

In order to understand this, one needs to recognize the difference between the "germ theory of sickness" and the "spirit theory of sickness." The spirit theory of sickness forces one to seek out the spiritual or emotional things in the sick person's life that may have gone wrong. In order to understand the importance of that, it is helpful to understand the role of "balance" or what is sometimes called "the harmony of the worldview." Sickness can be caused by imbalance. Wellness is regained by restoring balance in the spiritual realm.

Fortunately, those involved in western medicine are beginning to realize more and more that sickness may be caused by what are referred to as "psychosomatic" illnesses – those created by non-organic causes. Western medical people are now saying that 50% of those in hospitals in North America are there for psychosomatic reasons. (Some estimates run as high as 80% or 90%.) Hence, the spirit theory of sickness is gaining some credibility in western medicine. Still, a person deeply immersed in western scientific medicine may experience culture shock when entering a situation where people hold to the spirit theory of sickness.

Is There Any Good News?

Churches that take the spirit world seriously have a better chance of dealing with problems of spiritism and demon possession than those that are limited by their scientific orientation. Those who resist often write off the realities of the spirit world. The western scientific worldview is not the answer to the deepest questions of the soul, but thankfully the power of the Holy Spirit **is**.

For those who are interested in this subject, I suggest reading *Defeating Dark Angels* by Dr. Charles Kraft. This book shows that a spiritual solution to the problem of spirit possession is available. Remember, through spiritual renewal—taking the work of the Holy Spirit seriously – the Church can become all that God intends it to be. The Holy Spirit can help us deal with the huge differences between the two worldviews.

QUESTIONS FOR DISCUSSION
Chapter 14

1. *To what extent are you an individual or corporate decision-maker? Do you believe consensus decision-making is valid?*

2. *Can you think of examples where non-western technology is just as appropriate as western scientific technology?*

3. *To what extent has the western scientific worldview influenced your conversion experience?*

4. *Discuss your views of the impact of the so-called "Enlightenment" on Western Christianity.*

SUGGESTED READINGS

Kraft, Charles H. *Christianity with Power*. Ann Arbor: Vine Books, 1989.

Kraft, Charles H. *Defeating Dark Angels*. Ann Arbor: Vine Books, 1992.

Also see the suggested readings for Chapter 13.

CHAPTER 15

ETHNICITY AND CROSS-CULTURAL
CHURCH PLANTING: WHY DEPENDENCY DEVELOPS

Note: In this chapter I use the term "ethnic churches" in a different way from contemporary popular usage in North America. "Ethnic" is often used when referring to Black or Hispanic churches. My usage is broader and includes churches which have an ethnic term in the name of the denomination, though it is not limited to such. I give examples under the section below entitled What is an Ethnic Church?

Introduction

Consider this key question: Why do many western mission societies have difficulty planting self-supporting or indigenous churches cross-culturally? The subject of ethnicity and cross-cultural church planting could very well be one of the most important issues related to the matter of dependency and self-reliance.

Identity Preservation

One reason westerners find it difficult to plant truly indigenous churches is that many western mission societies are seeking to preserve the identity of the denomination they represent. If they are successful in doing this, the churches they plant will probably not be seen as indigenous in their communities. They may have the identity of the so-called "mother church" but not the identity of the society in which they are planted.

I recognize that is a rather strong statement, so let me hasten to describe what I mean. I begin with the premise that an indigenous church should look and act (culturally) like the society of which it is a part. The alternative to this is to have a church that looks and acts like the society from which the missionaries came. The problem I am referring to has particular relevance to what are sometimes referred to as "ethnic churches."

What is an Ethnic Church?

When I use the term "ethnic church" I am referring to one that often has an ethnic name in its title – e.g., Scottish Presbyterian, Anglican, Dutch Reformed, German Lutheran, or American Baptist. Of course, there are many other churches that don't have an ethnic name in their title, and they are also ethnic churches. These include the Mennonite Church, for example, which is closely tied to its German background, or the Brethren in Christ Church (also with a German background), the denomination to which I belong. I would classify this church as an ethnic church, because of the German background of many of its members. As with many other ethnic churches, thankfully some positive changes have been occurring in recent years.

When missionaries from ethnic churches go out to plant churches cross-culturally, many of them attempt to preserve the identity of the denomination of which they are a part. To repeat what I mentioned above, I believe that the extent to which they are successful in preserving that identity, to that same extent the church they plant is not likely to be indigenous to the society in which it is planted. One North American mission executive said that his purpose in planting churches in Latin America was to preserve the distinctives of his denomination in North America.

The Concept of an Indigenous Church

A truly indigenous church has its roots deep in its own culture. It is a church that sees itself as the body of Christ **in its own society** (*self-image*). People see it *in that society* as a legitimate and wholesome local institution to which they feel they can belong (*community image*). It stands to reason that a local church that tries to mirror its sending church will be less than an indigenous church in its own community.

What are some of the characteristics of a non-indigenous church? Often non-indigenous churches are looked upon as "borrowers." They borrow *language* and *church structure*. And they often borrow *theology* or *doctrine*. Almost every church planter thinks that the doctrines that he or she teaches are truly Biblical. In reality, one's Biblical theology or doctrine (while rooted in Scripture) can be somewhat different from someone else's Biblical theology or doctrine (which they also feel are rooted in Scripture). It is not unusual for both to think that they are theologically correct.

Unfortunately, ethnic churches which plant non-indigenous churches often plant dependent churches—churches which need various forms of assistance to exist. This can certainly be seen in the construction of church buildings. Have you ever noticed that when church buildings are built with foreign money and by foreign people, they have an uncanny resemblance to the structure of the sending church? In East Africa churches built by the Greek Orthodox are stone structures that look very much like Orthodox church buildings elsewhere. You will see a similar thing in other denominations. A church building may have a divided chancel, for example, because the sending church has a divided chancel.

The Dependent Church

Dependent churches, planted by ethnic churches through their overseas mission societies, are often not free to make decisions because whatever they decide must be acceptable to the church at home. Such a church is not likely to be locally owned and operated – my description of something truly indigenous.

Sadly, if a non-indigenous church has a "borrowed faith experience" it might not be meeting the deepest needs in the society where it is located. And when that happens, members **may not** have a deeply satisfying spiritual experience. Such church members are hardly candidates to reproduce their church elsewhere. American Christians may emphasize Christ dealing with guilt and loneliness. Another society may be struggling with the need for power and deliverance in the face of spirit activity. If missionaries' teaching is based on their own cultural background, the needs of those they seek to serve may never be met.

Consider how this affects music in the church. There are ethnic churches in North America that sing hymns which came from the "old country"—perhaps from Germany or Holland. This means that in America they are borrowing not only the music from Holland and Germany, but in some churches even borrowing a clothing style worn by people in Germany 400 years ago. Why is this? Many times it is because these people have come to feel it is a Biblical mandate, that it is a more spiritual way to dress (or sing). Since they inherited this foreignness, they may find themselves passing on that same foreignness to others. When such churches send out missionaries, they sometimes carry with them those German hymn tunes—even if they were not always joyfully sung at home! In other words, music which came from the "Old World" to the "New World" has now been carried to the "rest of the world." This results in people in African churches singing German hymn tunes instead of music that comes out of their own culture and background. Good theology should be expressed in hymns and other forms of worship; but if hymns and other such things are imported, worship most likely will not be authentic.

Imagine for a moment that people in Africa carry the good news of the Gospel to some other part of the world. Will they (or should they) take those German hymn tunes with them? You can see that at some point it is important that the cycle of carrying along "foreign" ethnic characteristics (music or theology) must be broken. A truly indigenous church learns how to break that cycle.

One of the best examples of breaking the cycle that I know about is the church started by the SIM in southern Ethiopia many years ago. This church grew into hundreds of thousands of members. I was told that in the early days when they had a quarter of a million members, they had only one hymn tune and all music in the church was sung to that one tune. There was no felt need to translate one piece of music after another from overseas.

This problem to which I am referring is sometimes compounded because local people use a five-note scale and the imported music is being sung to an eight-note scale. Imagine the dissonance that results. In some cases local music is not permitted in the church because it represents what the outsiders consider to be pagan or unspiritual. In fact, it may be thought by the outsiders to be associated with spiritism. While in some cases this may be true, some form of local music should be found and dedicated for use in the church.

When *church structure* is borrowed, it is often too expensive to maintain—let alone pass along. I referred to this in earlier chapters.

Additionally, some non-indigenous churches may be dependent on someone else's *vision*. One church in Central Africa began cross-cultural evangelism because the mission agency said it needed to be done! The vision for outreach wasn't born in the hearts and minds of the local people; it happened because an outsider indicated that it was the next thing to do. Therefore, this local church was not truly *self-propagating*, one of the marks of an indigenous church. While a missionary ought to introduce the importance of the Great Commission, the challenge is to see it become a passion of the local church—not something being done because the missionary says so.

What is the alternative? The alternative is for the Holy Spirit to fill local people with a desire to take the Good News to those still waiting to hear it for the first time. They would then *own* the vision. This once again points us to the need for spiritual renewal.

Avoiding a Non-Indigenous System

How then can cross-cultural church planters avoid introducing a non-indigenous system? This brings us to a very practical issue in missiology: How does one decide what is an essential part of one's Christian experience? In other words, what is a legitimate part of the Christian faith, and what is simply cultural?

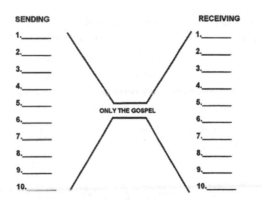

In my accompanying diagram you will see numbers listed on the right and on the left. Numbers represent cultural characteristics. (This could actually be 1000 rather than just 10.) The list on the left represents characteristics of the sending church and on the right, the receiving church. Consider what kind of things are on these lists.

Item 1 might be the kind of clothes church members wear. Item 2 might be the kinds of things they use when they eat a meal—knives, forks, chopsticks or fingers. Item 3 might be the language used when they speak or worship; item 4 might be their kinship structure. Number 5 may have to do with one of the church doctrines such as baptism. Number 6 may have to do with the form of communion used in the church. One could continue down that list with many other things.

The challenge for anyone going into cross-cultural ministry is to go down through that list and ask a very important question: Is this item essential to the Christian Gospel or not? Let's take number 1, for example—the kind of clothes one wears. The Bible does not teach that clothes should be a determining factor in whether a person is a Christian or not, apart from the concept of modesty. Even the concept of modesty varies widely depending on what culture one is in. In this process one is simply asking whether each item has anything to do with the real meaning of the Christian gospel, or is it simply part of one's own culture. Even the 11:00 o'clock church service on Sunday morning—as sacred as some may think this is—must be evaluated in terms of Christianity or culture.

Of course, there is the most important issue of coming to Christ and making Him Lord and Savior. There are other issues of importance such as repentance and conversion, being filled with the Holy Spirit, and some form of baptism or communion. As we go down the list, we might be able to eliminate 995 of the 1000 items as being cultural, but five of them must be recognized as being essential to Christianity. It is these five essentials that should accompany me through the small channel as I take the Gospel cross-culturally. The rest, as much as possible, I should *try* to leave behind.

I acknowledge that it is often impossible to leave many of those cultural things behind. My problem is not with the person who finds it hard to leave some things behind. My problem is with the person who doesn't think it is *important* to leave any of those cultural things behind. And of course, the biggest problem is with the person who *isn't even aware* of the cultural list and tries to carry everything through the channel.

Moving over to the right hand side of my diagram, we find a list that represents those who are to receive the Gospel. They also have a well-developed cultural list. Number 1 may be their way of wearing clothes. Number 2 may be their way of eating (knives and forks, chopsticks, or fingers). Number 3 may have to do with their marriage ceremonies. Number 4, 5, 6 and 7 represent other things about their religion and society. They also have a thousand things that are part of their culture. Here is the challenge: How many of those things are simply cultural and can remain—*should* remain—as people come to the Christian faith? And how many things will need to be replaced when people accept the Christian Gospel as their new way of life?

Unfortunately, too often missionaries look at that list belonging to the receiving culture and decide to condemn it outright, saying that the thousand things on that side simply need to be replaced. In fact, as westerners, we have often concluded that if people want to know the Christian Gospel, they should simply "come over to our side" and imitate the thousand things on our side. Then, we assume, they will be Christians just as we are. When western ethnic churches plant churches cross-culturally, this is far too often the direction in which they move.

I once shared this concept in a missionary conference where a former missionary to Japan was present. He raised his hand and said, "In Japan, we did not invite people to come from the right and imitate us on the left. We sucked them backward through that small channel!" Of course, this meant stripping them of the many things they needed to be an authentic indigenous expression of Christianity in their society. What he said might sound humorous, but it is quite an apt description of what has often happened.

Churches as Foreign Replicas

Newly planted churches that are replicas of the sending church have often been denied the privilege of retaining the things that make them unique. This is a serious matter because it denies people the privilege of holding on to the things that are good in their society. When this happens, their own self-respect is denied.

If we condemn most of the things in that right hand column, we may be condemning some of the very things that God ordained to hold that society together. Think of " culture" as the list of things that help to hold a society together. Think of them as wholesome ways of making decisions, of accomplishing projects, of caring for people, of giving to others and so on. If we simply condemn or destroy those things, we may destroy *the glue that holds society together*, which is my definition of culture.

What is the danger of indiscriminately condemning things in someone else's culture? An anthropologist once said, "When you teach children that the values their parents hold are invalid, you are sowing the seeds for dissolution in that society." Imagine teaching children that the views their parents hold are invalid! Who of us would want someone to come into our society and tell our children that their belief in Christ is wrong, and that they should give it up? We would take serious exception to that! The alternative is to introduce the claims of Christ to the parents and let them introduce the same to their children. Respecting the God-given position of parents in society is the healthiest for all concerned. That is why Professor Tippett advocated presenting the Gospel to elders in the society so that it becomes a safe place for children to believe.

But as missionaries, we are prone to go into a society and tell children that what their parents believe is wrong. Then we encourage the children to learn about Christ and stand up for their new faith regardless of what their parents say. In the process we are driving a wedge between parent and child. Surely there is a better alternative.

Returning to the diagram, there are things on that right hand side which will need to be given up. If, for example, the people on the right hand side are involved in idol worship, demon possession or child sacrifices, then such practices are inconsistent with the Christian gospel. Perhaps there are five or six things in that thousand which *will* need to be given up because they are not compatible with Jesus' teaching — or not compatible with the concept of the one God with no other gods before Him. But that does not mean condemning all the things that hold a society together.

Let's consider one example. What is the alternative to child sacrifices, something one might find on the right-hand side of my diagram? Professor Tippett used to say that if you minister in a sacrificial society where you know sacrifices of one kind or another are being performed, the Good News of the Gospel is that there is a Biblical alternative. A missionary can go to them with the Good News of the Gospel and say: "In the time of Abraham and Isaac this practice was being carried out. In fact, one of our ancestors (Abraham) was told to go up to the mountain and sacrifice his own child; and just as he had lifted up the knife, God intervened and said, 'STOP. I'm changing the rules. You don't need to do that any more.' Remember that Abraham was going to make that sacrifice because God told him to do so. But this time God changed the rules saying, 'Use a sheep instead.' And so for many years God was satisfied with the blood of sheep as a sacrifice for sin. But then there came a time when God said, 'I'm no longer satisfied with the blood of sheep. I am going to provide another sacrifice – human, yet divine.' And that was Jesus. The blood of that sacrifice was made on the cross of Christ, and that sacrifice was made once and for all." That is the essence of Good News for those who live in a sacrificial society. In this way we are not just condemning a cultural practice, but providing a viable alternative.

Dr. Tippett then went on to say, "And where do you learn about this? You learn about it in the book of Hebrews." He would ask a Bible translator, "Have you translated the book of Hebrews yet?" And they would reply, "Oh, that's a very difficult book. I can't translate that yet. I will leave that one until last because of the difficult language related to issues of sacrifices." I can remember hearing Dr. Tippett say, "If you live among people in a sacrificial society, you should consider translating the book of Hebrews early on, because that may be just the story they need to hear. The book of Hebrews might be the most helpful book in the New Testament for them to see that Christ was the eternal sacrifice once and for all." He allowed for the fact that perhaps Luke and Acts should be first, but he did not agree that Hebrews should be left to last.

Suggestions for Cross-Cultural Church Planters

1. **Preserving the cultural identity of a sending church is a fallacy** in cross-cultural church planting. It is in losing one's life that it is preserved (Matthew 10:39). An ethnic church that thinks it will lose its life unless it is reproduced the same way in another society misunderstands the concept of cross-cultural church planting.

2. **Inter-ethnic mission societies,** which bring together missionaries from different denominations, have a better chance of starting an indigenous church than ethnic churches which seek to preserve their own identity.

For example, if missionaries from Mennonite, Presbyterian and Methodist Churches join together with a few Christian Reformed and Anglicans to do church planting in West Africa, that would be similar to SIM International. In that case, SIM would not start a church that is like the Scottish Presbyterian, the Mennonites, the Baptists, or the Dutch Reformed. It plants what they call the Evangelical Church of West Africa. In this case, SIM is what one might call an "inter-ethnic mission society" — starting a church in West Africa not directly related to any of the denominations represented in the SIM. That is one way to overcome the ethnic orientation of sending churches.

One word of caution is in order, however. An inter-ethnic mission society can also develop a theological sub-culture which is just as problematic as the ethnic churches out of which they come. Of course, this must be avoided because it can have the same effect on cross-cultural church planting as a theologically bound ethnic church.

3. **It is important that cross-cultural church planting is not left in the hands of denominational loyalists.** Denominational loyalists are by nature preservers of identity. Often they are maintenance-minded, and the churches they plant cross-culturally may have little chance of being indigenous.

I once suggested to a mission executive that when his society opened a new field in Latin America he might consider joining with another denomination that was going into the same country about the same time. His response? "But we want to preserve our distinctives." Remember that "our distinctives" are often cultural and not necessarily theological or Biblical in nature.

4. Denominational mission executives should **consider training cross-cultural workers in inter-ethnic institutions** rather than in denominational schools and colleges. I suggest this because denominational training institutions tend to be places where

conscious efforts are made to preserve identity. A missionary studying in the training school of a denomination different from his own could have a valuable cross-cultural experience which would be helpful in learning about multi-cultural Christianity.

Inter-ethnic Mission Societies and Reproduction

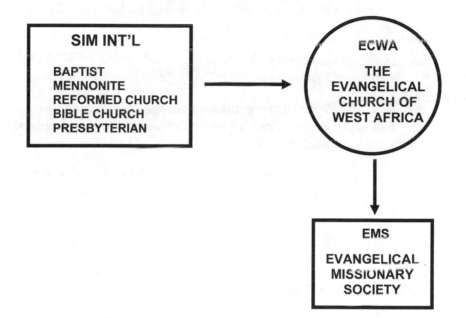

Looking at the accompanying illustration you will see that the SIM in West Africa moved out to plant the *Evangelical Church of West Africa* (ECWA) which in turn started the *Evangelical Mission Society* (EMS) which now plants churches in other places. This is the way churches create mission-sending agencies, which in turn start churches that launch their own mission sending agencies. One problem resulting from the dependency syndrome is that many mission-established churches have yet to start their own mission-sending agency, even after being in existence for a century or more.

Further thoughts on this subject can be found in Chapter 19, *Avoiding or Overcoming Dependency in Cross-Cultural Church Planting.*

QUESTIONS FOR DISCUSSION
Chapter 15

1. *To what extent does your church have characteristics which are peculiar to the culture of which it is a part?*

2. *To what extent has your church borrowed its language, theology or structure?*

3. *Is the music in your church indigenous? Are people in your society writing any new music?*

4. *How can people hold very different views and both think they are Biblical? To what extent is some "theology" cultural and without a Biblical basis?*

5. *Is a New Testament identity possible or desirable? Which parts of a New Testament identity are transferable to today and which are not?*

6. *Are inter-ethnic mission societies valid? Are they helpful when trying to avoid theological and other forms of dependency?*

SUGGESTED READING

Kraft, Charles H. *Christianity in Culture: A Study in Dynamic Biblical Theologizing in Cross-Cultural Perspective*. Maryknoll: Orbis Books, 1979.

Luzebetak, Louis J. *The Church and Cultures*. South Pasadena: William Carey Library, 1970.

Heibert, Paul. *Anthropological Insights for Missionaries*. Grand Rapids: Baker, 1985

(Plus scores of other books which one will be asked to read in a good cross-cultural missionary training program.)

CHAPTER 16

THE ROLE OF BUSINESS
PEOPLE IN SELF-RELIANCE FOR CHURCHES

Introduction

This chapter reflects the importance of the role of business people in relation to self-reliance for mission-established churches. For too many years we have overlooked or sidelined this important resource for the church. This chapter is not about Business as Missions, which is equally important when it comes to involving business people in the Great Commission. Here, I am limiting my thoughts to how business people can be part of establishing a healthy self-supporting church.

Mobilizing Business People

Mobilizing business people in the church, both men and women, is one of the key elements in making the transition from dependency to self-reliance. A successful transition requires a change in the mentality of both **church leaders and business people** if the change is to be successful.

On the African scene, frequently there is distrust in the business community regarding the church. Business people sometimes feel that the church is poorly managed economically. This causes business people to look upon the church as a begging community. This, of course, affects both the self and community image of the church. If non-believers look at the church as a poorly run institution begging for its very existence, how can they have respect for it? This often negatively affects the influence for Christ that the Church should be having in the community.

What is the Charitable Mentality?

Sometimes, however, Christian business people suffer from the same mentality as church leaders. It is interesting to note how many times business people enter a non-profit organization's boardroom or church committee meeting and leave behind the sustainability mentality they normally use in their businesses. It's as if, when they walk through the door of the church, they become charity-minded and seem to leave self-reliance principles behind. Why is this? Why do business people, who would never consider begging for their existence in business, enter into the church and begin to think in terms of getting money overseas for their church?

In East Africa the Board of Directors of a major Christian institution was considering how to raise funds locally. They began a number of projects to raise money in the community and were proceeding quite well. All of a sudden the institution received a significant grant from overseas. When the grant arrived, the business people on the board looked at each other and said, "Why do we work so hard to raise money locally when it comes so easily from overseas?" Remember, these are the same business people who would not think like that in their own businesses. How sad that the "easy money" sidelined the good they might have done in their own community.

Is the Money Available?

The question must be asked: Do church members in Africa have the money to do what God is asking them to do?

I refer again to the quote I gave earlier from Dr. David Barrett who says that if Christians in Africa gave just two percent of their income, they could pay all of their bills. He enlarges this to say they could pay for their pastoral training, pastor's salaries, build their church buildings, do their community development projects and buy computers if they want them — from just two percent of the income of Christians in Africa.

All of this points to the fact that the church may just have more resources available among its members than we might think. Of course they would have to begin to think creatively and with sound Christian stewardship. Then why do church members often not give a fair portion of their income to support what God is asking them to do?

Giving Among Business People

In Chapter 8 I dealt with some of the reasons why giving fails. I won't repeat what I said there, except to re-emphasize that the lack of giving can frequently be traced to the spiritual basis from which church members make decisions. Business people are no exception. If they are soundly converted, they will be motivated to give to the church out of love for the Lord. The reverse is also true. Don't expect those who are not soundly converted to give joyfully and generously to the work of the Lord.

A church administrator in Tanzania, whom I met in Dar es Salaam several years ago, did a calculation in his diocese and concluded that if everyone paid their tithe to the church, the church would have 100 million Tanzania shillings left over at the end of the year, after paying all their bills. It goes without saying that in many places business people with a heart for true Christian stewardship could solve the problem of dependency on outside funding if they decided to do so.

Some time ago, I learned about an economic development meeting that took place in Baltimore, Maryland. Christian business people came together to discuss various aspects of Third World economics and what they as Christians might do about global conditions. Among those who attended were American business people as well as some from Africa and elsewhere. Much to the surprise of some, eleven Tanzanian Christian businessmen were in attendance. They came completely at their own expense, to join in the discussions. That is some indication that the Church in that part of Africa has money to do things if they decide to do them. It was a surprise to some in attendance that the Tanzanian businessmen were not subsidized to get to that meeting.

At a subsequent meeting of the same group, several business people from the Democratic Republic of Congo participated. Someone asked them who paid for them to be there. (Notice the assumptions with which we often begin.) The men from Congo responded by saying, "Excuse us, but we are diamond merchants, and we have paid our own way to come here." What does it say about the paradigm on which we function when such things seem unusual?

The Widening Gap between the Rich and the Poor

The gap between the rich and the poor is particularly evident between the Northern and Southern hemispheres. But beyond that, there is a widening gap between the wealthy elite and many who are less well off in societies in the Southern Hemisphere. One has only to travel through East, Central and Southern Africa and observe the lifestyle that some African Christians have chosen and the gap between the *haves* and the *have*-nots becomes quite apparent.

Looking at this Biblically, it is not pleasing to God when some continue to accumulate simply for their own benefit. Laying up an inordinate amount of earth's treasures is frowned upon in Scripture (Luke 12:16-21) and should not characterize Great Commission-minded Christians. What is the alternative?

I met an American businessman several years ago who was chairman of the Missions Committee of his congregation. His congregation supported about a hundred cross-cultural missionaries – a considerable number for just one congregation. When he gave his testimony, it went something like this: "We have missionaries who live in very ordinary houses in many places around the world. Even though I could afford to live in a much better house than I do, I decided I should not live in a house which is better than the houses in which our missionaries live." In other words, he was practicing the concept of perpetual jubilee which I mentioned earlier. He willingly limited what he needed for himself, considering that what he earned beyond his own needs should be for the benefit of others.

Practical Suggestions Regarding Business People and Self-reliance for Churches

1. **Church leaders must make sure that people are not confused about the purpose of the church**. One of the problems in mission-established churches in Africa is that the concept of "business" and "church" has become intertwined. Churches sometimes run stores, farms, development projects, hospitals, and schools. The community looking on—and sometimes the members of the church—are not always clear about what the church is supposed to *be* and *do*. As I said in an earlier lesson, church-run businesses, whether they succeed or fail, tend to have the same impact on the church. If church-run businesses succeed and make a lot of money, the members may sit back and let the businesses earn income for the church. If they fail, members will not want to "bail out the businesses" with their tithes and offerings.

To clear up this confusion, the Presbyterian Church in East Africa made the decision to put church work under clergy and "profit and loss" institutions under Christian business people who were members of the church. This kind of re-structuring makes good sense to a businessperson. I am suggesting that this sort of thing may need to be done if business people are to gain respect for the church and become involved financially in its future.

In too many mission-established churches everything is under one umbrella, with church leaders responsible for everything. Bishops and moderators and other church leaders find themselves consumed with how to manage businesses. In Acts 6:2-4 the disciples decided to put some things into the hands of lay people so that they could give attention to prayer and the ministry of the word.

2. **Business people and church leaders must recognize that they NEED each other.** *Together* they can strategize to communicate the Good News. Unfortunately, there are often differences of opinion between church leaders and people in the business community. This is why some business people stay away from the church. They do not understand – or like – the way the church works. They may have different roles, but they should have the same goal—to share Christ's love with a waiting world.

3. **Both business people and church leaders need to promote spiritual renewal.** This may mean confessing their hostility toward each other, confessing their lack of trust and lack of cooperation. In the East African revival, about which I have given several illustrations earlier, one of the things that happened was the coming together of people who said, "We have not trusted each other. Let's begin to walk together in the light of Christ." When business people and church leaders are willing to do that, disillusionment related to the church can become a thing of the past.

Business people should not give up on the Church. They should help to steer it into a larger, living community of faith where it has a dynamic prophetic role to fulfill, not just in the small community in which God has placed it. The Church can and should have a prophetic role in the wider community, even the nation or continent. We all know that the African church has the potential to provide spiritual leadership and encouragement for people, not only in their immediate communities, but also within their nations and on the wider world scene.

Spiritual renewal can lead business people to voluntarily and joyfully give back to God something of what He has given to them. That should be considered good news for the Church!

4. **Church leaders must show that they are dedicated, hard working shepherds in charge of the flock of God.** Sometimes the business community looks upon church leaders as not being fully employed and not being busy or diligent. Most business people earn their money through diligence and wise decision-making. They know the penalty for anything less. They know that they wouldn't make a profit if they weren't diligent. They also know that they can't beg others to give them money. They would not survive, and they know that instinctively.

Church leaders must not fall into a pattern of thinking that they deserve to be rewarded for anything less than the highest service to their people! In Ezekiel 34 the Lord gives shepherds a very serious warning about caring for their sheep. In order for church leaders to have the respect of the business community (and God's approval), they must demonstrate both spiritual dedication and hard work.

5. **Business people must make sure that there is economic justice in the way that they gain their wealth.** Christians should not be in the business of taking advantage of others through the way they earn a living. Unfortunately, that is not always the case even among church members. In many African societies when a person gains wealth in an unscrupulous way, resentment follows. In fact, one definition of sin in an African society is a "broken relationship." And one of the ways relationships are broken is when someone gains more and more at the expense of other members of the extended family. Christian business people should set an example of how that can be avoided.

In West Africa a businessman had a farm of a few acres which he brought under cultivation. As time went along he increased the amount of land he farmed. When he had about 65 acres under cultivation he decided that was enough for himself and his family. In the process he noticed that many of his neighbors were not making an adequate living from their land, so he began to ask what his responsibility was toward his neighbors.

He decided to buy a tractor that he would rent out to others so they could till their land more efficiently. He also arranged for a truck to deliver produce to the town for the other farmers. It was a co-op arrangement in which all shared the expenses. The result was that his decision to limit the growth of his own farm resulted in **four hundred** other farmers improving their standard of living. It is this kind of impact that a committed Christian businessperson can have on the society around him. And, as was learned in other places, when Christian stewardship is coupled with increased income, the Church can be a beneficiary.

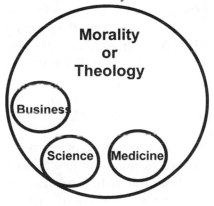

Christian business people should be in the forefront of showing how to live by God's principles. They can set an example in the community by avoiding injustice in the way they employ people, and they can challenge other business people to do the same. Such practices might not always give the best economic return, but in the Kingdom of God, returns are measured with a different measuring stick.

6. **What is the great temptation for business people?** One great temptation is for business people to make personal gain a higher priority than the Kingdom of God. Using the attached diagrams, Dr. Paul Heibert reminds us that there are several ways to look at business, science, medicine, law and education. If we make the primary frame of reference business or science, etc., then our morality may be too weak to judge the business, science, law or medicine. The alternative is to reverse the order, and put morality or theology into the larger frame of reference and let it judge our business, science, law, education or medicine.

What happens when the order is not right? Suppose for a moment that **science** is the primary frame of reference. With our scientific knowledge it is possible to make atomic weapons or to perform abortions, but one's morality is too weak to tell us that this does not measure up to God's standard. In the business world, if the primary frame of reference is **business**, then one can make as much money as possible, even though it may be at the expense of others because one's morality or theology is too weak to judge the business activity.

In terms of **law** there may be legal loopholes that we can use to gain something for ourselves. If the primary frame of reference is legal, we will look for such loopholes. If, however, the primary frame of reference is morality and theology, then that will judge whether or not we are doing the right thing. Morality will help us know whether something is morally defensible even if it could be done legally. *Christian business people need to make sure that their primary frame of reference is the Kingdom of God.*

One of the results of changing that primary frame of reference is that business people may not make as much money as they did before. I am frequently asked about this with the following question: "What should wealthy Christians do with all the money they earn?" I tried to answer that question in chapter 4. I begin by asking Christians to review how they get their money in the first place. This brings economic justice (morality) into the equation.

7. **The church must uphold God's standard before business people by church leaders setting an example.** If church leaders become desperate for money because their church is in financial difficulty, they may be tempted to do things that are questionable. If they engage in practices that are illegal or lack integrity, that sets a poor example for business people, whether believers or non-believers.

8. **Business people can help the unemployed through such things as revolving loan funds.** There are unique opportunities for business people to do very practical things in a community. And as I have said before, a businessperson doesn't even need to be a Christian to realize that unemployed people are not good for society. Crime rates go up when the unemployment rate rises. So even non-Christian community people can be challenged to do good in the community. But remember that even in the setting up of such things as revolving loan funds to help the unemployed, local resources are preferred over foreign resources.

Some years ago a trust in East Africa was established to help unemployed people find employment. Local businessmen set it up with their own money. They lent out a small amount of money such as 400 Kenyan shillings. In those days that was enough to buy a bicycle. A person would become employed and then repay the loan. The money was then lent out to someone else. In some cases the person who repaid the loan was able to borrow again. This trust worked very well. Many people were employed through that process. The funds came in and went back out, and the scheme had more than a 90% repayment rate.

Then, unfortunately, someone decided that it was such a good thing that what the trust needed was more cash. So they brought in 500,000 US dollars to add to the existing loan fund. Sadly, that large amount of foreign funding went out into the community and did not come back.

Large sums of money from the outside are often not monitored with the same watchful eye as are local funds. My point is that when business people put in their own funds, they are more highly motivated to make sure the project is run well. It is true that local funds can be misused, but it is much more likely that large sums from the outside will be misused in a way that local funds are not.

9. **Business people should consider having a prophetic ministry on larger economic issues.** I referred earlier to an economic meeting in Baltimore, Maryland. One of the purposes of that meeting was to give Christian business people an opportunity to

speak out on economic issues that the world is facing. Business people who are Great Commission-minded Christians will realize that spreading the Gospel is their opportunity, challenge and privilege. But they will also recognize an opportunity to do something about what Dr. Arthur Glasser calls the cultural mandate — to do something about injustice and poverty. All of this comes within the scope of the Christian responsibility for committed believers. First, comes the evangelistic mandate; second, the cultural mandate.

So western and non-western business people can come together, sit down and talk about the economic issues the world is facing. Together they become a great force for good as they crusade against economic injustice. Together they can make a difference.

In summary, local business people can help promote self-reliance through their own churches in order to break unhealthy dependency. They can also go on beyond their local community to influence national leaders and have an impact in the wider world.

A Lesson from Latin America

Sometime ago, one of the major economic magazines in North America did a story on evangelical Christians in South America. They showed how Christians had changed their communities for the better. Christians in business *can* make a difference. And if churches are to move toward healthy Spirit-led self-reliance, it will be done by evangelizing, recruiting and motivating business people.

QUESTIONS FOR DISCUSSION
Chapter 16

1. *In what ways do you feel business people and church leaders need to find better ways of cooperation?*

2. *Do you agree that business people sometimes shift their mentality when making decisions about the church or other non-profit organizations? Discuss.*

3. *What do you think is the reason for the widening gap between the "haves" and "have-nots" in our world?*

4. *What can business people and church leaders learn from each other?*

5. *What can a church leader do to show that he has a ministry worthy of his salary?*

6. *How can business people and church leaders develop a prophetic voice to the government and wider secular community?*

SUGGESTED READINGS

Greenleaf, Robert K. *Servant Leadership: A Journey into the Nature of Legitimate Power and Greatness.* New York: Paulist Press, 1977.

Befus, David R. *Where There are no Jobs: Enterprise Solutions for Employment and 'Public Goods' for the Poor.* Miami: LAM, 2005.

Introduction to Part Two
Eight Chapters and Three Appendices

Introduction

This section contains additional writings by the author on issues of dependency and self-reliance among mission-established institutions. Most of the author's writings before the video series was produced (in 1996) were covered in the text of the video series itself and are now in Part One of this text. Two of the following articles were written before the video series was completed in 1996. They are *Reflections on Several Bible Societies in Central Africa* (Chapter 22) and *Stages of Missionary Development* (Appendix C).

I acknowledge that there will be some repetition of anecdotes in these articles. I have tried to keep these to a minimum. This is because these articles were each prepared for a special purpose, such as a conference or an invitation to prepare an article for publication. Repeating an illustration reflects three things: 1) the importance that I as author attach to it. 2), it provides an opportunity for positive reinforcement as one gets to see the illustration in possibly a new light; and 3), repeating it here might be helpful to those who have not read an earlier part of this book.

Something to Remember

If healthy churches are planted, the Gospel will be well represented in each community where it exists. If weak unsustainable churches are planted, they will divert funds from places where the Gospel has not yet been preached. Unfortunately, planting dependent churches increases the burden on an already overloaded system. Planting self-sustaining churches multiplies the efforts we are all making to see the Gospel of Christ preached to a hurting, needy world.

I trust the following articles will increase your understanding of how to avoid or overcome the dependency syndrome.

CHAPTER 17

What Triggers
The Move Toward Self-Reliance?

Introduction

As one begins to think about the move toward self-reliance among mission-established churches an intriguing issue emerges: *What triggers the move toward self-reliance?* While there is much more to be learned about the dynamics involved, one thing has become clear. The event that triggers the change is different—sometimes very different—in different places. From what we have learned so far, the following are a few examples of the kind of things that trigger the move toward self-reliance.

1. First, for some, there is **a direct revelation from the Lord**. There are at least five South African church leaders who have testified to some special revelation—sometimes supernatural—in getting the message that their funding should be found locally and not overseas. Remember the story of the "buffalo man" which I gave in chapter 2.

   A second example is a church leader in South Africa who had an ambitious goal of raising 100 million South African Rand for a ministry that God laid on his heart. While on a visit to England he met business people whom he thought would help him to achieve the goal; but the Lord spoke to him saying, "All the funding you need is with business people in your own community in South Africa."

   A third South African leader visited North America and decided that he would seek to raise the funds he needed from **non-white churches** in the USA. He thought that would be a noble thing to do. However, every time he visited a congregation, the Lord spoke to him and said, "Don't ask these people for any money. Instead, bless this congregation by putting something into their collection." He said he found himself putting in twenty dollars here and fifty dollars there from his own funds. He obeyed the Lord and eventually ran out of money to give away. He then returned to South Africa to look for the funds he needed among his own people. He now testifies to how God honored his obedience, and the resources needed to buy a large building in the Capetown area were raised at home.

2. Another way that self-reliance is precipitated is **through divine intervention.** This happens when God removes outside funds and outside personnel, sometimes against the wishes of those involved. This happened in Ethiopia in 1938 when, at the time of the Italian invasion, expatriate missionaries were forced out of the country for a period of five years. They left behind about a hundred believers and upon their return found that the one hundred had grown to ten thousand. A similar thing happened in China in the middle of the 20th century when missionaries were forced to leave. Thirty years later it was estimated that the one million believers had become fifty million without outside funding or outside missionaries. More recent estimates put the number of believers in China as high as a hundred and twenty million by the year 2000. Similar stories could be told of Mozambique where part of the church began to thrive when outsiders on whom it had become dependent were removed through no choice of their own. The life of the church following such divine intervention could well depend on what kind of teaching about Chrisitan stewardship was done when the Gospel was first presented.

3. A third way the church learns to stand on its own two feet is through **sound teaching of those who sow the Gospel seed**. This happened in Irian Jaya among the Dani people where missionaries consciously and conscientiously applied sound indigenous principles when the church was started. So positive was the result that the Dani people began sending out their own missionaries at their own expense within a decade of hearing the Gospel. This inspiring story can be found in *Torches of Joy* written by John Dekker. Sadly, one reason that many churches become dependent is that missionaries often know little or nothing about the indigenous principle or how to promote it. One church in New Guinea was founded on sound teaching about Christian stewardship and at the twenty-year celebration sent air tickets to America so that the first missionaries could be present for the festivities.

4. A fourth way that churches become self-supporting is through **sound teaching and practices promoted by committed and creative local church leaders**. In Kenya, Zimbabwe and South Africa there are examples of church leaders who decided it was time to change the system on which their church functioned. Led by the Holy Spirit and sometimes exercising sheer determination, they led their people through a process of change. This process included finding local resources to replace the foreign funding on which they had come to depend.[1]

5. A fifth way, and one that has often not had good success, is **a one-sided plan initiated by missionaries** or donors who created the problem of dependency in the first place. In a few cases it has worked, though it has often been less than satisfactory. In this scenario outsiders become aware of the dependency they created and then introduce something like a ten-year plan so that over a period of time outside subsidy is reduced and eventually cut off. The assumption is that local resources will be found to replace the foreign funding. The reason this often fails is that, while the shift may take place in the minds of the outsiders, it does not necessarily take place in the minds of local church leaders and their congregations. Using my term for that phenomenon, *true psychological ownership* does not necessarily transfer. On the positive side, there have been situations in which the ten-year plan was set aside early by local people only a few years into the process because psychological ownership did transfer. In at least two cases, local leaders took full financial responsibility after only three years and therefore discarded the rest of the plan. When that happens, it points to the importance of the transfer of psychological ownership.

6. A sixth way the transition toward self-reliance sometimes occurs is where **outside funding is arbitrarily cut off**. Sometime ago a government official in the Middle East was reflecting on the amount of foreign aid his country receives from the West. His conclusion was this: "I think that our country will not learn to stand on its own two feet until it feels the shock of being deprived." Arbitrarily cutting off the funds seems like a harsh way to deal with the problem of dependency. One way that mission societies

---

[1] Details of several of these stories are given in chapters 1 and 2 of this book.

explain their rationale is to tell those in dependent churches that the funds they have been receiving are needed to preach the Gospel where it has not yet been preached. This would include countries in the 10/40 window and elsewhere. After all, it can be rationalized that some believers have been subsidized for a hundred years or more while others are still waiting to hear the Gospel for the first time. Great care must be taken when arbitrarily cutting off outside funding. That very act could well be interpreted as one more act of paternalism by the outsiders. Finding an appropriate way through the process will demand the guidance of the Holy Spirit.

7. A seventh way churches become self-reliant is **through widespread and genuine spiritual renewal**. For many years a church in Northeastern Africa was dependent on a church in North America. Then within a short period of time something dramatic happened. First came persecution and the church went underground. In the midst of the suffering, the Lord provided valuable lessons of survival. When the period of testing ended, the church emerged with a vigor it had not known before. In the process, church leaders began to testify to what was happening to the finances of their church. Shortly after receiving their new lease on life, outside subsidy dropped from 95% of the church's budget to 45%. Later the subsidy was down to 15% and continued to drop. In this case the church was taken through a process of refining and discovered that they could joyfully give what was needed to carry out God's work in their communities. Not surprisingly, the spiritual renewal also resulted in a dramatic increase in church membership.

8. Another way the church makes the move toward self-reliance is **through serious restructuring of the institutions inherited from the past**. The Presbyterian Church in East Africa took bold steps to restructure how its work should be done. They made self-reliance a theme in church business meetings. Even their worship times included singing a song about how a small bird learns to exercise self-reliance. Their church newspaper is called "Jitegemea", the Swahili word for self-reliance. In the restructuring process, businesses of the church were put into the hands of business people and issues of church administration, growth and evangelism were put into the hands of church

leaders. Most importantly, church leaders were aware of the leading of the Holy Spirit as they restructured the church. These positive changes were made in the face of criticism from outsiders who had difficulty appreciating the restructuring which was initiated and carried out by local leaders.

9. Yet another way that the transfer toward self-reliance is precipitated is **through a positive shift in attitude that occurs among missionaries.** This happens when insightful missionaries recognize that the time for change has come.[2] Instinctively and often with considerable courage they can do the right things which help to foster change. In one case, it was as simple as a seasoned missionary consciously taking a back seat while local people accepted the privilege of managing their own affairs. In cases such as this, wise and committed outsiders not only anticipated change, but they helped to precipitate it by the things they did or perhaps more importantly, did not do. Missionaries and mission executives have found that they can precipitate change simply by not being present when local decision-making is done. This may seem like a small change to make, but the consequences can be dramatic because it might just be what triggers the move toward local psychological ownership. This is quite different from item five above in which the solution may be arbitrarily imposed by outsiders.

Conclusion

There are many factors which affect the process leading to self-reliance for mission-established churches. These factors include such things as cultural differences, missionary attitudes, church doctrine, economic conditions, and the prevailing political situation, among many others. The best news of all is that the change from unhealthy dependency toward self-reliance is possible. That has been demonstrated over and over again. It should encourage church and mission leaders everywhere to become aware of the dynamics at work in the process and become aligned with what the Holy Spirit is in the process of doing.

---

[2] One story about a missionary demonstrating this change in attitude can be found in the testimony of Tim Michell. It can be found along with other articles on the WMA website.

CHAPTER 18

MAXIMIZING THE
BENEFITS OF SHORT-TERM MISSIONS

Introduction

A burgeoning interest in Christian missions has produced a new interest in short-term service. This has resulted in thousands of short-termers going out across the world, some under the direction of the Holy Spirit, some for their own benefit (as on a glorified vacation), but all, hopefully, for the benefit of those they seek to serve. Peterson, Aeschliman and Sneed in their book *Maximum Impact Short-Term Mission* (STEMPress: Minneapolis, 2003) say there are now at least one million going out each year into short-term mission service (p. 243).

For the purpose of this article, I have divided short-term missions into two categories: 1) **short visits of two to six weeks** by those taking a "working vacation" (or holiday); and 2) **longer visits of six months to two or three years**. Longer STMs (Short Term Missions) are most often taken by young volunteers, professionals on sabbatical, or retired persons willing to give a year or two of service. However, the major emphasis of this article will be on the shorter visits of two to six weeks.

The effectiveness of short-term missions has been written about in various missionary publications in recent years. (A brief list of books and websites appears in the bibliography of this article.) The main purpose of this article is to deal with something that one does not see addressed in any of the books I have read on short-term missions. I am referring to the relationship between short-term service and the possibility of creating unhealthy dependency on outside people and funding. In this article I will make various suggestions regarding how to avoid dependency on short-term mission trips. Included among these will be suggestions regarding sound cross-cultural practice.

At the outset, **I wish to emphasize that short-term workers can have a positive experience and at the same time make a positive impact on the community to which they go.** The fact that too often short-termers have counterproductive experiences or are ineffective is my reason for drawing attention to the subject.

What Happens when Good Will Turns to Ill Feeling?

My first encounter with short-term missions was in Central Africa in 1961.[1] While there I learned about a North American program created to send university students on a six-week visit to Africa to assist in humanitarian projects with the purpose of "building goodwill between the youth of two nations."

As part of this program a group of Americans and Canadians came to Bulawayo, Zimbabwe (then Southern Rhodesia) where I lived and worked. About four weeks into their six-week visit the group suddenly left. I heard about their premature departure and went to the building site to ask what happened. Since they were from North America, I thought it was good to learn why they left early. The local builder in charge of the project gave the following explanation:

> What the Americans didn't know is that we here in Africa also know how to build buildings. It isn't that they didn't work hard. The trowel was too slow to put mortar between the bricks, so they used their bare hands to speed things up. But they must remember that we built buildings before they came, and we will build buildings after they leave. Unfortunately, while they were here, they thought they were the only ones who knew how to build buildings. Finally things got so bad, we had to ask them to leave.

Obviously this short-term mission was counter-productive to "building goodwill between the youth of two nations." Ironically, when I visited the site some months later after the building was complete, there was a bronze plaque beside the entrance saying, "This building was built by the youth of Southern Rhodesia, the United States and Canada to foster goodwill between the nations." Sadly, it turned out to fall short of its goal.

---

[1] I was there on a two-year short-term program with my denomination – the Brethren in Christ Church. I later returned to serve in Central Africa as a full-time missionary for another five and a half years.

In a **second** incident, a group of North Americans helped to build a school building in West Africa. A local church in West Africa accepted their offer to provide manual labor from North America in order to complete the project. The Americans moved in and worked daily under the direction of one of their own members—a building contractor from North America who accompanied them. In situations such as this, the local builder in charge of the project usually steps back while the "experienced" North American directs the work.

When the Americans left, they had a good feeling about "what we did for them." And truly a building was left behind. Some time later, I interviewed several of the Americans who participated in that short-term project. It was not surprising that some of them looked back with a rather dubious feeling about their contribution. One was so embarrassed about the arrogance the short-termers displayed that the suggestion of another mission trip to build another building (this time in Asia) seemed almost repulsive. Indeed, thankfully not all short-term efforts are like this. The challenge is to avoid the "great white outsider" syndrome.

A **third** incident involved a church building erected in a rural part of Ecuador by well-meaning North Americans. On one occasion a group of short-termers saw the well-built building and asked about it. Local people said, "We refer to this as the *gringo* church. Gringos came from North America and built it, but we do not use it. We have our own places of worship."

A **fourth** incident occurred in Guyana, South America. A missionary told how he had taken a group of young people from North America to Guyana to build a church building. After three weeks of dedicated effort, the building was at last completed and presented to the local people. The North Americans returned home convinced that they had made a good contribution to needy people. Two years later the missionary, now back in the USA, got a letter from the people in Guyana. It read, "The roof on *your* church building is leaking. Please come and fix it." The importance of this is well understood by those who are familiar with issues of "ownership."[2]

---

[2] For more information on ownership and other issues related to dependency, see Chapter 1

A **fifth** incident occurred in West Africa where a short-termer was working in a two-year assignment. She served in an area where a medical doctor—turned church planter—was trying to get a local congregation to increase their awareness of missions and evangelism. He was elated when the pastor reported that their annual missions conference increased the total offering from forty-five dollars last year to sixty-one dollars this year. It was truly a time for rejoicing. The congregation even began to plant a new church some kilometers away. As the short-termer was about to leave, she took pity on the congregation and gave them what amounted to her life savings – six thousand eight hundred dollars—to build a new church building. Imagine, the impact of that sum of money thrust into a situation such as I just described. The result was that the pastor simply began to ask where he could find more of that kind of money. One can only feel compassion for the missionary who had been teaching principles of self-support. He saw his efforts at raising awareness about the importance of local resources go down the drain. Unfortunately, many short-termers have no idea of the impact that kind of giving has on those they try to help.

Is it Really that Bad?

By now you have probably concluded that these five illustrations represent a bleak picture of short-term mission efforts. Lest this cast an aspersion on all short-term mission trips, I suggest that we compare these negative experiences with sound missionary practices which lead to the planting of healthy, sustainable churches in cross-cultural situations. Allow me to illustrate in the following way.

Missionaries have successfully planted churches cross-culturally in many parts of the world where they earned the right to be heard. This has come to be known in missionary circles as "incarnation." Those missionaries learned local languages without expecting the people to whom they ministered to learn their language. They paid attention to the cultural elements to which the Gospel would need to speak. They exercised creative listening in order to be heard when they did eventually decide it was time to speak.[3]

---

[3] By contrast, short-termers feel they must speak within the short period they have whether they have done any listening or learning.

And what was the result? In some places, people movements to Christ followed.[4] This meant that significant numbers of people came to Christ and whole societies were changed. This kind of cross-cultural evangelization will hardly occur when the time frame is a two or three-week visit into and out of a society, with little knowledge or understanding of local language and culture. Short-term missionaries will hardly have opportunity to experience a people movement because, like many missionaries, they don't know what one is or how it works.

Can there be a positive short-term experience? Some programs such as YWAM (Youth With A Mission) and YES (Youth Evangelism Service – a Mennonite sponsored program) have demonstrated that there IS a wholesome way to prepare for short-term missions.[5] Both programs require in-depth discipleship training, sometimes as much as three months or more. One young woman having gone through such training, went to Indonesia several years ago when Christian/Muslim conflicts were very much in the news. The group she was with spent their time in prayer and intercession, relating to local people and learning as much Indonesian language as they could. They played with children orphaned in the religious conflict, taught English and had discussions with local teenagers, taxi drivers and even Muslim clerics. They were so well accepted that Muslim leaders invited them to teach English classes in the mosque! At the end of their time in Indonesia, *Christians and Muslims came together in a local church to thank them and bid them farewell* – so great was the respect for those young people and what they had contributed to the community! This could hardly have been done in a two-week

---

[4] For those who are interested in what a "people movement" is I recommend two sources, among many others. One is called *People Movements of Southern Polynesia* by Alan R. Tippett. Chapter 7 particularly gives the rationale for a people movement and how it works. The other resource is the video produced by New Tribes Mission entitled *EE Taow* which shows how seriously one missionary in New Guinea studied the language and culture before inviting people to make a decision to become believers. The people movement that followed was dramatic. Short of a miracle, discipling a people group this thoroughly can hardly be done during one two-week short-term mission trip.

[5] It needs to be recognized that since YWAM and YES participants are trained in different locations, the quality of their experiences may very well vary. Much depends on the quality and experience of the trainers and the ability and commitment of those being trained.

period and especially without the kind of cultural sensitivity they learned during their training.

Before sending out His disciples on a short-term ministry assignment, Jesus told them, "Be wise as serpents and harmless as doves" (Matthew 10:16b). Short-termers and long-term missionaries alike would do well to remember these words when venturing into cross-cultural ministry. Both will find that listening, learning and "being" are essential to an effective ministry.

The Alternative Demonstrated by YWAM and the Mennonites

Some time ago I was asked who is doing short-term missions right. I wish I had been quicker to respond and tell about the YWAM-DTS program and the Mennonite YES program to which I referred earlier. The following are some of the strengths of these programs:

- In both programs the participants are given a serious introduction to cross-cultural issues. This includes information on how people in other religions think and worship.

- They include training in spiritual warfare, something the average westerner often knows little or nothing about.

- The training also raises awareness about how we as Americans are viewed in the eyes of the rest of the world.

- Participants are forced to examine themselves as individuals, including personal strengths and weaknesses. This means learning to understand not just themselves, but also others on the team with whom they will serve. By the time such young people reach the point of ministry, they have had some of their potential personal problems confronted.

If anyone wants to give young people a wholesome cross-cultural experience in short-term missions, this kind of training is essential.

Why do Negative Experiences Occur in Short-Term Missions?

Obviously the purpose of short-term mission trips is to provide a positive spiritual experience for both the givers and the receivers. In the previous examples that I gave, applying a few simple rules to the training of short-termers could well have changed a negative experience into a positive one. Unless appropriate training is given, more and more short-termers will have less than satisfactory experiences for themselves and those they try to help.

First, in the preparation of short-termers, the anticipation of "doing good" for someone else is frequently overplayed. Americans are to be commended for their willingness to help those whom they perceive to be in need. Our worldview includes a substantial portion of charitable or philanthropic concern. Some of it is driven by the benefit of a tax-deductible receipt, some by a spirit of adventure, but much of it is genuine compassion. "Doing" (what we accomplish) is often in conflict with the importance of "being" (who we are). This important distinction could well be at the root of the problem. Someone once referred to such people as "human doings", rather than "human beings."

The importance of *doing* may be inspired by the need to report "what we have done." It is hard to raise support – even for short-term missions – based on *being*. Yet there is something about our witness which is greatly enhanced when people see us for who we are, rather than for what we do. In the book *Mack & Leeann's Guide to Short-Term Missions* (pgs 72-76),[6] there is an illustration of a group of young people who went to Kenya on a short-term mission. One of the young women was assigned to work in the home of a church leader in which the wife was about to deliver a child. The young woman found herself doing laundry, preparing meals and cleaning the house. She wondered how she would ever report this menial type work to those back home who gave financial support to help her get there. When all was said and done, however, expressions of gratitude by the local people proved that her servant attitude was worth it all. In this case,

---

[6] See Bibliography for details

"being" spoke louder than "doing." Her willingness to serve left a lasting positive impression on the local people.

Imagine how we in America would feel if people from another country—like Germany or Korea—came to our church and took over our Summer Vacation Bible School, asking us to serve as their interpreters because they did not speak our language. What if the illustrations they gave our children about how to live were, for the most part, culturally irrelevant? And how would we feel if while these "foreigners" were with us, they dominated our schedule and made it difficult for us to get our work done? Sadly, this is often the impact of poorly planned short-term mission trips.

Frequently short-termers go out with an air of superiority because of the assumptions which we as westerners hold. We assume that short-termers have something important to say to the rest of the world, even if they are young and inexperienced, compared to those among whom they go to serve. In some places where short-termers go, the Church has been in existence for decades (maybe a century or more) before short-termers arrive on the scene. Our judgment of the local people may be affected by our need as westerners for a certain standard of cleanliness or adequacy of shelter—based on what we feel is appropriate. Those we are trying to serve may not share those same felt needs. Little wonder that sometimes outsiders are often either envied for their wealth, or resented for their cultural insensitivity.

Second, the attitude that an "outsider" can do the job better than "local people" is often at the heart of how we as westerners view ourselves. Take away our sense of superiority and you cut at the very heart of who we think we are and why we believe we exist. This kind of arrogance has enormous implications, not only for the Christian movement, but also in international affairs. It should not be surprising that such attitudes can lead to the negative feelings many non-westerners have toward us as Americans. A sense of superiority has been instilled in us since the day we learned to speak English. Our songs, sermons, educational system and political speeches all reinforce this idea. To say that such assumptions are deeply engrained in us would be an understatement.

What are the implications of this air of superiority for those involved in cross-cultural missions? Perhaps those who fly airplanes into tall towers are trying to tell us something about how the rest of the world sees us. The scripture is clear that as God's people, we are to demonstrate a broken spirit and a contrite heart. The rest of the world may be trying to show us that our arrogance is not compatible with the Christianity we profess.

A **third** reason for the often-negative aspects of short-term missions is that westerners often give the impression that our wealth is the secret to helping people come into right relationship with God. I have written extensively on this subject in other places. I will deal with this more in the suggestions given later in this article. While this is not the place to deal in depth with issues related to finance, suffice it to say that unless we learn to recognize who is truly poor, and how to help appropriately, the danger is that misunderstanding will arise and an otherwise good short-term experience will have negative consequences.[7]

It is true that someone must help with the tremendous needs of a hungry, hurting and dying world.[8] Our challenge is to find a way to help that does not leave others with the impression they are too weak, too helpless and too uninformed to help themselves. Frequently, dependent churches are living in the midst of resources which are adequate, not only for themselves, but also for the work God is calling them to do.

A **fourth** reason behind negative short-term mission experiences relates to the matter of ownership. Too often, outsiders unwittingly become "owners" of the projects on which they work. I once had a conversation with a group of short-termers and posed the question, "Whose project is this that you are working on in [South Africa]?" The answer I got was revealing. "*Oh, we let the local people help us with the project.*" It is this spirit which is behind the statement I made earlier – "the roof on *your* church building is leaking."

---

[7] As of this writing there are about ninety articles on this and related issues on the WMA website www.wmausa.org. Regarding who are actually poor, I recommend chapter 20 entitled *Searching for a Meaningful Way to Help the Poor.* See also, *Missions and Money* by Jonathan Bonk, listed in the bibliography.

[8] For more on this subject, see the article on the WMA website entitled *I Believe in the Local Church.*

A **fifth** reason for negative short-term experiences is that short-termers most likely have inadequate training for the complex task of communicating the Gospel cross-culturally. In the video series entitled the *Vision for the Nations*, Dr. Lloyd Kwast gives the following different aspects that are important in cross-cultural communication:[9] oral, written, pictorial, kinesics (body movement), audio, silence, artifactual, touch, optical, spatial, time, olfactory (smell) and oculesics (eye contact). What chance do most short-termers have of knowing the importance of these factors in cross-cultural communication? Little wonder that those in whose culture we find ourselves are often offended by the kinds of things we do. Unfortunately, most of them are too kind to tell us of the many ways we break the rules, even as we are trying to communicate something as important as the love of God.

An Alternative Demonstrated by a Civic Organization

Western Christians could learn something from international civic organizations. Several years ago I attended a meeting of a local civic club. The speaker of the evening gave a presentation on his six-week trip to India in a "youth" exchange program. (He was a "youth" of 35 years of age, and an owner of a substantial farming operation in the United States.)

Several things impressed me as he spoke. First, he did not say one negative word about the culture of India or how things were done there. He did not talk about how terrible the food was or how unsanitary the conditions were. Rather, he spoke positively about visits to factories, farms, and communities and about the hospitality he received in the homes of host families. As he spoke, I asked myself how a secular organization could send out half a dozen Americans who would come back with such a positive experience and wholesome report?

---

[9] Every short-term team should be required to watch the video series *Vision for the Nations* before they set out for cross-cultural service. It is available through the William Carey Library at www.perspectives.org.

How did the Civic Organization Pull it Off?

First, this group went specifically to learn. They were not expected to tell how it was done in America. They were told to learn how things were done in India.

Second, they were not isolated on Western style mission stations or in Western hotels from which they could look down on the culture from a high-rise building. They lived humbly and with gratitude in homes of their Indian hosts.

Third, their orientation before leaving for India prepared them to be learners. It must have been refreshing for the people of India to entertain Americans who left their air of superiority at home.

One wishes that short-term mission groups could learn a similar kind of humility. It would be helpful if we, as westerners, came to realize that our ideas are most acceptable to others when we are most accepting of theirs. The Christian missionary movement would do well to take this to heart in relation to both short-term and long-term missions.

Suggestions for those doing Training for Short-Term Mission Projects

The following list of suggestions is not by any means exhaustive. In a short article such as this, one can only begin to scratch the surface. However, with short-termers, one at least needs to begin with the basics, which is what I am trying to do here.

1. Anyone promoting short-term mission projects should make it clear that those going to serve are *learners*. It is one place where on-the-job-learning is legitimate. This is especially true where there is little or no cross-cultural training provided beforehand.

   One of the more disturbing trends in short-term missions today is the anti-intellectual attitude that "simply going" is the important thing. This is evident among those who feel that for every hour of preparation, thousands and perhaps millions will be sidelined while the world goes into eternity without Jesus Christ. This can be documented in the writings of those who promote short-term missions.

I am one of those who "simply went" without cross-cultural training. I am convinced that many of the issues I am dealing with in this text could have been avoided if people like me had been given proper missionary training.

2. Short-termers – especially those without cross-cultural training—should be told that they are *guests, not specialists*. Short-termers often go to places where the Gospel has been preached for decades—and sometimes centuries. In such places young people should not be told that they are taking the Gospel there for the first time. One complicating factor is that those paying for the trip want to know that the Gospel is being preached. In reality, the short-termers may find themselves "preaching the gospel" to mature leaders in the church who themselves are capable of being trainers – if the visitors were in the frame of mind to be learners.

3. Short-termers should be made aware of the dangers of simplistic answers to complex cultural issues. How can one who has never lived in or studied a culture know how to respond to complicated issues such as work ethics, marriage customs, or elements of faith where religion is characterized by incredibly delicate and complex issues? How can one speak about the Good News of the Gospel to animists unless he or she is familiar with the basic tenets of animism? I speak from experience, because I went to serve among animists in the early 1960s without any understanding of what an animistic worldview is. Chances are slim to none that short-termers will be familiar with such issues in another culture.

When one begins to understand and appreciate the complexity of someone else's worldview, it becomes unthinkable to argue against the need for training cross-cultural workers as suggested in the quote from Peterson, Aeschilman and Sneed above. If a young person came to his pastor and said, "I think God is calling me to be a medical doctor", would anyone simply say, "Just go for it; you don't need medical training. As long as you are called and sincere, go practice medicine."

Much of the dependency we see in churches around the world is the result of well-meaning people who went out to serve without so much as a basic knowledge of the indigenous principle—

including the fact that churches can be self-supporting from the very beginning. There are plenty of examples to show that this has happened.

4. Short-termers should be reminded that their own testimony has validity but also that it should be shared discreetly. They should be reminded that their own testimony might not necessarily be normative for the rest of world. People in many parts of the world simply do not come to the Lord the way some North Americans do. What might be more important than giving one's own testimony would be to listen to the testimonies of the people to whom the short-termers go. Being willing to listen could communicate that we as westerners can actually listen as well as speak.

5. Short-termers should be told that *who they are* is far more important than *what they do*. (This is good advice for long-term missionaries as well.) The problem is that many times short-termers feel they must justify going so many miles and using so many dollars by having something tangible to show for it – like a finished building or a show of hands after an evangelistic event. It could be that this *desire to have something to show* is at the root of our ineffectiveness as short-termers. It is why learners, with the right attitude, might actually accomplish more than activists who must leave something visible behind.

6. Short-termers who feel that they must have something to show for the time and money spent might consider other alternatives. For example, it is much cheaper (though maybe not as glamorous) to have a cross-cultural experience in an inner city in North America. There are cities where non-English languages abound. Even here, it is important that one go with the attitude of a learner.

    It is also possible in a nearby North American urban setting to develop a long-term relationship and not just to make a foray in and out, never to go there again. One can even learn a foreign language by associating with those in an inner city. This kind of experience is an ideal proving ground for those thinking of long-term cross-cultural service. If one survives an inner city experience and enjoys it, that is a good sign that long-term cross-cultural service might be rewarding and effective.

7. Every short-termer should be reminded of the difficulty posed by our relative wealth compared to that of the people whom we visit. One of the temptations of short-termers is to become overwhelmed by what appears to be poverty when looking at the rest of the world from our perspective.

Here it is helpful to distinguish between *absolute* and *relative* poverty. People living in *absolute poverty* most likely will need outside assistance or they will not survive. This help may need to be given in the form of medicine, food, shelter or the like. *Relative poverty* – the kind many short-termers encounter – means that people may not be as well off as we are, but they are quite capable of surviving in the society and surroundings where God has placed them. Those who live in relative poverty are often susceptible to the kind of dependency we should all seek to avoid.[10] It is easy to give people the impression that since their houses or church buildings are not as good as ours, they need financial assistance for an upgrade. When outsiders give that impression to the person living in relative poverty, local people may begin to long for something they did not know was a need.

Short-termers should be reminded that their compassion must not result in doing for others what they can and should do for themselves. Sometimes the difficulty is knowing how to define the line between absolute and relative poverty. Leaders of short-term mission groups would do well to reflect on issues such as this before going on a cross-cultural venture.

8. Short-termers should be told that a good learner will not only listen to those in the community where they are visiting, but they will seek to learn about the place they are going. Reading *Operation World* or some other book about the country or local communities will give the short-termer an appreciation of what they will encounter. It has often been said that the longer an outsider stays in one place, the more he realizes how little he understands. This often doesn't dawn on short-termers because

---

[10] Even when trying to help those in absolute poverty, care must be taken so that long-term dependency does not develop. For further information on this, see Chapter 20 <u>Searching for a Meaningful way to help the Poor</u>.

time is so short; they feel they must to act, whether their actions are wise or not.

Another area of required reading for every short-termer relates to cross-cultural communication. Here is where the skills of a good learner can be developed. Every short-termer should be required to read a small book by Drs. Tom and Betty Sue Brewster entitled *Bonding and the Missionary Task: Establishing A Sense of Belonging.*[11] Everyone considering cross-cultural service – long-term or short-term — should read and digest the contents of this little book.

9. A second way to get good training for short-termers, especially the leaders of short-term missions, is to take the course *Perspectives on the World Christian Movement.*[12] The course has been revolutionary in introducing the missionary heart of God to those interested in serving Him wholeheartedly. Among other things, there are lessons on cultural and Biblical issues that will help to better inform those leading short-term missions.

10. Be careful to check the motives for a short-term mission trip. The following notice in a church bulletin shows how questionable motives can sometimes be.

> [Our congregation] is sponsoring a women's only mission trip to beautiful Guadalajara, Mexico! We'll spend the week of June 11-18 in Guadalajara (also known as the shopping capitol of Mexico!), where we will have the incredible opportunity to minister to, pray for, and teach women in a vibrant church community. And this trip isn't a "rough-roach-in-your-bed" kind of experience either – we'll be housed in nice clean hotel rooms, eat lots of salsa, and have plenty of time to shop! Our hope is to take at least fifteen women (including teenage daughters) on this Mexican Ministry Outreach . . . we trust that God will expand our hearts for Him as He expands

---

[11] It is published by Lingua House (1982) and is available from Academic Publications Summer Institute of Linguistics, 7500 West Camp Wisdom Road, Dallas, Texas 75236.

[12] Information on this course is available through the US Center for World Mission in Pasadena, California. Simply visit their website www.perspectives.org, and the times and locations of courses will be available. In the year 2006 six thousand people enrolled in Perspectives courses across North America.

our ministry to the women of Guadalajara. If you're
remotely interested in this great commission adventure
– or if you're just in the mood for Mexico after all this
winter weather – call for more details about this fantastic
outreach opportunity.

How do we expect to get the right people and engage in appropriate ministry when the benefits are portrayed in this way? Thankfully, there is an alternative. It is to encourage such a group of women to go as learners, not teachers (and especially not as shoppers). They can be told that they are going primarily to listen and learn. They should be told that living among the people might not be so bad after all. And what if they did experience a roach or two? It might give them a little appreciation for how another part of the world lives.

11. Whenever possible, keep short-term mission groups small. Imagine the impact when a large group of outsiders descends on a small community or congregation. Their presence is obvious, potentially disruptive and can easily cause embarrassment. Smaller groups are easier to place in homes. They are easier to talk to. They are less likely to stand out like the proverbial sore thumb in a community. In terms of a work team, a small group is less likely to outnumber the local volunteers who should retain ownership of their own project.

12. One ideal way to look at the size of the group is to consider a team small enough to be easily accommodated in the homes of local people. They will be guests in homes, rather than a large group that needs special catering. By all means, do not take along someone who will do the cooking for the group. Also, let the building project be in the hands of the local builder, not one brought along from the outside.

Conclusion

There are many good reasons to consider short-term mission trips. When done well, short-term missions can be a blessing to those in both the sending and receiving societies. However, in order for the experience to be beneficial for both sides, it is necessary to build into the process the right attitude from the very beginning. This right attitude, coupled with good training in cultural sensitivity, could well turn an otherwise negative experience into one that is positive. When done right, a servant attitude may develop which will turn some short-termers into life-long missionaries or life-long supporters of missions. Doing it right from the beginning is worth all the effort it takes.

Bibliography

Bonk, Jonathan. *Missions and Money.* Orbis Books: Maryknoll, NY, 1992.

Brewster, Thomas and Elizabeth. *Bonding and the Missionary Task.* Lingua House: Dallas, 1982.

EE Taow. (A video produced by New Tribes Mission, 1000 E. First St., Sanford, FL 32771, USA).

Greene M.D., H. Lee. *A Guide to Short Term Missions.* Gabriel Publishing: Waynesboro, GA, 2003.

Johnstone, Patrick. *Operation World.* OM Publishing: Carlisle, Cumbria, UK, 1995.

Petersen, Roger; Aeschliman, Gordon; and Sneed, R. Wayne. *Maximum Impact Short-Term Mission.* STEMPress: Minneapolis, 2003.

Stiles, J. Mack & Leeann. *Mack & Leeann's Guide to Short-Term Missions.* InterVarsity Press: Downers Grove, IL, 2000.

Tippett, Alan R. *People Movements in Southern Polynesia.* Chicago: Moody Press, 1971.

Websites: There are many websites that have information on short term-missions. I recommend putting the term "short-term missions" into an internet search engine and you will find many websites related to the subject. The following are only a beginning of what is available:

www.shorttermmissions.com

www.missionfinder.org/summer.htm

www.experiencemission.org

CHAPTER 19

AVOIDING OR OVERCOMING DEPENDENCY IN CROSS-CULTURAL CHURCH PLANTING

Introduction

To say that there is more than one way to do cross-cultural church planting would be a considerable understatement. Consider, for example, the following successful church planting effort.

An African American shop foreman, Mr. R, decided to take an evening course in theological education. This was in addition to his six ten-hour days working in a factory. The professor asked each one in the class to create and carry out a practical assignment as part of the coursework. Mr. R decided that his project would be to plant a church in his spare time in fulfillment of the course requirement.

He began by organizing a Bible study while continuing to work sixty hours in the manufacturing plant. The Bible study grew into a congregation. When I was first told about this church there were 350 people in attendance. Mr. R was serving as the senior pastor – and *still working sixty hours in the factory*. Obviously there was not an unhealthy dependency – even on the pastor.

Not all church planting efforts are this successful and encouraging. In fact, some new congregations take many years to get on their own two feet. It sometimes seems like they will never become self-supporting.

What follows is an effort to look at a few of the factors that result in healthy church planting. Some consideration will be given to those practices which result in long-term dependency — with suggestions for resolution.

A Personal Word of Experience

As a missionary living and working in Zambia in the 1960s, it was my privilege to be involved in three different church plantings. To my regret, in one of them I actually served as the first pastor. That should have been the privilege of a local person.

One thing I learned very early on was the importance of identifying local resources. In the second church planting in which I was involved, the matter of local resources surfaced at the very beginning. The church people in the community asked us as missionaries to provide a building for them. During the discussion the pastor from a nearby congregation listened to the request and interrupted by recounting his own experience. The following is the story in his own words:

"Several years ago our congregation decided to build our own building. We wanted to do it all with our own labor and at our own expense. Our purpose was to be able to go to the larger conferences of the church and tell other people that 'we built our own building at our own expense.' However, the missionaries decided that we should accept their offer to put on a metal roof which they would pay for with missionary funds from overseas. We reluctantly agreed and the missionaries actually came and put on the roof for us at their expense. The result was that we could no longer say that we built our church building with our own resources." (I regret to say that I was one of the missionaries who went there that day and helped to put on that roof.)

Upon hearing this pastor's story that day in 1967, I determined that I should never again be part of taking away the privilege that rightly belongs to those who can and want to do things for themselves. Little did I know at the time that three decades later my ministry would be primarily raising awareness about how such well-intentioned efforts help to destroy local initiative.

Patterns in Church Planting

In church planting efforts, it is important to ask an important question from the beginning. Is it intended that this new congregation will be like the congregation or denomination which had the vision to plant it? Or, will this new congregation intentionally be planted among those who are culturally different? If the population to be reached is different, is it a little different or very different? These factors will have a bearing on which church planting approach is most appropriate. This brings to mind the terminology E1, E2 and

E3 introduced by Dr. Ralph Winter. E1 is church planting among *people just like us*. E2 is done among those who are *near cultural neighbors* and E3 is done among *those who are culturally very different* from those with the original church-planting vision.

Dr. Winter put Hispanic church planting into the E2 category as near neighbors though that could be debated. Whereas, because of the cultural distance within the USA, Navajo church planting is clearly E3. One could debate where lines should be drawn, but suffice it to say that differences should be taken seriously. In fact, even when language and culture seem on the surface to be the same, considerable differences might exist. That is why more and more congregations in North America are including both traditional and contemporary options in their Sunday worship. At first glance, both might appear to be E1, but clearly there are cultural differences and preferences to be considered. Those who ignore this reality lose good people from their congregations unnecessarily.

In church planting there are cultural and financial implications depending on which choice is made. Let's begin with the cultural. If E1 is the objective, it may be possible to take a significant number of people from an existing congregation in order to get the new congregation started. They are already like the people they are trying to reach. It might be decided that half of the congregation will go into the new church planting, giving the new effort a financial jump-start. Mature believers who are accustomed to contributing to the church will help to make financial viability a possibility very early on. It may be quite in order to begin an E1 church planting with a significant number of such outsiders.[1]

Church planting is not as straight forward if the new congregation being started is E2 or E3. In this case, if the new church planting is to be like the society in which it is being planted, one will not want a significant number of outsiders coming onto the scene with customs and mores unlike the people who are to be reached. To avoid this happening, one denomination in the USA decided that in E2 and E3 church plantings no more than two couples from an existing congregation should become part of the new church

---

[1] One side benefit of taking a significant number from the existing congregation is that it makes space for the original congregation to grow. This is an alternative to building a new or larger building every time the old one fills up.

planting. Hopefully the few who participate will be culturally sensitive as well.

Becoming aware of this principle in E2 or E3 situations has many ramifications. In cross-cultural church planting one objective should be to ensure that the new congregation would have its own identity and not that of the outsiders. Why is that identity so important? It is to ensure that the new congregation will be a place for people in that society to feel at home. Otherwise, potential members might get the feeling that they are joining something that belongs to someone else—and they would be right.

There are also significant financial implications regarding the planting of E2 and E3 congregations. Decisions made in the early stages will determine whether the new congregation develops—or avoids—the pitfalls of dependency.

There are several finance-related factors to keep in mind in the early stages of E2 and E3 church planting.

- **First**, it is possible to encourage new congregations to develop their own financial base from the beginning. This is critical, especially if a congregation does not have the jump-start from a significant number of people brought in from the outside.

- **Second**, a congregation which consists primarily of new believers needs to introduce the concept of Christian stewardship from the time of conversion. If new believers begin a pattern of looking to others rather than to their own resources, then the dependency problem is on its way.

- A **third** implication is that without an adequate financial base, there will be little funding available to pay a pastor, provide a building or send out missionaries.

The health of the congregation for years to come could well be determined by what the leaders recommend and implement from the beginning. In other words, there is no substitute for avoiding a spirit of dependency from the beginning.

The Importance of Ownership

One of the more important factors to be considered in the early days of church planting is the issue of <u>ownership</u>. If those who begin the process advocate local ownership from the beginning, the oftentimes messy process of transferring it later on can be avoided. "Early ownership" might not be the quickest way to plant a new congregation; but for its long-term health, it is likely to be one of the most important. For example, local owners who want to preserve their own dignity will not be looking to outsiders every time they want to develop another part of the project. They will set their own agenda, which might include borrowing to build. But, even borrowing will be an honest obligation which they will "own."

Ownership means that people in the new congregation will have something to say about who pastors them, how much that one is paid—if at all—and whether that person will hold other employment and for how long. If outsiders decide those things from the beginning, the syndrome of dependency already has a foothold.

Local ownership has many implications:

- It means avoiding from the beginning a well-paid outside church planter that local people cannot afford. The transition from outside to local funding for such a salary can become an enormous barrier to cross once it is established.

- It means avoiding outsiders having pity on the new believers to the point that they think they have nothing worth giving back to God.

- It means stimulating new believers to have a vision of growth that will keep the blessing within their fellowship, rather than surrendering it to older, wealthier believers who live and worship somewhere else.

An Illustration from East Africa

A church-planting story from East Africa will help to emphasize the point of starting out right and avoiding the spirit of dependency. An African missionary was sent from his church in Nigeria to work in Tanzania. He was given an air ticket and a small amount of money to get started. Upon leaving Nigeria he was told, "This is all the money we have, so you will need to plant a church very quickly and teach the people to give because that is how you will be supported." That is a low-budget church planting strategy designed to avoid the problem of dependency. I am happy to report that the Nigerian missionary was not in Tanzania very long until he started fourteen congregations — all without financial support from the outside.

This points to the importance of starting out right. But, what about those who have inherited a dependency-ridden situation started by someone else a generation or two ago? The problems that were created did not appear over night and, most likely, will not be resolved over night. This means seeking the leadership of the Holy Spirit and finding the route of spiritual renewal and spiritual growth in order to restore dignity to a congregation which should be able to stand on its own two feet.

Raising Awareness about Existing Dependency

Everyone involved in situations where dependency exists will need to become aware of how serious the problem is. In fact, some people will need to be convinced that there is even a problem. There are those who don't see any problem with one part of the body of Christ leaning on another – even for long periods of time. After all, they rationalize that it is the responsibility of one part of the body to care for another. In this case, the challenge will be for those who are dependent to realize that they too have an obligation *and privilege* to put back into the Christian movement some of what God has given to them.

There is another place where awareness about dependency will need to be raised. Those who are perpetuating dependency through their good intentions are most likely getting a good feeling from the contribution they are making. They, too, will need to be convinced that long-term dependency is not healthy. Experience has shown that there is hope for those on both sides of this fence – those who are dependent and those who are perpetuating the dependency. In both cases, awareness about the dangers and long-term implications will need to be raised if progress is to be made.

The Magnitude of the Problem and the Magnificence of the Solution

It is important to acknowledge the MAGNITUDE of the problem. The following sketches show part of the picture:

- One small denomination in Pennsylvania planted a single congregation in Latin America. Over the years the well-meaning people from Pennsylvania invested more than a million dollars in that one congregation. More than that, the congregation could not seem to grow beyond fifty members – after a million dollars and more than a decade of existence.

- Another denomination planted many congregations among Latin Americans investing several million dollars. They are still waiting for those congregations to become aware of their privilege of supporting the church planter who serves them. Denominational leaders are frustrated by the lack of financial ownership reflected in the new congregations.

- Someone calculated that congregations planted in Europe by American missionaries cost an average of a million dollars each. They hardly ever grow beyond a hundred in attendance and are often pastored by the missionary who started them or a missionary successor.

- Church planters going into the Former Soviet Union have created serious dependency in as little as two or three years. Some are wringing their hands asking what to do now. Sadly, some do not see it as a problem and are glad to make the funds available for as long as it takes. One North American congregation just sent a quarter of a million dollars for church buildings in the Former Soviet Union (FSU).

But this bleak picture is only part of the story. What about the MAGNIFICENCE of the solution?

- An American mission society decided to do church planting in the Former Soviet Union. Such awareness was raised regarding financial responsibility that the new believers offered to reimburse the missionaries for the expenses they had in bringing the Gospel to them. That reflects the magnificence of the solution.

- In another situation about two hundred congregations were planted in Papua New Guinea. Twenty years after the founding of the church, some of the missionaries were already back in North America. On the occasion of the twenty-year anniversary, the church in New Guinea sent air tickets to the missionaries in America inviting them to return for the celebration. When they arrived in Port Moresby, local church leaders provided hotel accommodation and put into the missionaries' hands some cash which they would need for meals while they were there.

- In an E1 church planting in the USA (Pennsylvania) a handful of believers met in rented facilities for more than a decade while they worked and prayed to build up the congregation. They made a commitment to give away to mission projects outside their congregation ten percent of all the funds they raised toward their own building fund. As they look upon their recently completed building, none would say that the road was easy. However, they were careful to retain ownership of the process throughout. They may have borrowed funds in the process, but always with the consciousness that "this church is ours and whatever is done must be handled by our own people."

What can one conclude from events such as these? It becomes clear that planting dependent churches is not inevitable. The secret is to find out what principles can be put in place from the beginning to help avoid long-term dependency.

Building the Concept of Self-Support into the Process from the Beginning

There is no substitute for avoiding the dependency mentality from the beginning. The following are a few suggestions regarding how to lay a sound foundation early on.

- Consider having a church planter who is earning a living just like the people in the congregation. Mr. R, in my opening story, sent a powerful message when he kept his factory job and delegated the work of the congregation to those in attendance. On the other hand, paying the pastor with outside funds makes people think that since he or she is being paid, "the work of the church" belongs to the one being paid.

- Consider renting or sharing facilities for as long as it takes. It helps to remember that the real *Church* is people, not improved real estate. But how does a congregation compete for attendance when others have spacious and comfortable facilities? Does it not come down to whether there is Life with an upper case "L" within the fellowship? If that Life is present, there may be little competition from the place where the facilities are better but where Life is missing. One of the ways to compensate for this in the early stages is to share facilities with those who have space to spare. It may mean meeting at unusual times, but always with the aim of ensuring that the new congregation maintains it own identity and feels good about supporting itself.

Something New versus Renewal

In some areas where new church plantings are undertaken there are existing buildings, perhaps with a paralyzed congregation in existence. Such a congregation might not be growing and in fact could be dwindling. Almost every denomination has congregations in this category. Unfortunately, the rationale is sometimes, "Why waste a good pastor on a place like that?"

An alternative to assigning such a place to death or ineffectiveness would be to consider spiritual renewal. **It is important to remember that even that which is new will someday need to be renewed.** Renewal should be acknowledged as a fact of life, and as important in some circumstances as beginning something new.

A Lesson from the Life of William Carey

Before William Carey went to India as a missionary he served as pastor of several congregations in England. In a place called Harvey Lane, Carey faced a unique challenge. He took over a congregation that was characterized by severe internal dissent. They had gone through three pastors in as many years. The congregation was said to be divided "three against two and two against three." Disputes included issues related to theology, among other things. Following Carey's short honeymoon period as the new pastor, the ugly reality became evident. When it became clear that normal patterns of discipline would not resolve the situation, Carey embarked on a rather radical process. He declared the congregation to be closed and only to be reopened after each member had an opportunity to declare his or her position based on Scriptural behavior. Some found they could not bend to the new standard and did not return. However, such a spirit of renewal followed that most responded to the challenge of the new beginning with repentance and renewed vigor. The church set aside days of fasting and prayer and soon a new gallery was added to accommodate the crowds who gathered to worship at Harvey Lane.[2]

It could be that an existing building needs only the transformation of those present – with the possible exit of a few – to become the basis for what could become, in effect, a healthy new church planting. Indeed a small building without a mortgage might already be in place. Of course, visionary leadership is the key ingredient if either revitalization or a new church planting is to be successful in a location like that. Without visionary leadership, both the existing congregation and any new church planting are doomed.

There is another alternative regarding the renewal of a stagnated congregation. This would be to place a successful pastor, perhaps one capable of leading a much larger congregation, into that location. At first thought, this might seem to be a waste of a good leader. Of course, it is not a waste unless the existing unhealthy spirit of the old congregation is left unchallenged. Or it might also be a waste if the location does not represent an available population on which to draw. In that case, of course, one would not do a new church planting in such a location.

Dealing with Dependency where it Already Exists

So far we have been primarily dealing with the idea of new church plantings or revitalizing older existing congregations. What can be done about places where well-meaning people in a previous

---

[2] This story can be found in the book *Faithful Witness: The Life and Mission of William Carey* by Timothy George (Christian History Institute, 1991), pp 127 ff.

generation planted churches that are perpetually dependent on outsiders? This is a complex issue and one to which there are no quick and easy answers.

Where do the Best Ideas for Change Originate?

Where dependency is entrenched, there may be a desire for change on one side but not on the other. If it exists on the side of those providing the outside resources, there are a few things that can be done to precipitate change. Upon reflection, one might be surprised at the number of options available to those who provide funding. The following are a few suggestions:

- **First**, there needs to be a willingness for attitude change on the part of the funders. Sometimes they hold the idea that subsidy will be needed forever. This assumption frequently fuels the dependency mentality. Without a change at the assumption level there is little hope for progress.

- **Second**, there is no substitute for adopting a spirit of anticipation about eventual change. One must begin to think about better days ahead. One must look forward to a time when local people will joyfully stand on their own two feet. During this process it will not be unusual for old feelings such as compassion, for example, to get in the way of real change. Of course, if compassion is needed, it should be exercised. How does the love of God dwell in those who have no compassion (I John 3:17)?

- **Third**, it may be necessary to ask whether inappropriate compassion exercised in the first place might be at the heart of the problem. This may mean distinguishing between "relative poverty" and "absolute poverty." In cases of absolute poverty, someone must help or those in need may not survive. In cases of relative poverty, local people might not be as well off as those who are trying to help, but they may well have something to give back to God, if they choose to do so.

- **Fourth**, it can be shown over and over again that those who *seem* to have nothing to give actually can give back to God from the little they do have. In 2 Corinthians 8 we read about Macedonians who *begged for the privilege of giving* "out of severe trial and extreme poverty." And when that happens, the God who receives from them becomes their provider. There are dramatic stories out of refugee camps and other situations of poverty where one would assume that people live in absolute poverty, yet they joyfully find a way of giving back to God from what he has entrusted to them. It is why the two small coins of the widow (Luke 21:2) represented so much by comparison. We must take great care not to do our giving in a way that destroys that initiative to give, however meager it might seem to us. This is an important reason to acknowledge the difference between *absolute poverty* and *relative poverty* which I have explained elsewhere.

- **Fifth**, in addition to anticipating change, there is *the importance of doing things that will precipitate change*. How can such change be precipitated? Ideally, the decision to move away from dependency is best initiated by those who are dependent. If initiating the process of change is by outsiders, it could well be perceived as another imposed solution from the outside. Paternalistic decision-making may be what caused the problem in the first place.[3]

What Kind of Things can Outsiders do to Precipitate Change?

- **First**, if congregations are dependent because of the lack of spiritual maturity, then there is no other place to begin. People who do not know the Lord or have no passion to serve Him are not likely to enjoy the benefits of being self-supporting. Without spiritual renewal or even sermons on the new birth, it is unlikely that they will ever joyfully put enough into the church collection to sustain themselves, let alone reach out to others. Both insiders and outsiders can preach such sermons. The key is to recognize when the lack of true spirituality is at the root of the problem.

---

[3] About twenty-five years ago a colleague and I tried to counsel a friend who was obviously getting into difficulty through the way he tried to help people. In defending himself, our friend made the following rather revealing statement: "How can you accuse me of paternalism? I treated these people like my own children and they did not appreciate it."

The need for spiritual renewal points to one of the major things outsiders can do to precipitate change – that is to *pray*. After all, this is a *spiritual battle* and no one is more pleased about the paralysis caused by dependency than Satan himself. We are reminded that this Gospel is adequate to bring down strongholds (2 Corinthians 10:4).

- **Second**, it might be necessary to remind dependent people about the unreached wider world. Assume for a moment that there is a cluster of congregations that could probably stand on their own two feet. However, through the efforts of well-meaning outsiders, they allowed someone else to subsidize their congregations long after it should not have been necessary. One could raise awareness about unreached people elsewhere and ask them to participate in reaching them. One could also ask if it is right to continue to send funds to a place where the Gospel has been preached for a long time while others have not had the opportunity to hear it for the first time.

- **Third**, those who hold the purse strings may need to examine their own attitude regarding the funding they provide. For example, people who represent funding sources should recognize themselves as people of power. They might precipitate change simply by declining to be present when local people engage in business discussions about the work of the church. Gracefully declining to be present when decisions are made can send the message that we (as outsiders) do not need to be a controlling or even an influencing presence in local decision making. After all, is it not in those business meetings when the funders are present, that the long lists of projects are brought out for consideration? It can be shown that the very presence of a person of means in such meetings distorts the decision-making process. Those present may be guarding their thoughts and words based on the fact that the funders might be offended. That is why the solution might be precipitated when the funders simply decline the invitation to be present when local decisions are being made. This is not always easy because such meetings tend to make the donor feel important – but they may also create or perpetuate dependency.

- **Fourth**, another way to precipitate change is to help raise awareness about the availability of local resources. This may be as simple as looking around at other churches or organizations functioning in the same area. Some of them may never have had the problem of dependency. Or perhaps they once had it, but now it is resolved. One way to do this is to stimulate conversation regarding why not everyone has the problem of dependency. This kind of investigation can be beneficial for both the funders as well as those trapped in dependency. It is not unusual for resources to be within arm's reach while people turn to those far away for subsidy.

- **Fifth**, it is helpful to remember that increasing income is only one way to move toward locally supported churches and other institutions. Cutting expenses is the other way to help make something manageable. This is important if outsiders created expensive projects such as buildings and programs that are only sustainable with outside resources. Precipitating change in this kind of situation is tricky business. But, it may include local people learning that they are free to close down expensive projects, even if they were the creation of some well-meaning people who may or may not still be on the scene. If the decision to close down projects is made by outsiders, it could reflect yet another form of paternalism. [4]

- **Sixth**, precipitating change can be done by making the vision of self-support the topic of sermons and other presentations at leadership conferences, retreats and annual general meetings. Speakers can be asked to describe the problem as well as the challenges of overcoming it. In my own experience conducting seminars on dependency over the past twenty years, I have found that such conferences might not produce instantaneous change; but as those in attendance

---

[4] For many more suggestions on how to precipitate change toward healthy self-reliance see Chapters 7 and 8 in which I deal with what missionaries and local church leaders can do to avoid or overcome the problem of dependency

discuss the ideas later on, change can begin to occur. The healthiest change might not be an abrupt change, but rather that which grows out of serious prayer and reflection over a period of time. I have been both astounded and gratified to hear what decisions were taken sometimes a year or more after we conducted a seminar on dependency. I should also add that I have seen instantaneous change occur. On one occasion in Mozambique before a two-day seminar ended, local pastors publicly confessed their dependency on outsiders and then formed a local committee to send out their first missionary. Since then, they have sent out several missionaries after not having done so in the first eighty years of having the Gospel preached among them. And the decision to do so was made in one short conference. We should not conclude that unhealthy dependency must go on forever.

Initiating a Process of Change

Professor Alan Tippett used to say that if outsiders created financial problems among mission-established churches, they should not simply walk away as if they have no responsibility.

- **First**, recognizing the role outsiders had in creating the situation would be a positive step.

- **Second**, engaging in frank discussions about the current situation may be necessary to get the process going.

- **Third**, it may take some humility to acknowledge that the altruism of outsiders is behind the dependency.

- **Fourth**, seeking the counsel of local people in solving the problem is an essential step in the right direction. This helps to break the pattern of paternalism which is what local people might sense if there is another solution imposed from the outside.

What about the Highly Paid Local Person Who Receives Foreign Support?

As churches are planted and local people assume positions of pastoral leadership, hopefully the ideal of self-supporting local congregations will develop early on. Sooner or later the salary of an outside paid church planter will become a concern. This is particularly true if the church planter — such as a missionary — is paid an inordinately high salary compared to what local pastors are able to get from their own congregations.

At this point great care must be exercised in dealing with the disparity. Unfortunately, it is not unusual for church planting missionaries to serve as pastors of one or more of the churches they plant. Then there comes the time for a local person to take over the congregation or the position. Of course, it is assumed that the outsider's salary will not be transferred to the new local person. The local congregation, having benefited from outside support of their missionary pastor or church planter, may resent having to pay the local pastor who is chosen to replace them. This is not a pleasant place for a new local pastor to step in. One such local pastor in Tanzania told me about his dilemma. He said that his congregation told him to go find his salary at the same place as the missionary. This reflects how serious the dependency mentality can be when it is not avoided from the beginning. It takes a little Christian grace, patience and some re-education to work through the implications.

Mission administrators who recognize such unhealthy dependency would do well to stop it before it becomes a way of life. Such a highly paid church planter or pastor paid from the outside might well be redeployed to another location at some distance. Conversations should begin about how to engage a local church planter or pastor willing to live on a salary and expense account commensurate with local resources. This is a complex subject that has implications for how missionaries are paid, where they put their weekly tithes and a host of other things too complex to deal with here. If the highly paid church planter or pastor is willing to remain in position, then he or she should be prepared to disclose his or her personal financial situation and adapt to the local level of support. In this way a potentially explosive situation might be avoided. Suffice it to say, that allowing an unresolved disparity to continue might not be the healthiest for all concerned.

How Much Time Should One Allow for Change?

One might assume that healthy change from dependency to self-support will take a long period of time. This may or may not be the case. It is helpful to think about the issue of "readiness for change." Professor Tippett used to say that when the appropriate psychological moment for change comes, it should be seized without delay. In fact, he said if that moment has arrived and is not recognized, the readiness for change may pass and a long hard struggle could follow. How does one recognize the appropriate psychological moment for change? Only those who are spiritually and culturally sensitive will be able to recognize the moment. This is too complex a subject to deal with adequately here. But it is one that certainly deserves attention if the time for change is right.[5]

Does anyone Believe in Interdependence?

A word is in order about the globalization process at work in our fast-paced world. It is not unusual in this day and age for North Americans to go throughout the world looking for those with whom they might link up as "partners in the Gospel." Sometimes this results in adopting existing independent churches into the North American denomination. This might be called "church growth by acquisition."

It is important to examine the reasons why this is done.

- **First**, such acquisition helps denominations grow at a faster rate than by normal church planting. It certainly looks good on paper, especially for the giving constituency at home.

- **Second**, the motivation might be that, as westerners, we can become providers for those who are less well off. In other words, this becomes a place for us – to put it crassly – to give our alms. Giving alms is valid if the situation is characterized by *absolute* poverty, but questionable in cases

---

[5] For further information on this, see Alan R. Tippett *Verdict Theology in Missionary Theory*. Also, see chapter 7 in this text.

of *relative* poverty – no matter how good it makes the donors feel.[6]

- A **third** motivation might be that we are genuinely interested in helping those who seek an affiliation with other believers in order to demonstrate "oneness in the Gospel." Some use the term "interdependence" for this process. In reality, given the economic disparity between the two parties – interdependency might not be the best term. As wealthy westerners, we might need something that others have, but it may be a kind of medicine which is hard to swallow. I am referring to the kind of humility and contrition that the rest of the world is waiting for us as Westerners to demonstrate.

One way to encourage *oneness in the Gospel* and *real interdependence* is the way it is described in East Africa. Leaders of the self-reliance movement there have coined the term "local-local interdependence." Their point is that interdependence for the sake of the Gospel is a noble ideal, but it is best done between those who are more or less equals. They say that if there are several clusters of churches in an area such as East Africa, the Caribbean or Central America, they might best demonstrate their oneness in the Gospel by sharing human and other resources with others in the area that are similar to them. In other words, interdependence is healthier among equals living and working in the same region.

How might this work? One church might have a Bible Institute, another a building big enough for large conferences and yet others a campground or printing press. Resources are then shared at the local level, oneness in the Gospel is demonstrated, and the Gospel of the Kingdom is shown to a waiting world simply by the unity displayed. Consider for a moment the alternative. If the only visible partnership is with wealthy churches overseas, the waiting and watching world might well become suspicious of what this Gospel is really about.

---

[6] On giving alms, I recently learned about one perception in a West African Muslim country regarding the US invasion of Afghanistan. The West Africans concluded that the USA needed a place to give their alms. This was reinforced when the President of the United States put out a call for every child in America to give a dollar to help the children of Afghanistan. It is helpful to look at the issue the way others perceive it.

Interdependence and Levels of Expectation

One of the problems with international relationships and interdependency has to do with levels of expectation. It is natural for everyone to expect to get something out of such relationships. Some clusters of churches identify with wealthy western partners in order to benefit financially. Many dependency situations have roots in this kind of expectation.

But there is another kind of expectation. This is on the part of the wealthy or western churches which seek the linkage for their own benefit.[7] They would like to see the new partners from other parts of the world "buy into" the psychological unity that we all believe should be part of the Christian Gospel. But when that "buying in" fails to happen, people on both sides of the coin feel let down. Wealthy westerners need to examine why it is hard for others to buy into psychological oneness with "our kind of people."

Why is it not enough for people to build their own ethnic identity or ethos as a church? Why should they have to become like us, to enjoy our way of life, to fit into our way of worship or church administration? This is one more reason to encourage churches in other parts of the world to find their fellowship and cooperation with those who are close at hand. The term I used above comes to mind – local-local interdependence. We might be able to reduce anxiety on both sides if such expectations were lowered. As much as we outsiders might wish, the way we do things just may not create "a place for others to feel at home."

It might be helpful to try to understand what it is like for outsiders to try to fit into our kind of ethnic church which has developed its own unique identity. Sometimes there is an unseen hand that makes outsiders feel that "belonging" is something they may never achieve. For example, an Asian who married into an ethnic church in Pennsylvania did her best to fit in. Of course, one hurdle for her was that she was considered somewhat exotic. Such special attention is enough to give one an uneasy feeling. But after some

---

[7] Korean churches are finding similar problems as they become active in world evangelization – especially given the amount of money they have available for missions. Nigerians who have changed the paradigm (as in my illustration earlier in this chapter) have not created such an expensive method of church planting.

years of trying to fit in, she came to the following conclusion: "I feel like I am interrupting a family reunion whenever I go to church gatherings."

Some years ago I learned about a young couple living in Southern California who felt the unseen hand every time they went to church. The congregation they attended was of Dutch (Holland) descent. People in the congregation all spoke English, but they were not aware of the little cliques they formed following the Sunday service each week. Their conversations were clearly for insiders and sometimes even the punch line of a funny story was in Dutch, not English. That would be enough to make any outsider uncomfortable. Outsiders simply laugh to be polite.

On one occasion this couple went home from the morning service and discussed their feelings during the noon meal, as had become their custom. All of a sudden, the husband hit the table with his fist and said, "That's it. We're staying; these people need us." Those in an ethnic church will sooner or later need to acknowledge the extent to which the unseen hand convinces outsiders that "this is not a place to feel at home." It becomes doubly important when those in an ethnic church seek to plant churches cross-culturally. It can be done, but it is a challenge requiring cultural sensitivity, understanding and an awareness of how the process feels to those who are different in background.

Conclusion

There is plenty of evidence to show that church planting without causing dependency is possible. Also, dependency where it exists has been shown to be curable.[8] However, in each case there may be a price to be paid. **First**, it may include a generous dose of humility and cultural sensitivity. **Second**, it might mean a serious time of reflection on how to get out of the current state of dependency in which congregations find themselves. **Third**, it might mean serious hard work over a longer rather than shorter period of time. Anyone looking for a quick and easy solution will probably be disappointed.

---

[8] For further information see an article on the WMA website entitled *Is there a Cure for Dependency among Mission-Established Institution?*

There is one thing about which I am convinced. I do not believe that seriously dependent churches are healthy, happy or honoring to the Lord. Whatever can be done to avoid or lift the burden will be a merciful thing for all who are involved.

CHAPTER 20

SEARCHING FOR MEANINGFUL
WAYS TO HELP THE POOR

Introduction

This article was first written at the request of the Salvation Army International headquarters in London. It was part of a combined effort to look at ministry among the poor--those whom the Salvation Army was originally established to serve, well over a century ago. I consider it a privilege to have been asked to contribute to this project.

What is Ministry Among the Poor?

When I first began to reflect on the dependency syndrome related to ministry among the poor, my thoughts turned to the issue of "good news for the poor" a term mentioned in Scripture. When I asked my computerized concordance to find all references to the poor, I found that depending on which translation is used, there are between thirty and forty references to the poor in the New Testament. Of particular interest to me are the references to the concept of "good news for the poor." I must admit that I never spent much time reflecting on just what this concept might mean.

The first thing I noticed is that preaching good news to the poor is listed along with a number of other things Jesus commanded His disciples to do. These include such things as curing lepers, opening the ears of the deaf, raising the dead and causing the lame to walk (Matthew 11:5). In another place, good news for the poor is mentioned along with proclaiming freedom for prisoners, recovering of sight for the blind, and releasing the oppressed (Luke 4:18). When a banquet is given, the poor are to be invited along with the crippled, lame and blind (Luke 14:13).

This is not a paper on Biblical exegesis, so I will not attempt to make all the distinctions that a Biblical theologian would make. Suffice it to say that Jesus was as concerned with the state of the poor as he was with those who suffered from disease, disability, oppression or incarceration. It is interesting that gifts to the poor are mentioned as a credit to those who strive to be spiritually upright, such as in the story about Cornelius (Acts 10:4,31). Paul himself included in his ministry collecting gifts for the poor and delivering them to the temple along with offerings (Acts 24:17). I assume that these were Paul's own personal offerings, not those which he collected from the Gentiles for the poor saints in Jerusalem (2 Corinthians 8 and 9).

To say that Jesus had a special concern for the poor would be an understatement. What interests me is that this concern is reflected in sentences that include the lame, lepers, prisoners and the like. It is amply demonstrated in the New Testament that deliverance was made available to those who had all manner of illnesses; and such things as freedom for those in prison were not only demonstrated, but also taken for granted (Acts 12:17). In spite of that, some who prayed for Peter's deliverance from prison were astonished that the Lord performed it.

One can only conclude that it is quite in order to pray that people will be set free from bondage. It would be a merciful thing for those in poverty to be delivered just as we earnestly pray for someone to be delivered from an illness or from wrongful imprisonment. Our God delights in delivering people from bondage, whatever the nature may be.

One Practical Illustration Regarding the Role of Prayer

Some time ago I was in Maputo, Mozambique where I was asked to conduct a seminar on issues of dependency and self-reliance. As often happens, I encountered people in the seminar who had down-to-earth experiences that demonstrated God's concern for us all. Time was given for anyone who wanted to testify to the grace of God among the poor. One pastor began to tell about the church in his community. He said that because of the depressed economy in his part of the country there were many unemployed people. His church was faced with what to do. They obviously had several options, one of which was to appeal to the government for assistance. Another was to appeal to aid agencies for whatever might be available from overseas. He testified that they decided on a rather different plan of action.

The congregation decided to begin a prayer meeting for the unemployed at 5:00pm three days a week – Monday, Wednesday and Friday. He said it was not long until people became productive in their various areas of employment – particularly the fields in which their crops were grown. These efforts were so blessed of the Lord that they soon had so much produce that it could not all be used locally. They then began to pray about ways to get the produce to markets in the capital city many kilometers away. The church put legs to their own prayers, and businessmen with big trucks donated their services to carry the extra produce to the city. How many times have we thought of a prayer meeting three times a week as a solution to the problem of poverty?

A Second Illustration

The causes of poverty are many and varied. Sometimes the roots are in a society so demotivated about helping itself that people simply turn to alcohol and crime as an alternative to productive work. Such was the case in Almalongo, Guatemala. Things were so desperate that the three town jails could not hold all the people the police were arresting. Spiritism had taken over the town; and poverty, alcoholism and crime were evident everywhere.

At a point of desperation people turned to prayer, inviting various churches to join in unified prayer. Imagine their surprise when a total transformation of society began to occur. Alcoholics were delivered from years of bondage. Prisons began to clear out and eventually every jail was closed! There was no need for a place to incarcerate even one prisoner. But something else also happened. The poverty of the community was exchanged for prosperity unlike anything they had ever known. Even the soil seemed to be "converted" and began to produce far more than it had ever done before. Vegetables grew in proportions never seen before. One man was seen holding a carrot the size of a man's arm. Again the problem of marketing the excess produce became an issue. So much progress was made that farmers began to buy huge Mercedes Benz trucks – with cash – to haul the produce to markets at a distance. This move from poverty, crime and alcoholism resulted from churches laying down their denominational differences and joining in concerted prayer. Prayer as an antidote to poverty might not fit the average five-year plan of an aid agency, but it is not unlike our Lord to respond to a crisis when people come humbly before Him.[1]

Above all else, what could the poor use most?

There are a number of things from which the poor would benefit if they were able to verbalize it. Some of the things they need might not be obvious to them, and they certainly might not be able to articulate it for anyone looking on from the outside. When I began to reflect on what might be missing among many who are poor, my mind turned to the concept of "margin." I concluded that the poor often don't enjoy the margin that is so much taken for granted by those who are much better off economically. It is margin which makes life tolerable; otherwise, life is reduced to mere survival.

I recently tried to help a family that lives in a constant state of hand-to-mouth existence. If there was ever a family that had little or no margin, it was this one. Every issue that confronted them was enough to put them over the edge. With five children in the house, there never seemed to be enough food. An illness meant that there was no reserve—financial or otherwise—with which to respond. Hence, that margin which healthy families count on--having enough to pay a doctor or hospital--was out of the question for this family. A simple car repair bill was enough to bring transportation to a halt. There was no financial margin to ensure that such crises could be handled.

But the kind of margin I am talking about is a luxury for many in our world today. Those who are stretched to the limit financially are without margin. Those who are physically at the end of their rope have no margin to give anything back to society. Some have no spiritual margin to handle one more episode of stress – perhaps resulting from one of the other areas of life where they are without margin. In short, life has become a battle for survival with no

---

[1] The story of Almalongo and several others are told in a video called *Transformations*. It is available through the Sentinel Group at www.sentinelgroup. org.

reserve to draw upon when rough patches occur. Truly for such people margin is a luxury. [2]

Why is margin in such short supply when it is so essential and longed for?

The surest way for anyone to build margin into his or her life is to learn about and practice the principles which God has laid down for mankind. It is in finding and following those principles that we discover the margin that would make it possible to move away from poverty, sickness, demon possession and depression.

What does this mean for those of us who preach good news to the poor? It means that truly good news for the poor is discovering that God's way and His principles are the surest way to find margin. In other words, His way is **the way out** of the poverty trap.

Another contemporary illustration

I recently learned about a growing segment of the Christian movement in an Asian country where believers are a tiny minority. This unbelievable growth is not occurring because church leaders are making it easy to get into the Kingdom of God. The philosophy of the leaders is that if one wants to identify with the Christian faith in this part of the world, he or she will need to learn God's principles and live by them. This means doing at least four things.

- **First**, everyone must pay his or her debts. Christians are honorable people who pay what they owe.

- **Second**, Christians must pay their taxes. Christians are to show nonbelievers in government that they are law-abiding citizens.

- **Third**, believers are taught from day one that they should tithe. No excuses are tolerated, such as being too poor to give back to God. Salvation from day one means that everyone gives something back to God from what He has

---

[2] For a good discussion of the concept of "margin" see a book by Richard A. Swenson, MD entitled *Margin: Restoring Emotional, Physical, Financial and Time Reserves to Overloaded Lives.* Navpress: 1992.

provided. It is a recognition that everything we have comes from God.

- **Fourth**, believers are taught that they should put some of what they earn into savings. This helps them to be prepared for the time when the harvest is lean and also gives them a way to help those less fortunate when a crisis arises. In short, the fourth principle is designed to build a little *margin* into one's life as a believer.

It may be surprising to learn that this group is growing rapidly in a country where the government and nearly a hundred percent of the population are not believers in the Christian way. It also makes one wonder why the Christian movement in other parts of the world is in such economic difficulty. Could it be that we have a generation of believers in many parts of the world who came into the kingdom so easily that they have not been required to follow God's principles? If so, little wonder they are not able to benefit from the margin that God has intended for us all. Maybe all of this has something to do with the assumptions we often begin with as Christians – assumptions which are quite different from the four mentioned above.

What Assumptions are Those?

We often assume that the poor have nothing to give back to God. This may be related to a second assumption which is that since those living in poverty don't have much *money*, they have little or nothing to give to God. This could well explain why in some churches the collection is taken in a velvet bag with a small hole in a wooden handle at the top. The only thing it is designed to receive is money – something the poor don't have in abundance. As one man in Africa said, you can't even put in a banana, let alone a cow or bag of maize. Churches that have broken dependency on outside resources have learned that a new kind of giving must be found if they are to get on their feet financially. Of course, that will mean changing basic assumptions about giving.

More practical illustrations

A few years ago I learned about a church in Rwanda that invited its members to bring whatever they had without emphasis on money.

They found that so many kinds of produce were brought that the church had to assign a previously unemployed person to collect and sell the produce the church was given. They also found in the process that a side benefit emerged. The side benefit was that they were able to help some truly needy people in the community from the produce given to the church. Imagine getting two benefits from one changed assumption. The church not only had increased income for its operation, but it was able to minister to those who were truly needy in their midst. In addition to the produce stand from which they sold the things members were bringing, they eventually created a cattle kraal for the animals that were given to the church. When the assumption about what could be given to the church changed, the "offering basket" was enlarged to the size of a cattle kraal!

Changing our idea of what goes into an offering basket has interesting ramifications. Some time ago I was in a congregation in Zambia which meets in the ballroom of a large hotel. They were raising funds for the sanctuary they hope to eventually build. That particular morning one of the elders was asked to make an appeal for the building fund. Among other things he put down on the floor a large hand-woven basket and then stood inside it. He told the congregation that he was putting himself into this offering basket. How about that for showing that the offering basket is for more than just money? We all sat in silence as we reflected on what it meant to make such an offering.

Assumptions are powerful things. Perhaps that is why Scripture tells us that as one thinks, so is he (Proverbs 23:7). If we say it can't be done, then maybe our prophecy will be self-fulfilling. Perhaps some day we will realize how much of the poverty of the Christian movement can be laid at the feet of those who have excused people from giving back to God even when their giving seemed small and insignificant. One woman in East Africa told how she discovered that if you give zero to God, He can multiply it and it will still be zero. She then asked what happens to a little when it is put into the hands of the One who can multiply without measure. It is how several small loaves and a few fish can feed thousands.

What does true help for the poor look like?

Anything short of giving God complete ownership and following the laws He has laid down, will not be truly good news for the poor. The question is how to encourage those who need this message to actually begin implementing it and benefiting from it.

Perhaps, a healthy dose of the good old-fashioned virtue of **hope** is a place to begin. People who want to find true margin in their lives must begin with the hope or belief that it is possible. Those who have margin know what hope is — especially if they have come from a previous place where hope was virtually unknown. One way to disseminate hope is to get those who know what margin is, to spend time talking to the poor — one by one, family by family, church by church or community by community — telling them how they learned to give ownership to God and follow the principles He has laid down. Without those principles, discovering margin might never be possible. Helping the poor in this way reminds one of the old description of effective evangelism -- one beggar telling another where to find bread.

What would happen if the church mobilized its members who have margin — or hope — to spend time in communities where people suffer from a lack of teaching on scriptural principles about life and how to cope with the world around us? Nothing would speak more effectively than for someone to hear from a fellow sufferer that this sickness can be overcome through the message "I did it and so can you", or "God helped me and He will help you, too."

Several Cautions are in Order

One caution is to make sure that those who know about margin in their lives do not make the goal look so high that no one can imagine attaining it. Hope is not hope if it is continually beyond reach.

Second, care must be taken so that margin does not become an end in itself. One of the problems with economic development is that sometimes, spiritual transformation is looked upon almost as a side benefit – not the primary issue. *When people improve economically and not spiritually, we end up with nonbelievers who simply have a higher standard of living.* When that happens the root causes of poverty are glossed over and such things as violence, hatred, greed, corruption, depression and many other societal ills go unresolved. Are these not some of the things which exacerbate the problem of poverty? So creating economic margin alone is not enough.

Third, as I continue to draw attention to issues of dependency and the need for healthy Spirit-led self-reliance in the Christian movement, there is one thing that frequently concerns me. I sometimes fear that someone will misunderstand what I am saying and use it as an excuse to hold on to what they have and not be concerned about the poor. Jesus reserved some of his harshest criticism for those who offended the poor. I also fear that some will think that I am promoting giving with the view to getting something in return. None of us should be found promoting health and wealth for its own sake. We should all – the poor included – give in gratitude for what God has done for us, and not for what we might get in return.

With all that I say about breaking dependency, we must recognize that our world is a very needy place. There are people whose families have been living on the edge—some in survival mode—for generations. Jesus commands us to help, and as Christians we must do what we can. Our challenge is to find a way that preserves dignity and does not create or perpetuate dependency. I invite you to join me in seeking to serve those in need in the most helpful way possible.

Conclusion

I am enormously encouraged when I see the effects of spiritual transformation that are occurring in our world. With it there is every reason to be hopeful for the poor – those who have little or no margin beyond survival. Without spiritual transformation, the battle with poverty will continue unabated, and we who work at it will find little in which to rejoice.

CHAPTER 21

MISSIONARY DEMEANOR AND
THE DEPENDENCY SYNDROME

INTRODUCTION

As with many things in life, when it comes to dependency, there are two kinds. One might be called unavoidable dependency and the other avoidable. Unavoidable dependency characterizes newborn infants. It also comes to everyone when we are no longer physically or mentally able to care for ourselves. Peter was told that a time would come when he would not even be able to put on his own clothes (John 21:18). Terminally ill people experience their own form of dependency which we all accept and understand.

When it comes to avoidable dependency there are also two kinds. One I'll call self-induced dependency. This may be the result of choosing to become dependent on drugs or alcohol, for example. This kind of dependency can be avoided or even cured as many people have learned—sometimes through sheer determination— other times through the direct intervention of the Holy Spirit. In short, people can usually be delivered from self-induced dependency if they want to.

The other kind of avoidable dependency is what one might call other-induced dependency. Children spoiled by materialism or with excessive money from their wealthy parents are in the category of other-induced dependency. One spouse sometimes does so many things for the other that when the first of them passes away, the one remaining is unable to care for themselves even though they have retained reasonable physical and mental health. This could be called other-induced dependency, however well-meaning it may seem when it is occurring.

For the past ten years I have been concentrating on the problem of dependency among mission-established institutions. I have concluded that this most often falls into the category of "other-induced" dependency.

Some Root Causes of Other-Induced Dependency

One of the factors behind dependency among mission-established institutions is *the western understanding of the Biblical mandate to evangelize the world*. I am referring to two mandates, both cultural and evangelistic, to bring the entire world under the authority of the Kingdom of God. It is symbolized in two political or theological doctrines. One is the Western Hemisphere concept of Manifest Destiny. The other is sphere sovereignty which led to the philosophy of apartheid in South Africa. Both of these have been powerful forces driving westerners to go out with a form of authority which, when not rightly handled, sowed the seeds for the problem of dependency in the Christian movement. If ever there was a need for a shift in western missiology, it is just on this point. It might be helpful to think of the shift being from the Mosaic "thus saith the Lord" to the Pauline "I beseech you therefore brethren."

A second assumption which sows the seeds for dependency among mission-established institutions has to do with *the way in which western missionary candidates are recruited and motivated*. One of the assumptions is that missionary candidates are being recruited to go out to do something significant among the world's poor, needy and unevangelized people. The emphasis here is on *doing something* which I believe often results in the development of the dependency syndrome. Without a proper understanding of how to help, Westerners end up doing things which others could do for themselves.

As a result of this doing, westerners often create projects, programs and institutions, which cannot be carried on or reproduced by those they are trying to help. Sometimes those who create this outside-induced dependency carve out a future from which they cannot seem to extricate themselves, if indeed they want to be extricated. If they don't really want to be extricated, a situation develops that thrives on **the need to be needed** on the part of the outsiders. The need to be needed is a very powerful force.

But let me return to the dichotomy between doing and being. What a missionary is going out **to do** is a very important part of how we raise prayer and financial support. For example, how much support could one raise if the pitch would be "I am going out **to be** rather than **to do**? I am going out to stand beside open graves and weep with others at funerals. I am going out to encourage other people to be all that they can be before the Lord. I am **not** going out to do what others can do for themselves." If a missionary thinks that support-raising is already difficult, try replacing all the rhetoric about "doing" with the concept of "being."

Admittedly this is an area fraught with problems. Some missionaries might hide behind just being as an excuse for their lack of productivity. Herein lies the challenge: How can one have a productive ministry without doing those things which create or perpetuate dependency? Admittedly, that is a subject too ponderous for this short presentation. But it is of critical importance if the dependency syndrome is to be understood and avoided.

Another way to look at the doing/being issue is to remember what we all learned about the difference between *advocates* and *innovators*.[1] Frequently when missionaries move from being advocates to becoming innovators it is then that the dependency syndrome gets its foothold. How much of the syndrome could be avoided if outsiders limited themselves to being advocates and permitted insiders to have the privilege of being the innovators? Again, this brief presentation is not a place for an in-depth treatment of that important subject.

This determination to do something is a very powerful force among western missionaries. Everyone wants to know what I am going to do as a missionary when I get to my assignment. This often results in the determination on the part of the western missionary to find something of which he or she can be in charge. Being in charge of something provides more impressive material for prayer letters to send home.

In chapter 6 I told the story of a missionary in West Africa who was smart enough to do the job, but not smart enough not to. It is an example of how important demeanor is for the missionary.

Missionaries have often taken leadership positions in the spirit of servanthood or so-called partnership. This is how they avoid being looked upon as uncooperative or unwilling to carry responsibility.

---

[1] We are indebted to Dr. Alan Tippett who introduced us to the important distinction between advocates and innovators in missiology.

It represents one of those fine lines that we often encounter in cross-cultural ministry. It may be that only an *astute, well-trained, culturally sensitive and Spirit-filled* missionary will have a chance of getting it right. If envy weren't forbidden in Scripture, we might all envy someone with those four qualities.

The secret is knowing how and when to gracefully decline when the offer of a position is made to us as an outsider. I personally found that the offer could be declined gracefully, with positive results. Something happens when local people discover that the outsider no longer gives the impression that he or she is the most capable person around. That is what consciously communicates that the privilege of leadership belongs to local people, even if it seems on the surface like "nobody wants the job."

Permit a personal illustration from my time in Zambia as a missionary. It was the custom there that any missionary visiting a congregation was normally invited to preach the morning sermon. This happened even when the missionary showed up unannounced and the pastor was ready to preach what he had prepared. I came to the point where I regularly declined such invitations to preach, saying something like this: "You preach better than I. Allow me to sit with the people and listen." In short, I was sending that all-important message that "you can do it—I will gladly listen." Eventually they stopped asking me and a new relationship developed between us.

There are a few creative ways to encourage local church leaders to begin to stand on their own two feet. It may mean some departure from the normal pattern of behavior on the part of the missionary or mission executive. The following are a few more lessons that I have learned.

As I have mentioned several times before, a missionary might make his or her greatest impact by declining the privilege of being involved in business meetings where decisions are being made, especially decisions about money. A church leader from Central Africa once said, "As long as there is one white missionary present in the meeting, we will vote the way he wants us to vote, even if he doesn't say anything. We will watch his eyes and we will know how we are supposed to vote."

In order to prevent this kind of silent, yet obvious and often powerful influence, I suggest that outsiders gracefully decline the opportunity to be present when local business is being discussed. Arrange to visit an elderly villager whom you haven't seen for a long time or simply take the afternoon to do some hospital visitation. The surprise associated with your willingness to be out of the meeting when important decisions are to be made might make a more powerful impact on local leaders than your presence ever could make. Naturally some local people will ask questions like, "Don't you care what we decide?" You can honestly reply something like this: "This is your church and it is your privilege to make decisions about your future and especially your day-to-day operations without my presence and influence." Part of the unspoken message on such an occasion is this: "You are not only free to make your own decisions, but you are free to do what you do without the promise of money often expected when I as an outsider am present."

I recently met with a group of area secretaries representing some sixty countries in which their large mission society is working. They were asking me how to raise consciousness among the leaders of some of their dependent churches regarding local ownership and decision-making. They especially wanted practical suggestions for them as mission executives. I asked how many of them sometimes visit the fields for which they are responsible. They all said they did. I then asked how many of them participate in business meetings with the local church leaders when they make such visits. They acknowledged that they did. All of a sudden it got very quiet when I suggested that might be part of the problem. It took a few seconds while the thought sank in. It is hard to imagine a mission executive from overseas not being invited to or not attending a meeting of local church leaders when he or she is in the area. After all, that is when real business is done, when the moneyed person from overseas is present.

I suggest that mission executives (and missionaries) take a look at that definition of "real business." Real business at a time like that is often when local people get out the shopping list and make a plea for so-called partnership. And then, in the name of global cooperation, commitments are made about how the outsiders will help to fund what remains of local vision. Sometimes even local vision is not very local.

How does one deal with the question about not caring which I mentioned earlier? The most caring thing one might do is to think so highly of the gifts, abilities and privileges of local leaders that the outsider wouldn't under any circumstance want to interfere. And when that attitude sinks in, sometimes a very powerful message can be communicated. It is an effective message generated from silence or absence, rather than the rather overpowering message which accompanies personal presence, personal influence and outside money.

Tim Mitchell is one missionary who responded to this kind of thinking. Several years ago he sat through a five-day seminar I conducted in a rural part of Transkei in South Africa where he served as a missionary. He listened to what I said about outsiders taking back seat positions and not needing to be present when important decisions are made. He made the decision to change his personal mode of operation. Now, years later, he testifies to the positive things that happened among local leadership when he receded into the background. It reinforces what I believe so strongly, that if you think being in charge of something is fulfilling as a missionary, you ought to learn the blessing that comes from not being in charge. Tim Mitchell learned that blessing very well.

Psychological Residence

In the matter of missionary conduct, I find it helpful to ask where outsiders have their psychological residence. By that I mean, where do they feel at home? We have all learned and often taught the importance of moving into the local frame of reference in order to carry out a valid cross-cultural ministry. This includes learning local language and maybe even dressing (or wearing one's hair) like local people do. That is what Hudson Taylor is said to have done. The aim is so that others do not need to come into our frame of reference or—to use my term—into our area of psychological residence, in order to learn the Gospel. That principle is simple enough. The challenge is to figure out how to function as an insider without bringing into the situation the power, authority and resources of the outsider which everyone knows we have as westerners. Unless that is avoided, the seeds of the dependency syndrome are sown and it may be next to impossible for anyone in the future to break this addiction.

I once met a missionary serving in Indonesia who modeled what I am talking about. He was a Mennonite by the name of Dan. The following is his story.

Dan was assigned to work with a local pastor in the capital city of Jakarta. The pastor with whom he worked did not have a motorcar, and Dan felt he should not have one either. So Dan traveled around Jakarta on a small motorbike so that his position would not be deemed to be higher than his colleague, the pastor. Dan said he and his wife often rode across the city on the moped arriving at a Bible study covered with the oily exhaust of Jakarta's diesel buses. But Dan was determined not to buy a car until the pastor bought one. Dan said the longer it went, the more it looked like the pastor was not going to get round to buying himself a car.

One day, however, the pastor said, "Dan, I have been thinking about buying a car. Would you be willing to go with me to help choose the right one?" Dan agreed to do so and they went off together. As soon as the pastor had finalized the deal, Dan said to his colleague, "Pastor, for some time I have been thinking about buying a car, too. Would you be willing to go along to help me choose the right one?"

There is no way to estimate the impact of that kind of demeanor on the part of a missionary. How many times is the western missionary forging ahead with the mandate of evangelizing the world with all the power, authority and money of the Western missionary society behind him or her, all the while running roughshod over local customs, decorum and sense of community! Little wonder that local initiative is stifled.

Think again about balancing the role and function of the outsider. It is not an easy challenge. It will certainly demand sound cross-cultural training — the kind to which I am sure all who teach mission studies are committed. Little wonder that those who have no cross-cultural training miss the importance of this kind of thing.

The Sense of Urgency Regarding the Task

If the demeanor of the missionary is so important, it points to the importance of cross-cultural training. But how do we balance the urgency of the task with the need for adequate cross-cultural training? Or how do we balance the urgency of the task with waiting for local initiative to develop? Let me suggest something which may help to move us in this direction.

Assume that all who are preparing for cross-cultural ministry accept that they need cross-cultural training. (I wish that were true, but let's assume it anyway.) Good solid missionary training might take several years of concentrated effort, if not a life-long commitment. Several weeks of training are more like immunization which convinces missionary candidates that they have had enough of that—now they can now get on with ministry. Little wonder they don't have the patience to wait for local initiative to develop.

Some of this tension might be resolved if those who are committed to the urgency of the task will also commit themselves simultaneously to the training. Fortunately, this is becoming possible more and more through distance learning which a number of institutions are pioneering these days. But what about those who aren't mature enough to go to any field far away from home anyway and would benefit from serious concentrated cross-cultural studies even in a classroom? With the help and creativity of those designing the study program, why not build active ministry into the process in a multi-cultural inner city situation near by? Here is the pitch: "Come study with us and begin your cross-cultural ministry now." Or better yet. "Are you eager to get to the field and begin your ministry? You can do it right now while you are studying in our training program." Remember, for the sake of the urgency, the studying, not the ministry, is on the side. That brings the urgency issue together with the importance of training. It also gives some candidates time to mature while they make their blunders closer to home where the expense and the consequences are not so great. And so far as the patience required for local leaders to come on board, perhaps this period of training will give the Christian grace of patience time to develop.

What about Paternalism and Missionary Demeanor?

Admittedly paternalism sometimes creeps into the heart of western altruism, and perhaps even more often into the demeanor of missionaries. There isn't time to develop it here, so I will just mention it in passing. We as westerners cannot imagine how our benevolence or altruism could possibly be at the root of the dependency syndrome. After all, we use money to solve many problems. Furthermore, we get such a good feeling from giving that we might not even realize when paternalism creeps in. Remember the statement I mentioned earlier, "How can you accuse me of paternalism? I treated them like my own children and they didn't appreciate it!"

What Hope is There for the Future?

Is there a ray of hope for this situation in the future? Is it not that today's and tomorrow's missionaries have access to training that was not available even thirty or forty years ago? If they take advantage of it, the Christian movement will certainly be better off in the next generation than it was in the last. Of course, the effectiveness of this depends on whether those teaching missions are familiar with the dependency syndrome and know how to help avoid it. This represents a challenge for many who are helping to prepare missionary candidates for service, especially those teaching in Bible Colleges and seminaries. Of course one needs a teachable spirit for training to be effective.

There is another ray of hope. It is in the new missionary force — especially from the non-western world — which is not so well endowed financially and therefore less likely to create and perpetuate financial dependency as the Christian movement spreads. As Dr. Arthur Glasser once said about the China Inland Mission: "We barely had enough money on which to survive as missionaries ourselves. We could not have spoiled churches with money if we wanted to."[2] When this subject came up in a recent gathering of retired OMF missionaries we heard his former missionary colleagues who had lived on meager income agree with resounding affirmation.

---

[2] For more on the wealth of western missionaries see Jonathan Bonk, *Missions and Money: Affluence as a Western Missionary Problem*, Maryknoll: Orbis Books, 1992.

Conclusion

Missionaries **can** speak and act with authority and urgency, and they **do not need** to create the dependency syndrome in the churches which are started. But it will take a new and sometimes radical approach for that to happen. It remains to be seen how many are prepared to pay the price for such innovation and how many have the courage and humility it will demand. After all, taking this approach means bucking a lot of history over the last century.

CHAPTER 22

REFLECTIONS ON SEVERAL BIBLE SOCIETIES IN CENTRAL AND EAST AFRICA

This article was originally written in the early 1990s. Some things have changed since then, but the general principles related to dependency are still applicable.

INTRODUCTION

In 1989 Dr. Lars Dunberg of Living Bibles International (now the International Bible Society) calculated that if all existing Bible Societies in the world worked at one hundred percent of their capacity between 1989 and the end of the century, they would meet only 25% of the need for Bibles during that eleven-year period. This causes one to reflect on what would have to be done differently in order to raise that percentage by ten, twenty-five or fifty percent. Considering that the 75% unmet need represents people without Bibles, the situation bears serious reflection.

In the past my ministry travel has brought me into first-hand contact with national and regional Bible societies in East, Central and Southern Africa. My interest in how well African Bible societies are doing is heightened by the other major emphasis of my ministry, namely, issues of dependency and self-reliance for churches and other Christian organizations in this part of Africa. This chapter is a result of those two concerns coming together.

One Bible Society Scenario

In the early 1990s the General Secretary of one African Bible Society reported the following overall picture of his situation: "Of our annual budget of 127 million units of currency, last year we raised 955,000 within our own country. That is about three-fourths of one percent of our budget. The other 99.25% came in the form of subsidy through the worldwide network of Bible societies of which we are a part."

In specific terms, he reported that they import and sell one local Bible in large quantities "at a price people can afford." He explained that the cost of production for that edition of the Bible is US$7.20. The Bible is sold for the local currency equivalent of US$1.00. The one dollar collected is not used toward the cost of production but rather for in-country costs such as storage, transport and profit margin for resellers. As a result, the US$7.20 production cost requires 100% subsidy from outside the country of destination, with the end-user contributing nothing toward the cost of production. One begins to get a glimpse of what lies behind the 75% unmet need calculated by Dr. Dunberg.

Little wonder that those in Bible Society circles are not able to realistically think about producing Bible concordances and other Bible study helps for the millions of African believers who could use them. Without doubt, change in the overall system will need to take place in order to produce the Bibles, concordances, Bible dictionaries and study Bibles Africa deserves. Until that change takes place, African Christians will simply need to wait.

The purpose of what I write here is to promote serious reflection on the kind of presuppositional change (or paradigm shift) that will need to take place in order to give African believers the Bibles and related literature they deserve.

The Shortage of Bibles and Blocked Cash[1]

When I first wrote on this subject (1992) one could not buy a Kikuyu Bible in Nairobi. Someone spent a week trying to locate a new Kikuyu Bible in Nairobi. (Kikuyu speakers represent the largest ethnic group in Kenya.)

Was it a shortage of funds in 1992 that caused the scarcity of Kikuyu Bibles? The answer is both yes and no. Along with many others, Kikuyu Bibles have been sold at a subsidized price in East Africa for a long time. Even so, a large amount of so-called "blocked cash" was accumulated in Kenya, just as in many other African countries at that time. It is difficult and often times impossible to get blocked cash out of a country so that more Bibles could be printed outside Africa.

---

[1] Since this was first written in the early 1990s, thankfully the blocked cash problem has been resolved in some countries. Of course, the economic situation in various other countries is still very grave, indeed.

The result is that the "system" is waiting for Bible societies and other charities in America and Europe to raise more donations (and lots of them) so that Kikuyu and other Bibles can be printed outside African countries. This also helps us to see why 75% of the need continues to go unmet.

An alternative is to begin printing Bibles in Africa using some of that blocked cash. This has been tried in the past but those responsible have not been happy with the quality of the final product. One Bible society director said that one such Bible was not bound well enough and did not last like the ones printed in the Far East. He then quickly added, "Maybe we gave up too soon. For fifty pounds worth of better glue we might have been able to do it successfully."

Even if printing equipment, paper and glue had to be imported, at least local labor would benefit. And since Africa has an abundance of labor, one questions why such jobs should continue to go to the Far East.

But I submit that more than jobs and blocked cash are at issue. In two countries recently (one in West Africa and one in Latin America), local Bible societies printed their first Bible in their own countries. One director said rather excitedly, "It took us a whole year and it was difficult, but we did it. It is our first Bible and we did it ourselves." That is the kind of excitement which is desperately needed throughout developing countries. Think how often people in Western countries have enjoyed the good feeling that accompanies giving the money, producing and distributing the Bibles and then went about telling what a blessing they received. That is what happens every time someone from Gideons International or a western Bible society speaks in churches or civic clubs across America and Europe. One urgent need is to transfer that good feeling to those who deserve the blessing of doing things for themselves. In the end, the Bibles may be on thicker paper and perhaps the bindings will not be quite as good, but that is part of the price to be paid in order to begin to close the gap on the 75% unmet need.

Analyzing Current Assumptions

One assumption that helps to keep the price of Bibles low in East, Central and Southern Africa relates to the Western perception of poverty. Most westerners who visit Africa are convinced that the widespread appearance of poverty means that unless Bibles are priced very low or even given away free, very few will receive scriptures. It is not unusual for western visitors to simply want to buy a stack of Bibles at a national Bible Society (at a highly subsidized rate, of course) and give them away free. Those who give Bibles free are contributing to a major part of the problem. They convince local believers that the Bible should cost little or nothing because, after all, **it is God's Word**. It does not occur to the local believers that somewhere, someone is paying US$7.20 for each Bible they get free. Nor does it occur to the overseas visitors that they are giving away highly subsidized Bibles.

Are Christians in Africa so poor they cannot pay for the Bibles they want or need? Actually, that is the subject of the rest of this book, but it bears some reflection in regard to Bible distribution. It is quite apparent that the first assumption that should be analyzed is that African Christians are too poor to pay their fair share of what it costs to run their churches and buy their own Christian literature, including Bibles.

Sometime ago I learned about a Bishop in Mozambique who was selling cheap bibles and also expensive ones. A woman asked to buy a Bible from him, and he told her that he did not have one that she could afford. She was somewhat offended by the nature of his assumption and asked how much an expensive one would cost. When he told her, she pulled out enough metical (Mozambican money) to pay for it on the spot. His faulty assumption was challenged on the spot. He later told the experience with some embarrassment for his faulty assumption.

A second presupposition which must come under review relates to the non-profit paradigm on which Bible societies and other NPOs in Africa function. There are several ramifications to this. One is the idea that NPO's need to exist only on "charity" and, therefore, sound business practices simply don't apply. Some service-oriented charities may not always be able to pass on the full cost of services; but in cases where a product such as Bibles is concerned, this assumption should be vigorously reviewed. In other words, the spirit of dependency or "you owe us something" which characterizes a non-profit "business" with a product is due for reconsideration.

Third, the problem may well be the mentality of boards of directors and trustees responsible for the organizations they are supposed to direct. How so?

Boards of directors for Bible societies and other NPOs in Africa are frequently made up of representatives of the churches they are meant to serve. It is not unusual to find that the board of an African Bible society, for example, includes bishops, moderators, Salvation Army officers and others who hold official positions in their respective churches – which are also charitable organizations.

When a non-profit board of directors consists of heads of other non-profit organizations, there is a potential conflict of interest. For example, when the board of such an NPO meets to strategize raising next year's budget, the discussion will be among those who have their own non-profit budgets to raise. "Conflict of interest" may be too mild a term to describe this turn of events.

Yet the problem is even more serious. What if the Bible Society board consists of representatives who come from churches which themselves are dependent on foreign funding and cannot stand on their own two feet? It is inevitable that such board members will conclude that their Bible Society will also have to appeal for major foreign subsidy just as churches do. Hence, there is little hope of such board members creating and promoting a balanced budget based on sales and local donations. Also, there is little chance that the Bible Society will get a contribution from their churches. It is more likely that the dependent church will be approaching the Bible Society for a handout of free Bibles from them.

In my experience, heads of other non-profit organizations do not represent a strong foundation on which to create a sound financial operation. Many years ago when I became head of a non-profit organization (World Mission Associates) I resigned from several other non-profit boards on which I served. I resigned in order to remove the conflict of interest since I would also be engaging in fund raising for our own organization. I know how it works. If one non-profit identifies a good funding idea or source, it will be attractive to others who are present.

Herein may be part of the solution to the dilemma facing Bible society boards in Africa. Are they not desperately in need of business-minded Christians who are not encumbered with their own non-profit budget to meet? Are Bible societies not in need of "can do" minded business people who do not expect handouts from overseas to balance their company budgets? Some of them know instinctively what marketing involves. They know that one cannot engage in poor marketing techniques, for example, and then fall back on foreign subsidy to make up the difference. Businessmen just can't afford to think that way.

SEVERAL CHALLENGES MUST BE FACED

First of all, there are several problems related to converting boards of NPOs from dependency-minded church men and women to business-minded church people. I do not minimize the difficulties involved in such a transition. First of all, church men and women have long held authority in how organizations such as Bible societies are organized and how they function. Relinquishing that control means someone must think through the implications with great care.

Second, the leadership of NPO's such as Bible societies must brace themselves for the approach that tough-minded business people will bring to the board of directors. First, a CEO will need to adjust his or her attitude toward foreign subsidy and the mentality behind it. Next to come under review will be the style of management that takes the eyes off the bottom line and allows anyone to conclude that "this is simply how charity works." Tough-minded, survivor-oriented business people have learned they can't resort to such fatalism and survive in the business world.

But the resources business people bring to the board can far outweigh the tough-minded questions they are bound to raise. Indeed, the change they represent is precisely what a Bible society or other NPO may need for their survival. Referring to my opening statement, their presence could represent the much-needed step toward closing the 75% unmet need for Bibles in the world.

In addition to competence and sound management, boards of directors and Bible society staff will need to be people of integrity. Dishonesty and unwise stewardship will, in the long run, affect both the ministry and the market that the Bible society should have. There are many examples of the importance of this in NPOs throughout Africa and elsewhere.

A **third** assumption that should be given serious consideration is the form (or quality) of scriptures being produced and distributed. The $7.20 Bible referred to above could well be equivalent to the $69.00 leather bound Bible in North America or Europe. Not everyone needs it or can afford it. The problem in Africa is that the Christian population has become accustomed to the nicer editions. Producing cheaper ones will take some adjustment in thinking. In 1992 in Zambia there was an interesting situation regarding the pricing of Bibles. A soft cover New Testament with thin paper and a nice red string was being sold for ZK50 [2] (Zambian kwacha) while one had to pay ZK85 for a can of beer in the market. The Bible was meant to give life and to last for years. The can of beer takes life and can be consumed in ten minutes. That difference in perceived value is worth reflecting on.

Fourth, new believers on university campuses in North America and England are often seen carrying well-used paperback editions of the Bible. Is it possible that African Christians could come to accept editions of the Bible that may not cost US$7.20 to produce in a foreign country, with foreign currency? Adjusting such long-held expectations will not be easy. However, the importance cannot be minimized. If African Christians insist on the nice $7.20 Bible, that option should be available to them at the full or near full cost. The cheaper paperback version should also be made available for those who still want a Bible but cannot afford the more expensive one. That would do much to move Bible production and distribution in the direction of sustainability.

To sum this up, the problem of heavily subsidized Bible societies was not created overnight and will not be resolved overnight. However, everyone involved must avoid a fatalistic mentality

---

[2] Remember that the value of the Zambian Kwacha was considerably different at that time from what it is today. The comparison is still valid.

which precludes progress toward closing the 75% unmet need. It might be helpful to think of ourselves as one of those who would not get a Bible because of the way the system currently operates. I do not believe, however, that the solution lies in continuing to raise millions of dollars, pounds and deutch-marks in the West to subsidize Bibles in the rest of the world. More Bibles will become available when the system is altered. The subsidy just may be part of why the gap got so wide in the first place.

Practical Suggestions for Adjusting the Paradigm on which Bible Societies Function

1. Reconsider the kind of people who are recruited to serve on Bible Society boards of directors. If necessary, put church leaders on an advisory board, allowing them to give input regarding translations or other matters of inter-church cooperation. Above all, seek to insure that their own dependency mentality is not transferred from their dependent church to the Bible Society board of directors.

2. Consider the possibility of having the General Secretary of the Bible Society get his salary directly from the churches. If four denominations each committed one-fourth of his salary, they would probably be giving more to the Bible Society than they are under the present system. In addition, churches would be more keenly aware of his work and better able to pray for him and the work of the Bible Society if they had a stake in his or her support. Other Bible society staff could be church-sponsored in a similar way.

3. Create a network of market-minded business people of integrity from the churches who will serve as board members and help to strategize sales and distribution of Bible Society literature. Seek to make use of business men and women as they travel throughout the country for other reasons.

4. Experiment with locally printed editions of Bibles at lower cost in an effort to provide an alternative to the present unrealistically priced, higher quality Bibles. In that way, the price can be raised on highly subsidized and more expensive Bibles. Those who want them can still get them if they are willing to pay the higher price. The additional amount they

pay will help to close the 75% unmet gap. It may be helpful to remember that in many African economies, expectations have been lowered considerably over the last several decades. For example, brown unrefined sugar has frequently replaced the more expensive white refined sugar. And, while it may not be preferred, in some places yellow maize has been used to replace white. As people use brown sugar and yellow maize, they look forward to the day when white sugar and white maize will again become available. Just so, in order to get a Bible of their choice, some people may have to buy one with a cheaper binding and cheaper paper until the time they can afford the more expensive edition.

5. One place to begin is to accept a "can-do" mentality at all levels of Bible Society activity. This will mean reviewing practices related to translation, production, storage and distribution. This mentality adjustment should include seminars for Bible Society staff and board members on their role in breaking unhealthy dependency. Board members must discover their potential in leading their Bible societies toward a more sustainable practice. It is not only the path to economic survival, but also the path to personal satisfaction and improved productivity. Until this happens, those waiting for the 75% unmet need to be filled will simply have to exercise patience.

Conclusion

Thankfully since I first wrote this article some positive changes have been made in Bible society circles. Several Bible societies have begun to produce Bibles in their own country. My purpose here is to encourage all who are concerned about the problem of subsidy and shortfall to engage in serious conversations at all levels, seeking to adjust the paradigm wherever possible. I especially encourage business men and women to have an increasing role in helping to turn around the prevailing mentality of dependency. I have no doubt that more Bibles will be available if that were to happen.

I gladly make myself available to meet and talk with anyone or group of individuals who wish to discuss the implications further. For those who are interested, I can be reached at the e-mail address given elsewhere in this book.

CHAPTER 23

ISSUES OF SUSTAINABILITY IN
MEDICAL MISSION INSTITUTIONS

Introduction

I have not been a medical missionary, although my wife and I have two children who were born in a mission hospital. I also had the privilege of working as a non-medical person alongside others in a large mission hospital in Central Africa. This was part of my experience as a missionary in Africa beginning in 1961 and continuing in one form or another there and elsewhere since then.

I currently serve as Executive Director of World Mission Associates and for the past twenty-three years have been dealing with issues of dependency and self-reliance in the Christian movement. Most of our research and writing has been related to East, Central and Southern Africa. However, many stories from other parts of the world are evidence that the phenomenon of unhealthy dependency is widespread. My passion is to help those who wish to either avoid or overcome unhealthy dependency in the Christian movement. For this reason my service is to church and mission leaders as well as to expatriate missionaries.

A Few General Lessons Learned

The following are a few lessons we have learned regarding unhealthy dependency in the Christian movement.

1. First, **the problem of dependency among mission-established institutions has its roots in spiritual issues**. Without genuine spiritual transformation, it is unlikely that people will generously and joyfully support their own church, let alone medical services or missionary outreach.

2. Second, **the road to dependency is often paved with good intentions**. Well-meaning outsiders, often driven by compassion, do for others what they might otherwise be able to do for themselves. Those seeking to do good don't always

calculate the long-term impact that indiscriminate giving can have on those they try to help. Indeed, the need to be needed compels many westerners to act without regard for the long-term consequences of their actions.

3. Third, **self-reliance has little to do with wealth or poverty**. Believers in many parts of Africa and elsewhere have demonstrated that when true psychological ownership transfers, great strides toward local sustainability can be taken. A church in South Africa made up of unemployed women and children was so transformed that now when they gather for an annual church conference, the collection can amount to the equivalent of one million US dollars.

4. Fourth, **many transitions toward local sustainability include a direct revelation from the Lord to the church leaders involved**. That kind of spiritual intervention stimulates local leaders to begin the move toward finding local resources. Space does not permit illustrations here, but this can be documented over and over again.

5. Fifth, **westerners often assume that their wealth is the missing ingredient in the spread of the Gospel or in doing healthcare or other community development projects**. Ironically, it is sometimes such funding that prevents leaders of churches and other local institutions to look for resources close at hand. It is simply easier to get outside funding than to develop a local funding base.

6. Sixth, **the transfer of psychological ownership must precede stewardship teaching**. Those who attempt to "demand" Christian stewardship, without first promoting a feeling of local ownership, find the battle to be very difficult. In medical mission institutions, if the prevailing paradigm is foreign (both personnel and funding), little wonder that local people who wish to be served feel they should not need to pay for the medical care they receive. The real test for ownership is to ask whether anyone on the local scene would step in if outside resources were threatened or cut off. If not, then true local ownership is most likely missing. And in that case, local support will be very hard to develop.

7. Seventh, **it is necessary to distinguish between those who live in absolute poverty and those who live in relative poverty,** something I have mentioned several times before. In many places where unhealthy dependency has a foothold, people live in *relative* poverty, not *absolute*. That means that they **do** have resources, but not in abundance when compared to the westerners who seek to serve among them. In such situations, outside funding can be counterproductive in mobilizing local support.

Dependency – Not A Terminal Illness

It can be shown that mission-established institutions mired in a state of unhealthy dependency do not need to remain on outside subsidy forever. In other words, such dependency does not need to be considered a terminal illness.[1] The question is whether or not those who are responsible are willing to engage in the serious restructuring that will be required.

What About Those Who Are Truly In Need?

There are places where climatic, political, economic and other conditions make providing health care for the general population difficult, if not impossible. In some places, people simply don't have food and shelter, and therefore don't have sufficient resources to pay for the medical services they need. What, if anything, can be done in such situations?

The first question to be asked is who should fill the gap and provide the services that are needed. I have dealt with this subject in other places, and time and space do not permit an in-depth treatment of it here. My short answer is that the best help is that which is within arm's reach or near by. Global resources are often thought of as being the first line of defense, whereas, in reality they should be considered the last, if local dignity is to be preserved. The challenge is how to find and mobilize resources in a way that will not make local conditions more difficult – which can happen when global

---

[1] For further information on this point, *see Is There a Cure For Dependency Among Mission-Established Institutions?* on the WMA website www.wmausa.org.

resources are used to meet a need that could otherwise be filled from local, regional, national or continental resources.[2]

Those who cannot pay for their own healthcare are most likely in need of increased personal income for other reasons as well. When that is the case, then concern for the whole person means that economic issues need to be addressed. This brings to mind the work of an agency in West Africa originally called Faith and Farm, the forerunner of what is now called RURCON, those who serve as rural development counselors in Africa.[3] The aim of Faith and Farm was to bring together spiritual and agricultural principles in an effort to address needs of both soul and body.

When Faith and Farm paid attention to issues of food production there were several gratifying side benefits. People not only had a better diet, but their family income improved. A further side benefit was increased personal income which resulted in increased income for the church. In dealing with issues of dependency in mission churches I long ago learned that improving personal or family income is only part of the challenge. Another important part is to ensure that Christian stewardship is built into the earning process. That is how the kingdom of God benefits the most. Without built-in principles of Christian stewardship, the economic standard might increase, but one ends up with wealthier non-believers than before. And wealthy non-believers have the potential to do more harm in the world than those who are not well off economically.[4]

Can Any Medical Mission Institution Be Expected To Stand On Its Own Two Feet?

At a conference held in Nairobi in 2000 about seventy medical officers, hospital administrators and others related to health care spent five days telling about their successes and failures regarding the sustainability of Christian hospitals. At the conclusion it was agreed that the syndrome of dependency may be widespread, but it

[2] For further treatment of this, see what I have written regarding the principle of geographical proximity in Chapter 10.
[3] RURCON is based in Jos, Nigeria.
[4] For further information on this and similar economic issues, see Chapter 20 entitled *Searching for Meaningful Ways to Help the Poor.*

is not inevitable or incurable. The following are a few illustrations from the lessons learned.

1. First, **some of the best examples of local sustainability were hospitals in countries where government subsidy was not available**. Two case studies from countries outside of East Africa were given and both, despite substantial government subsidy, were struggling for their existence. Other hospitals (in places like Kenya) were able to exist on nearly a hundred percent local resources. This was *in spite of* the fact that government subsidy was not available. Conclusion? Sustainability is not tied to the availability of government funding.

2. Second, **there is no substitute for local "ownership."** Several illustrations are in order.

    a. One hospital in Kenya succeeded in recruiting Kenyan trained medical doctors from an East African university. Hospital staff developed a relationship with doctors in training and followed them through their educational experience until they were ready to serve. The transition out of medical school did not cause an overseas "brain drain", because they went to serve the hospital that was courting them. In this hospital there were four Kenyan medical doctors – supported by the hospital from local resources. The hospital got 95% of its funding from local resources.

    One other factor is of significance. The financial viability of this Kenyan hospital was the presence on staff of four **debt counselors** who went into the surrounding villages to counsel those who were required to pay for the healthcare they were receiving from the hospital.

    b. Tumutumu Hospital (a Presbyterian institution) in Kenya fell into economic difficulties and was threatened with closure. Those providing funding from overseas developed donor fatigue and issued an order to close the hospital. It was then that local people threw up their hands and said, "How can someone from overseas tell us that our hospital should be closed? Let us take it over to see what we can do." (This is a good example of the transfer of psychological ownership which I mentioned previously.)

The transformation of Tumutumu Hospital is nothing short of astonishing. Local people from the Tumutumu area went back to the place where the Gospel was first brought to them from overseas – a suburb of Nairobi called Kikuyu. That was about a hundred and fifty kilometers from Tumutumu Hospital, the one threatened with closure. A band of concerned individuals began the 150km march from Kikuyu to Tumutumu. Among them were medical personnel as well as pastors and other believers. As they marched toward Tumutumu they held roadside clinics and evangelistic meetings in the evenings. People along the way asked why they were marching and were told that they were trying to save their hospital. Through this effort they raised awareness and invited others to join them.

So successful was their effort that the hospital is now 95% supported from local resources. Facilities were refurbished, and new equipment was installed. It soon became a showpiece for other hospitals in Kenya. Staff from other hospitals came to learn about the transformation of Tumutumu Hospital.[5]

c. A third transformation took place at Clinica Biblica, a mission-run hospital in Costa Rica. This hospital was also started by missionaries who over the years developed what one might call "mission fatigue." Similar to Tumutumu, it was the mission that recommended closing the hospital. In the 1970s local people in Costa Rica asked if they could take over the hospital in an attempt to breathe new life into it.

So successful was the transition to local ownership that it has become a model medical institution in the region.

---

[5] A more complete story can be found on the WMA website at *www.wmausa.org* under the title *The Transformation of Tumutumu Hospital*.

Clinica Biblica recently launched an expansion program costing some **twenty-three million dollars**. There were several major side benefits of this transition to local ownership.

1. First, it stopped draining funding from the mission agency—funding which could be used for the spread of the gospel, rather than balancing the budget in a church or mission-run institution.

2. Second, services to those in need were significantly increased in both quality and availability.

3. Third, the new "owners" established a fee scale in which middle and upper class people needing treatment helped to subsidize those who were unable to pay. This is similar to North American hospitals which treat the poor either free or at a reduced rate, made possible because of the income they receive from middle and upper class clientele. As much as forty percent of Clinica Biblica's services were redirected to those who are otherwise unable to afford medical care.

d. A third illustration comes from Madagascar. I only recently learned about this transfer of ownership and so do not have very many first-hand details. However, in the 1970s, the mission hospitals of the London Mission Society were put under local ownership and have been self-supporting ever since. I am awaiting further details on how the transition and subsequent budgeting were handled. Such transitions will help us to understand the dynamics involved in attaining sustainability.

Observations

1. In each of the examples above it is possible to find things that are not ideal. For example, some will say that after the transfer of local ownership, spiritual ministry in the hospital deteriorated. In fact, there is no guarantee that spiritual ministry will be effective simply because outsiders run a hospital with heavy

outside subsidy. I refer again to the matter of spiritual renewal which is at the heart of avoiding or overcoming dependency.

2. The most effective local ownership is where parachurch institutions (including Christian hospitals) are under independent board leadership. One of the first questions to be asked is whether the final authority for the hospital rests with church leaders or with qualified business people. Remember the church is to be run on tithes and offerings. Institutions such as hospitals should be run on a profit and loss basis.

3. On a related issue, it is not uncommon for church leaders to want a hospital, clinic or other development project because of economic side benefits for the church. Interestingly, the benefits to the church might well be temporary or even counter-productive in the long run. Following a ten-year period of outside funding for development projects one bishop in East Africa actually discovered that his church members were giving less than before the assistance began.

4. Short-term medical missions can have a positive impact on local health care, but too often that impact is minimal. One study done in Central America showed that the **annual** expenditure cost of short-term medical missions to one country was fourteen million US dollars, and that there was no appreciable change in the quality of overall healthcare in the country.

    One way the short-term medical experience can benefit medical missions is through the visit of specialists who are able to bring expertise and respite to overworked medical staff in busy mission hospitals. That brings true relief. If those on short-term teams are not specialists, they may end up taking time and energy from medical staff who are already overworked and yet feel obligated to create something meaningful for the visitors to do.

    On the positive side, it is possible for short-term medical teams to make a positive contribution in other areas. Several teams going to Uganda included those who were specialists in Emergency Medical Training (EMT). They were so effective in giving that kind of training that a nation-wide program resulted in which Ugandans were trained to provide that kind of service. Soon after the training began, lives were being saved which would have been lost previously.

Short-term medical teams should be aware that the service they sometimes give is in competition with local practitioners who may be trying to make a living through a privately owned clinic. Since some short-term medical teams provide medicine and services free of charge, they may have an adverse effect on the private clinic nearby. Remember that the private clinic is a fifty-two week enterprise based on profit and loss – not a two-week enterprise based on overseas charity.

5. Of significance in medical missions is the matter of attitude and demeanor. Some mission hospitals are managed and sustained by outsiders who create an atmosphere that makes it difficult to attract locally trained medical personnel – particularly medical doctors. A hospital in Central Africa had five expatriate doctors on staff but could not get one locally trained medical doctor to join the staff. When local church leaders were asked about this, their reply was, "No local doctor in his right mind would work there." The five expatriates created an atmosphere that simply was not a place for a local medical doctor to feel at home. In some cases, the outsiders bring in so many supplies and outside funding that they make themselves indispensable. Indispensable people can develop a demeanor that does not allow other people to feel at ease.

What Can Be Done To Promote The Transfer To Local Ownership?

Every situation is different from every other. Therefore, it is not possible to prescribe one cure that is suitable for all. Having said that, the following are a few general suggestions.

1. The first step is to positively **anticipate a change to local ownership**. If you don't want it to happen, it is unlikely that it will.

2. Second, **precipitate the change** by doing things that will lead local people to discover the benefits of local ownership. This means proactively working toward change. It will take some skill, creativity and a great deal of patience. Not all efforts to

precipitate change will be successful. But, if no attempts are made, little change can be expected. Most importantly, try to figure out how to precipitate change in a non-paternalistic way.

3. Third, **learn all you can about how positive change takes place**. Find out how Dr. Dan Fountain and his colleagues led Vanga Hospital in Congo to local ownership and effectiveness.[6] On the World Mission Associates website (www.wmausa.org) there are scores of articles with suggestions about how to avoid or overcome unhealthy dependency. Of particular interest, note what I say in chapter 17 entitled *What Triggers the Move toward Self-Reliance?*

4. **Be prepared to do serious restructuring, if necessary**. There are two ways to balance a budget. One is to increase income. The other is to reduce expenses. Restructuring may be essential in order for the institution to become locally sustainable. Some programs created during the days of heavy outside funding may not be sustainable as an institution moves in the direction of local support. For example, decentralizing an institution can be an important part of cutting costs as portions of the workload are shared with smaller units at a distance—units which have lower overhead costs. (This would be true of a move in the direction of village clinics.) When the institution is decentralized, so is the expense budget, and that can be a major side benefit of the restructuring process.

5. **Don't expect someone to hand you a ready-made solution** that you put on like a glove. Such solutions will rarely be useful. But, with a willingness to learn and under the direction of the Holy Spirit, positive changes can occur. The illustrations of transformed hospitals, which I gave above, are evidence that it is worth the effort required to make it happen.

Conclusion

The world in which we live is desperate for available and improved healthcare. To paraphrase a researcher at a large children's

---

[6] Look in any good source of books for the writings of Dr. Dan Fountain, former missionary to Congo.

hospital in London, "Our greatest need is not for more research and technology. We already have more information than we are able to manage. The real need is for a new way of doing what we already know how to do."

Of course, this means being willing to adjust the paradigm on which we function. And such a shift is why new attitudes and procedures regarding sustainability among medical and other institutions are so incredibly important.

CHAPTER 24

AIDS AND ORPHANAGES IN AFRICA

Introduction

For the past twenty years or more I have been researching and producing materials on issues of dependency and self-reliance in the Christian movement. My efforts have been primarily in East, Central and Southern Africa but elsewhere as well. Through interaction with church and mission leaders in other parts of the world, I have learned that unhealthy dependency in the Christian movement is a worldwide phenomenon.

Inspiration Behind This Article

This article is about AIDS and dependency brought to my attention by two articles that came across my desk recently. One was in a recent issue of *Christianity Today* in which students at Wheaton Academy in Illinois raised a quarter of a million dollars for a village in Zambia. They helped to build a clinic and "provide food for the children for a year"! The other publication I read is a web article entitled *Priorities: Orphans or Air Conditioning?* by Marvin Olasky in which he tells about an orphanage project in Namibia that receives $11,000 a month from a supporting church in the USA. All of this set me to thinking about the kind of help being given by outsiders.

One of the questions that keeps surfacing is what to do about the rising problem of AIDS – particularly AIDS orphans in Africa. Medical, government and church structures are under enormous strain as is the extended family system. In some places, the population is being decimated to the point where only young children are left in the villages. Heroic accounts are told about how well some children are coping in the face of unbelievable challenges.

All of this means that AIDS-related problems are on the increase, prompting Christians to ask what they should do to help. Various solutions are being tried far and wide. In Uganda, positive results are reported from a campaign to promote behavior change. In other places African churches are instituting programs to help their members show compassion toward those who are suffering. In some instances westerners are convinced that western-style orphanages are the best response to this growing challenge.

This heightened interest brings e-mails to my desk. Missionaries and mission executives are asking what westerners can and should do with their resources that will hopefully avoid unhealthy dependency. What follows is not a comprehensive treatment of the subject. That needs to be done, but hardly in a short article like this. Given that limitation, the following are a few comments and recommendations.

OBSERVATIONS ON THE AIDS CRISIS

First of all, AIDS should be considered a "social sickness", not primarily a medical problem waiting to be solved. That is the conclusion of Drs. Jacques Kriel and Willem Sayman who, a decade or so ago in South Africa, produced a small book entitled *AIDS: The Leprosy of Our Time*. Their position is that venereal diseases like gonorrhea and syphilis, despite treatments that are available, are still prevalent in many parts of the world. Drs. Sayman and Kriel contend that behavior change is the most significant factor in dealing with the problem of AIDS. They maintain that even if a so-called "cure" were found, without behavior change the problem would continue to be widespread. They believe that a closed sexual relationship — faithfulness to one's spouse (or spouses in the case of polygamy) — is the only remedy for the spread of AIDS. That is the single most important thing known to stem the growth of AIDS infections.

Their conclusion should be confirmation for the church and the message of fidelity that Christians have to offer. Sadly, in many places where the epidemic is prevalent, one spouse may be faithful and the other is not. Hence, the faithful spouse becomes infected and suffers the life-threatening consequences of AIDS. But since fidelity in marriage is the best-known recourse, thankfully the church has that message.

Second, what should be done for those who are suffering from AIDS in their families? Here again, one should not be surprised that the church holds an important key to meeting the challenge. A congregation of Africans in England has so many people dying of

AIDS in that country that they have a "bereavement officer" assigned to help families with repatriation, funeral services, etc. One church in Zambia has a Department of Compassion. This includes people who go throughout the churches teaching family members how to deal with those who suffer from the full effects of AIDS. They teach what precautions to take in working with AIDS victims and how to help relieve the suffering. One of the most important things they do is help alleviate the problem of fear which distorts the picture through a lack of understanding. Simply helping people know the difference between having the AIDS virus and having full-blown AIDS is an important part of their effort. The message of the church represents an alternative to unrealistic fear.

The **third** challenge relating to AIDS is what to do about the increasing number of orphans. Because the innocent are suffering, this breaks the hearts of compassionate people far and wide. Good people simply feel compelled to help. This makes westerners with charitable intent want to use their resources to get involved and do *something!* Hence, the building of orphanages becomes an attractive option for them. One reason that westerners are attracted to orphanages is that our culture has often used "institutions" to deal with problems in society. Orphanages, prisons, homes for the elderly, and rehabilitation centers for those in substance abuse are among the kinds of institutions we have established.

Western-Style Orphanages And Other Resources

One reason that orphanages become attractive to westerners is that donors can see *visual* evidence of their investment. Not only can they see the pictures; they can go to visit what their resources have provided. Marvin Olasky's article shows how rewarding that return on someone's investment can be.

As well-meaning outsiders, westerners often do not realize that they are bypassing other resources that could be used if they were identified and appropriately mobilized. One of those resources is the extended family – a God-given institution for caring for the young, elderly, crippled, unemployed and those suffering from illnesses such as AIDS. If the extended family is allowed to disintegrate or is rendered ineffective, one will end up with the kind of homelessness and alienation that we see on the streets of western cities. Homeless people on the streets of western cities often have

no viable working relationship with members of their own family
– immediate or extended.

I frequently meet homeless people on the street and engage them
in conversation about their family connections. They often say that
they are no longer welcome at home, or that their family lives far
away and no one cares about them anyway. The result is that such
people turn to charity, the government or to appealing for alms
on the street—or all three of these options. If the current trend of
disintegrating families in North America continues, imagine what
the situation will be like thirty or forty years from now. More
and more people will be on the streets depending on charity or
government support as a result of the disintegration of the family
structure.

The Extended Family and the Local Church as Resources

Unfortunately, the extended family in Africa is not the strong safety
net it once was. It has been weakened by people moving to cities
where they do not have affordable housing or fields where they can
grow food for themselves or their families. In fact, many people
in cities are unemployed, adding to the already strained extended
family system. Add to the weakened family system the challenge
of AIDS, and one can see the disaster that is unfolding in many
parts of Africa.

But the extended family system is not the only God-given resource
for society. The local church is also God's provision for those in
need around the world. I have written elsewhere about this in an
article titled *I Believe in the Local Church*.[1] I attempt to show that
the church represents the hands and feet of Christ in the world,
doing what He would do if He were here in person as He once was.
The true motivation for church planting should be to multiply His
hands and feet as God's people in communities around the world.

Is the church adequate to meet the needs of the world where it
exists? In many places, the church empowered by the Holy Spirit,
is adequate to do Christ's work in the world. In other places,
however, because of the way churches were started, they are not
contributing to the cause, but are draining from it. In other words,

---

[1] This article is available on the WMA website www.wmausa.org.

churches are often born "handicapped", while those planting them assume that they will never be able to stand on their own feet. In chapter 1, I give attention to two kinds of fatalism behind the dependency mentality. Unless that fatalism is challenged, the Christian movement will continue to be plagued with churches that are born handicapped.

Given the prevalence of handicapped churches, one begins to see the scale of the tragedy. Think of it this way: into the world of already dependent churches there comes a crisis with the magnitude of AIDS. The church is now expected to reach out to the many orphans in their communities, even though they have not yet learned how to support themselves from their own resources. Fortunately, this is not true of all churches for there are some admirable examples for the encouragement of us all.

Little wonder that outsiders feel they must step in and build orphanages with foreign resources. After all, if they consider local believers too poor to build their own church buildings without outside assistance, how could such churches ever be expected to build their own orphanages if, indeed, orphanages are deemed to be the right solution?

I used the term "deemed to be right" because institutions such as orphanages were unknown in pre-Christianized Africa. It was the family that cared for orphans, the widowed, unemployed, and the elderly. In light of that, what is an appropriate solution to the problem of AIDS orphans in Africa? I maintain that it is to rediscover the role and importance of the extended family and the local church. Admittedly, both the church and the extended family are stretched beyond their ability to carry the current burden of AIDS in Africa.

What Is The Role For Outsiders?

In light of this, what should well-meaning outsiders do to help in the face of this crisis? Outsiders might consider helping to strengthen extended families so that they can better carry the load they already have on their shoulders. This can be done by helping to increase food production, stimulate job creation and get appropriate job training. Things like revolving loan funds can help to improve family finances. This is not the place for an extensive treatment of how to help the poor as I have written further on that in Chapter 20.

The second thing outsiders can do is become aware of the factors that contribute to the mentality of dependency. Will local churches ever be able make their contribution in the Christian movement if they are considered to be handicapped with no possibility of change?

One should be aware that solutions such as this will require long-term commitment and involvement by those who are culturally and spiritually sensitive. The current trend toward short-term missions and "quick fix" solutions — financial and otherwise — will not be adequate for a challenge of this magnitude.

Who Owns The Project?

One way to test the appropriateness of establishing an orphanage is to ask who will own the project. Sometimes such institutions receiving heavy outside funding are psychologically "owned" by the outsiders who fund them. Outsiders decide how much funding will be made available and how it will be spent. They sometimes decide who is worthy of being employed to work in or manage the institution. Perhaps they decide what kind of furnishings will be provided. In the case of an orphanage, they may even decide which children qualify to live there. It may not even strike them as inappropriate that the children in the orphanage have better accommodations than those living in the surrounding villages!

What is the alternative? Outsiders who truly want to help will pay attention to this important issue of "ownership." They will ask questions like the following: Whose idea is this? Does it have local support? Are local people making any of the decisions related to the project? Would this project be sustainable if the donors decided to go elsewhere to do their charitable giving?

I recently learned of an African church leader who appealed for over one million US dollars to build an orphanage in Central Africa. The appeal was for help with the 40,000 AIDS orphans in the part of the country where he lived. For a while it looked like an aid agency was going to provide the funding. When I learned about this, I asked another senior church leader from the same country how he would deal with the problem of so many orphans. Without batting an eye, he said he would look for forty thousand families who would each take one of the orphans. Of course, this brings us back to the strain already on the extended family system. But, if the family system does not remain intact, then multiplying orphanages could become an expensive alternative of choice for generations to come.

An Observation Is In Order

The suggestions in the last few paragraphs may not seem like good news for well-meaning people from the USA or Europe who want to do something for AIDS orphans in Africa. Indeed, they might feel that the emphasis on local decision-making could lead to inefficiency and eventual loss of control by the outsiders. After all, the orphans need help now. Outsiders might also fear that funds designated for orphanages will be sidetracked to some other project like a vehicle for one of the church leaders. Since the donors cannot risk that kind of thing happening, they might hesitate to relinquish control of a project such as an orphanage.

All of this brings us back to the importance of resolving the mentality of dependency. If local people are raising and spending their own finances, they can use those resources for whatever they want. Indeed, their own ingenuity means that much cheaper solutions will often be found. But on the matter of outside resources, it is true that outside funding in Africa and elsewhere has been misappropriated. It is also true that when that happens, the job does not get done well, or it simply does not get done at all. But misappropriating the Lord's resources happens in far more places than among African churches! The bottom line question is, "What does one do when there is apparent misuse of what is being given, whether from local or foreign sources?" That is a discussion for another time and place, but a necessary one to be sure.

At this point a word about urgency is in order. There are some in need who will not survive without substantial assistance. This is what relief aid is about—rushing in to help those who must have assistance now. My point is that while some are called to meet urgent needs, real help for the long-run also needs to be given consideration. Indeed, if long-term assistance had been planned for in advance, the affects of some disasters could have been minimized. The challenge is to avoid having orphanages meet only a short-term need or a very small part of the overall need while long-term challenges go unmet.

A Cautionary Word Is In Order

It is one thing for someone like me, living a long way from African villages decimated by AIDS, to reflect on the best way to help those in need. It is another thing for an African family to sit by the bedside of loved ones who are deteriorating physically, knowing that the solution to the AIDS problem is nowhere in sight. I do not underestimate the difference between where I am and where they are. Having said that, it is clear that unless well-meaning people learn how to help appropriately, unhealthy dependency will result and outsiders will continue to build clinics, orphanages, church buildings, Bible institutes, and development projects far and wide. And some will do that without regard for the feelings of those who should have true ownership. Unfortunately, some western Christians consider this to be normal and have not indicated that they want to see the problem resolved.

I long for the day when churches and families in Africa and elsewhere will be so strong that they will say to outsiders, "Wait, wait. Give us a chance to see if we can do it for ourselves." Donors far away who truly want to help should not be discouraged when they hear statements like that. They should rejoice! In fact, it is possible for them to test their motivation right now by asking if they would ever like to hear those words or not.

Conclusion

So then, the **first** and most urgent challenge is to work at the root cause of the spread of AIDS. That means advocating a change of behavior to slow the growth of the epidemic. The Biblical message about fidelity in marriage is the place to begin.

Second, attention must be given to the root causes of poverty, a contributing factor to many social diseases. This means promoting nutrition, education and economic justice wherever possible. These are the kinds of issues I recommend dealing with in the article mentioned previously — *Searching for Meaningful Ways to Help the Poor*. The church and those who wish to help AIDS orphans should look at sustainable ways to help affected families support themselves.

Third, there is little hope for the Christian movement in some places unless the mentality of dependency is dealt with. Those who provide outside resources where local resources could be used may be giving short-term assistance, but doing long-term harm.

Fourth, this is a superficial treatment of a subject that demands much more reflection, prayer and planning. I welcome all who have the interest and capability to join in writing about their experiences for the benefit of others who are concerned. Together, we can make a difference where otherwise any one of us might have limited understanding of the issues.

May the Lord help everyone involved – those in need, as well as those with the resources – so that suffering people get the help they so badly need.

APPENDIX A

Annotated Bibliography:
Issues of Dependency and
Self-Reliance in the Christian Movement

Introduction

I am sometimes asked how to avoid or overcome dependency in cross-cultural church planting. Unfortunately there are no quick and easy answers. The first reason is that the conditions behind dependency are as varied as the cultures in which the Gospel is being preached. Second, the problem has its roots in the basic assumptions often underlying cross-cultural Christian ministry. These assumptions are powerful, and the effects can be felt for generations of church planting.

So, one answer does not fit all. Therefore, I encourage every serious-minded cross-cultural worker to embark on a learning expedition. Turn to the Scriptures and to historical and contemporary books on mission studies. I know of no shortcut to avoiding or overcoming dependency in church/mission ministry.

Serious reading is the place to begin. Follow that with thought, prayer and discussion with one's colleagues. Of course, seeking counsel from professionals may be an important part of your search. It is important to learn all you can so that unhealthy dependency can be avoided from the beginning, whenever possible. What others have learned can help us to avoid repeating the mistakes of the past. But this means a lot of work – serious reading and digging into the issues – looking for clues that will be helpful.

The following annotated references are only a few suggestions, but they are enough to get started in the reading process. You will find that many good books have a bibliography in the back of the book, a built-in mechanism for finding more good references. Every bibliography is a clue to what the author thinks is important – and a clue to other reading on the horizon. It soon becomes apparent that the horizon is virtually unlimited.

Regrettably, I am not able to satisfy the person who wants a quick fix to the problem of dependency in church-mission relations. Some may have such answers; but knowing the complexity of the problem, I am not the one to ask for the quick fix. However, for those who are serious, the following are a few places to begin. The rewards of avoiding or overcoming dependency are worth the effort.

I must emphasize that this is a very limited list. Many more entries could be made. Also, the annotated portion of this bibliography does not include related topics such as poverty, partnership or the effects of international aid. (Nor does it include fundamental books on cross-cultural missionary work.) Each of these areas has material related to the problem of dependency and self-reliance. A few entries (without annotation) in these specialized areas are listed at the end.

Read and enjoy.

The Bible

There is ample evidence in Scripture that God's people are expected to give back to him a portion of what he has given to them. Refugees traveling from Egypt to the Promised Land gave so much toward building the Tabernacle (Exodus 35) that they were told to stop bring contributions. At the time of the building of the Temple (1 Chronicles 29), people gave willingly. And when they were finished, they ended up on their faces in worship before the Lord. Out of severe trial and extreme poverty, the Macedonians begged for the privilege of giving (2 Corinthians 8).

Scripture shows that even those who are in relative poverty usually have something they can give back to God. It is true that the scripture commands us to help those who are poor, including widows and orphans; but it also includes an example of a poor widow who gave the last coins she had. The scripture is also filled with admonitions to the wealthy to contribute to Kingdom ministry. In other words, encouragement is given to both rich and poor about giving back to God some of what He has given to them.

Missionary Methods: St. Paul's or Ours, **Roland Allen**

This seminal work is fundamental to any understanding of the missionary principles behind avoiding dependency in cross-cultural church planting. It is as basic to understanding missionary practice as the germ theory is to understanding western concepts of medicine.

Roland Allen wrote his books in the early part of the 20th century. He predicted that it would be decades before people would take his writing seriously. That is exactly what happened when, in the 1960s, his books began to be published in earnest. This volume had five printings in the 1960s.

If one is looking for encouragement regarding how to use outside funding for cross-cultural church planting, it will not be found here. Allen, who served as a missionary in China between 1895 and 1903, learned from first-hand experience the often-negative effect that outside funding can have on cross-cultural church planting. In the foreword Bishop Leslie Newbigin says:" . . the reader should be warned that he is embarking on a serious undertaking. Once he has started reading Allen, he will be compelled to go on. He will find that this quiet voice has a strange relevance and immediacy to the problems of the Church in our day."

The Spontaneous Expansion of the Church, *Roland Allen*

A related book by Roland Allen is *The Spontaneous Expansion of the Church and the Causes which Hinder it*. This is "must-reading" for every serious missionary. It cautions against taking too high a profile at the beginning of cross-cultural church planting by involvement in such things as the appointment of local elders, etc. It is also a powerful reminder that success in cross-cultural church planting is not related to the number of workers involved. Allen makes the statement (page 19) that "a thousand thousand [missionaries] would not suffice; a dozen might be too many." That should inject a little humility into our role as missionaries.

Missions and Money: Affluence as a Western Missionary Problem, **Jonathan J. Bonk**

The following paragraph appears on the back of the book:

This insightful, deeply probing book on the problematic relation of mission and money zeroes in on difficulties that occur when the evangelizer is relatively affluent and living among the poor. Drawing on his Mennonite heritage and the gospel's profound ambivalence towards money, Bonk demands we confront fundamental questions: do contemporary western missionaries – despite their sincerity – subvert the gospel and hinder its enculturation, because of their relative wealth? Does the wealth of the missioner eventually lead indigenous converts to feel hostility – either consciously or unconsciously – towards the missioner?

"Missions and Money" is an extraordinary book that requires all Christians involved in mission to third-world countries to be true to their biblical roots – to live simply.

The Indigenous Church, Melvin Hodges

This small book first appeared during the 1950s. It is short and to the point: "Outside funding is not the secret to cross-cultural church planting." I first read this when I was a missionary in Zambia in the 1960s. I picked it up recently and read it again. I was again inspired and found that many of the things I have been saying over the past fifteen or twenty years are nearly direct quotes from Hodges' little book. I must have absorbed more of it than I realized at the time.

Hodges was a missionary with the Assemblies of God denomination in Latin America. He saw the effects of both good and bad mission practices. Now his name is almost synonymous with the term "indigenous principles."

Mission in the Way of Paul (With Special Reference to Twenty-first Century Christian Mission), Christopher Little

This is a doctoral dissertation done in 2003 at the School of World Mission (now School of International Studies) at Fuller Theological Seminary, Pasadena, California. This work comprises two emphases. The first is a thorough biblical study of the missionary practice of the Apostle Paul. Little makes the point that the way the Apostle Paul did his work (*orthopraxy*) is as important as what he said about the Gospel (*orthodoxy*). Therefore, Little says, imitate the missionary *practices* of the Apostle Paul!

The second part of this important work (chapter 6) is an analysis of what Little calls the International Partnership Movement (IPM). In it, he reviews the contributing and dissenting voices regarding issues of dependency, self-reliance and "partnership" in the Christian movement.

The Great Omission, Steve Saint

Steve Saint is the son of martyred missionary, Nate Saint, who, in 1956, died at the hands of the Waodani people (then called the Aucas) of Ecuador. After growing up among the Waodani, Steve became a businessman and later on when back to live among these people. He saw in a graphic way the effects of dependency that had set in over the years. This book (particularly chapter 3) gives significant insight into this problem. More than that, it gives hope for those who want to find a new and better way of doing cross-cultural ministry. Steve is an excellent communicator, and you will not be disappointed reading what he has to say about living and working with people like the Waodani.

Steve also published an article highlighting the problem of dependency in *Mission Frontiers* (May-June 1998). See the list of articles below.

Materials available through World Mission Associates

The team of World Mission Associates has been producing articles and recordings on issues of dependency and self-reliance for the past twenty or more years. On their website (www.wmausa.org) there are about ninety articles on the subject. I have written most of them, but there are also a number written by African and other writers.

WMA also produced an eight-hour video series on dependency. It is available in various VHS and DVD video formats (NTSC, PAL, SECAM) as well as on audiocassette and audio CD. This video series includes a 125-page Study Guide. It has been used by missionaries and church leaders in group-settings with discussion following. This is no substitute for proper missionary training, but will hopefully serve to whet one's appetite for serious training. (The first sixteen chapters in this book are transcribed and edited from the video series.)

Dependency and Its Impact on Churches Related to the Baptist Convention of Zimbabwe and the Zimbabwe Christian Fellowship – Dr. Robert Reese (Unpublished Doctoral Dissertation)

This study investigates the origins of the problem of dependency in Zimbabwean churches planted by American evangelical missionaries, showing how historical factors contributed to attitudes that fostered dependency. Dependency is a deeply engrained attitude of many Zimbabwean churches, and of the missionaries that founded them. The study centers on two case studies: the Southern Baptist mission work that started in colonial Rhodesia (now Zimbabwe) in 1950, and the mission work of some families from the Churches of Christ that started in independent Zimbabwe in 1980. Research centered in southwest Zimbabwe where the author was a church planting missionary with the Churches of Christ from 1981-2002. This dissertation can be acquired through University Microfilms, Ann Arbor, Michigan.

Articles and Periodicals

There are frequently articles on dependency and self-reliance appearing in contemporary missionary and other Christian publications. The following is a brief list of articles that one can find on line or in previous issues of the periodicals.

"Stop Sending Money!" Robertson McQuilkin. *Christianity Today* (March 1, 1999).

"Cutting the Apron Strings." Glenn Schwartz. *Evangelical Missions Quarterly* (January 1994). Reprinted in *Mission Frontiers*, Jan-Feb 1997.

"When the Mission Pays the Pastor." David Allen. *Evangelical Missions Quarterly* (April 1998).

"Fighting Dependency Among the 'Aucas'." An interview with Steve Saint. *Mission Frontiers*, May-June 1998.

"Looking at Missions from Their Side, Not Ours." Steve Saint. *Mission Frontiers*, May-June 1998.

"How Missionary Attitudes Can Create Dependency." Glenn Schwartz. *Mission Frontiers*, May-June 1998.

The Church in Africa: Making Its Way from Dependency to Self-Reliance. Zablon Nthamburi. *Mission Frontiers,* Jan-Feb 1997.

What Hath our Western Money and our Western Gospel Wrought? William J. Kornfield. *Mission Frontiers,* Jan-Feb 1997.

It's Time to Get Serious About the Cycle of Dependency in Africa. Glenn Schwartz. *Evangelical Missions Quarterly,* April 1993. Reprinted in *Mission Frontiers,* Jan-Feb 1997.

Don't Chase Buffaloes. Glenn Schwartz. *Mission Frontiers,* Jan-Feb 1997.

A Champion for Self-Reliance. An interview with Glenn Schwartz. *Mission Frontiers,* Jan-Feb 1997.

Avoiding Dependency – Mobilizing Local Resources. Glenn Schwartz. *Mission Frontiers,* Sept-Dec 1998.

Can Foreign Funding be Used in Support of Indigenous Missions? Glenn Schwartz. *Mission Frontiers,* Jan-Feb 1999.

The Papua New Guinea Bible Church. Gerald Bustin. *Mission Frontiers,* April 2000.

Going South of the Border for a Short Term? Rick Johnson. *Mission Frontiers,* June 2000.

True Local Ownership Through Micro-Credit. Joseph Richter. *Mission Frontiers,* September 2000.

When Two Bikes Split the Church. Christopher Little. *Mission Frontiers,* December 2000.

Is There a Cure? Glenn Schwartz. *Mission Frontiers,* March 2001.

From Dependency to Fulfillment. Glenn Schwartz. *Evangelical Missions Quarterly,* July 1991.

An Open Letter on Giving in Kenya. Gideon Kiongo. *Mission Frontiers,* June 2001.

Short Term Mission Trips: Maximizing the Benefits. Glenn Schwartz. *Mission Frontiers,* March-April 2004.

Note: Some of these articles (more than eighty in all) can be found on the World Mission Associates website – www.wmausa.org.

Books on Poverty and Related Issues

The following represent only a small sample of the books available regarding international aid and the poor. It does not mean that I agree with everything each author has to say, but each one is eye opening regarding international aid and related economic issues. Many more entries could be made to this list, but here is a sampling.

Befus, David R. *Where There are no Jobs: Enterprise Solutions for Employment and 'Public Goods' for the Poor.* Miami: LAM, 2005.

Bolling, Landrum. *Private Foreign Aid.* Boulder: Westview Press, 1982.

George, Susan. *How the Other Half Dies: The Real Reasons for World Hunger.* Harmondsworth: Penguin Books, 1976.

Hancock, Graham. *The Lords of Poverty: The Power, Prestige and Corruption of the International Aid Business.* New York: Atlantic Monthly Press, 1989.

Madeley, John. *Trade and the Poor: The Impact of International Trade on Developing Countries.* London: Intermediate Technology Publications, Ltd, 1992.

Hughes, Dewi and Matthew Bennett. *God of the Poor: A Biblical Vision for God's Present Rule.* Carlisle: OM Publishing, 1998.

Jayakumar, Christian. *God of the Empty-Handed: Poverty, Power and the Kingdom.* Monrovia: MARC Publishing, 1999.

Museveni, Yoweri. *What is Africa's Problem?* Kampala: NRM Publications, 1992.

Olasky, Marvin. *The Tragedy of American Compassion.* Washington: Regnery Publishing, 1992.

Tangri, Roger. *The Politics of Patronage in Africa.* Oxford: James Currey Ltd., 1999.

Yamamori, Tetsunao, Bryant L. Myers, Kwame Bediako, and Larry Reed, editors. *Serving with the Poor in Africa*. Monrovia: MARC Publications, 1996.

APPENDIX B

GLOSSARY OF SPECIAL TERMS

The following definitions are given to assist those who are not aware of the special vocabulary used in mission studies or what is often called missiology. The definitions are not meant to be highly technical.

10/40 WINDOW: The area between 10 degrees and 40 degrees above the equator extending across North Africa, the Middle East, South Asia and much of East Asia. It is estimated that 97% of the people living in this area have not been evangelized.

AFRICAN TRADITIONAL RELIGION: The primary religion of the spiritist or animist. The formal practitioner is a specialist in healing, divination, and providing guidance to those who depend on him or her. This practitioner may or may not be a herbalist. Many practitioners specialize in the manipulation of spirits.

ANIMISM: Used to describe the worldview of those who believe that "spirits" reside in everything: people (including ancestors), rocks, wind, trees, rivers, etc.

APARTHEID: Describes the policy of so-called "separate development" which the South African government used to support white minority rule. Aspects of this policy were evident for several hundred years, but it was only formally adopted as government policy in the mid-twentieth century. The government of South Africa officially discarded apartheid as official policy in the early 1990s when the country became a multi-racial and multi-party democracy.

APPROPRIATE TECHNOLOGY: Used to describe ways of doing things that are appropriate to the society in which they are placed. Inappropriate technology is often too expensive or too complex for those who are supposed to benefit from its use.

BASIC PRESUPPOSITIONS OF LIFE: These are assumptions which all of us have but which are often difficult to identify or define. They determine how we make decisions on the spur of the moment. It is often easier for someone else to identify my basic presuppositions than it is for me to identify my own.

CHURCH GROWTH: This term means different things to different people who use it. As used in this series, it refers to the movement that began in the 1960's primarily through the inspiration of Dr. Donald A. McGavran. It refers to a comprehensive way of understanding the growth and spread of the Christian movement.

COLONIALISM: Describes the spirit with which countries in Europe, North America and elsewhere set about to possess or "colonize" many places in other parts of the world. It often included imposing government and business practices in a way that benefited those doing the colonizing. In fairness to the colonizers, the process did provide employment and infrastructure through the building of roads, communication, western educational systems and other things which still benefit so-called Third World countries today.

COMMUNITY IMAGE: How people in the community view the church.

CONCENTRIC CIRCLES: Circles within circles are called concentric circles.

COSMOLOGY: Another word for worldview. It describes how people look at and seek to interpret the world around them.

DEPENDENCY: Most often used to describe those in society who are unable to care for themselves. That includes small children, handicapped people (both mentally and physically), the elderly, etc. As used in these lessons, however, it refers to those who allow someone else to carry them along financially and, some times, administratively.

DIVINATION: Describes the way in which a practitioner of traditional religion determines how something will take place in the future.

ETHNICITY: The characteristics of a given ethnic or people group.

E-O EVANGELISM: Used to describe outreach among nominal church members. There is no increase in church membership when they come to Christ because their names are already on church rolls.

E-1 EVANGELISM: Used to describe outreach among non-believers who are in the same cultural group as those doing the evangelizing.

E-2 EVANGELISM: Used to describe outreach among non-believers who are culturally "near neighbors." They may speak a related language though it might not be mutually understood. An example would be German, French, English and Spanish people who have a similar cultural background even though they may not be able to understand one another's language.

E-3 EVANGELISM: Used to describe outreach among non-believers who are very different from our own cultural group. Their language, customs and worldview are completely foreign to us. These are our culturally distant neighbors.

EVANGELIZATION: For our purposes, evangelization takes place when the Gospel has been presented in such a way that those hearing it are capable of making an intelligent decision—yes or no—regarding Jesus as Lord and Savior.

EXCLUDED MIDDLE: This term is used to describe an important area of life experienced by many spiritists or animists. It is the spirit world of healings, demons, spirits, etc., between the High God above and Jesus who walks with us day by day. For a diagram see chapter 1.

EXPATRIATE: Technically this term refers to anyone outside his or her own country. It is frequently used to describe missionaries who are not citizens in the countries where they serve.

FATALISM: This is the negative attitude which believes there is no solution to a problem or no way out of a dilemma.

GERM THEORY OF SICKNESS: Used to describe the western understanding that sickness is normally caused by bacteria or germs. This leads westerners to search for the "what" and "how" causes behind illnesses. Non-westerners often search for the "who" and "why" reasons for illness.

HARAMBEE: A social event in East Africa in which participants set a goal to raise funds for a church, community or family project. It is an attempt to make giving an enjoyable social occasion, often including a spirit of friendly competition in the buying and selling of donated items such as fruits, vegetables or cooked meals.

HERBALIST: A person who provides traditional remedies for illnesses. Such a person uses "herbs" (parts of plants or trees) and may or may not practice spiritism.

HOMOGENEOUS UNIT: Used to describe a group of people having a common set of characteristics. They may speak the same language, participate in the same profession or have a similar cultural background.

INDIGENEITY: Describes the state of being indigenous, or locally owned and operated.

INDIGENOUS: Those things belonging to the people of which they are a part. Non-indigenous practices are those which have been imported or borrowed from the outside.

INTER-ETHNIC MISSION SOCIETIES: Used to describe mission societies with missionaries from many churches cooperating in the spread of the Gospel. Such a society may have missionaries from the German Lutherans, Dutch Reformed, Anglican and American Baptist denominations.

JUBILEE: The Biblical concept found in Leviticus chapters 25 and 27 and Numbers 36. It was a system built into society for the periodic redistribution of wealth. It included returning land to the original owners, freeing slaves, and forgiving debts.

MARGINAL CHRISTIAN CONVERSION: The term used to describe those who are only minimally committed to Christianity. They are the most vulnerable to taking on another religion or returning to their previous belief system.

MISSIOLOGY: Term used to describe cross-cultural mission studies. It was first used by Catholic missionaries but has come into common usage by Protestants in the last half of the twentieth century.

MOBILIZING: Refers to the concept of encouraging and equipping people to become active in evangelization or missionary activity.

MULTI-INDIVIDUAL DECISION: A term used to describe many members of a family or extended family deciding to become Christians at the same time. It differs from group conversion in that individuals have a choice in whether or not to join others in the process.

PARA-CHURCH ORGANIZATIONS: Christian organizations which are not directly related to any one church or denomination. They might be referred to as non-denominational or sometimes inter denominational organizations. Examples of para-church organizations include Bible societies, World Vision, Scripture Union, Campus Crusade, and many others. This term would not be used to describe an institution (such as a Bible institute or hospital) directly under the control of one church or denomination.

PARADIGM SHIFT: Pronounced "para-dime." A paradigm is a framework into which we fit ideas we hold to be valid. It provides order for arranging how we look at our world. When one changes the primary way he or she looks at the world, we call that "paradigm shift." The most profound paradigm shift for the Christian is the conversion experience.

PEOPLE MOVEMENT: Refers to the conversion experience of more than one person at time—usually a family or clan. It is not the same as a mass movement in which some members of a society may feel themselves coerced into agreement. Rather the term is best defined as a "multi-individual decision"—a real possibility in societies where communal decisions are often undertaken after discussion. For a good description of the concept of people movements see Chapter 7 in *People Movements in Southern Polynesia* by Alan R. Tippett.

PERPETUAL JUBILEE: Sometimes used to describe what Jesus had in mind when He said, "Do not lay up for yourselves treasures on earth" (Mark 10:21). It includes helping those who are in need, recognizing that it is better to give than to receive (Acts 20:35). In short, it does not allow for the accumulation of large amounts of earthly possessions.

POWER ENCOUNTER: The best-known scriptural example of a power encounter is the story of Elijah and the prophets of Baal on Mount Carmel. The phenomenon occurs when the power of God is demonstrated in the midst of "the powers." It can be seen in the film "Peace Child" (story by Don Richardson) when a special stone was passed around demonstrating that its magical powers were no longer effective.

PROPHETIC MINISTRY: As used in these lessons this term refers to speaking out on important issues which communities and their governments need to hear. It may be thought of "forth-telling." The term is not used in this book in the sense of foretelling events which one thinks may happen in the future.

RESTRUCTURING: The term used to describe the changing of the church structure so that it becomes compatible with the society in which it is located.

REVIVAL: A spiritual renewal among believers—such as the East African Revival.

REVOLVING LOAN FUNDS: Refers to the establishment of small loan funds which are managed for the benefit of people who need help to start a business. It is assumed that, unlike grants, these funds will be repaid and then re-used for the benefit of others.

SCAFFOLDING: The term used by Dr. McGavran to describe mission societies in relation to the churches they start. He claimed that this was not meant to remain forever, but rather to be taken down and moved elsewhere as soon as appropriate.

SCHISM: Refers to the division of churches into groups or factions. Many African Independent churches were started by such a schism.

SELF-IMAGE: How we view ourselves or how a church views itself.

SELF-RELIANCE: As used in these lessons this term refers to the Christian movement looking for local rather than foreign resources in order to do what God is calling His people to do. It does NOT mean that people do not rely on God.

SPIRIT THEORY OF SICKNESS: Unlike the germ theory, the spirit theory of sickness concludes that there is a spiritual reason behind most, if not all, illness. This is believed to be true even when western medicine gives a carefully constructed scientific explanation for an illness.

SPIRITISM: Similar to animism — the belief that a spirit resides in everything.

SPIRITUAL AWAKENING: Dr. J. Edwin Orr, the famous researcher on revivals and awakenings used this term to describe what happens among masses of unbelievers when they are brought to readiness for spiritual change. He reserved the use of the term revival for a spiritual renewal that happens among believers.

STOREHOUSE GIVING: A concept of giving which insists that tithes (especially) and offerings should be brought first to the church or "storehouse." When this is done, gifts or offerings may be given to other organizations. The concept is based on Malachi 3:8.

THREE-SELF PRINCIPLE: Used to describe indigenous or independent churches which stand on their own two feet. Such churches are often described as being self-supporting, self-governing and self-propagating.

TICKET SYSTEM: The system used to record the regular giving of church members in southern Africa. It was often a small amount compared to the income of the individual. The concept was first applied by John Wesley in England and is still in use in some parts of Africa and elsewhere.

TITHING: Based on the Biblical concept of giving back to God 10% of what one earns. For the Biblical usage of the term see Leviticus 27:30 and Malachi 3:8.

WORLDVIEW: Used to describe how people view and seek to interpret the world around them. Another word for worldview is cosmology.

APPENDIX C

STAGES OF MISSIONARY DEVELOPMENT:
A STUDY IN CULTURAL ADJUSTMENT

(Hopefully this will help some missionary to laugh at him or herself and make it through another day until better days dawn.)

Introduction

Individual and family stress often result from involvement in cross-cultural ministry. Sometimes the stress is minor and one sails through the various stages mentioned below with vibrant colors flying from the masthead. At other times a cross-cultural worker feels the effects of the culture shock so severely that discouragement prevails, ministry ends and the one involved retreats from service with any number of psychological side effects.

This paper is an attempt to bring to light some of the symptoms, causes and cures for the culture shock experienced by cross-cultural workers. The symptoms are many and the stress is real. The effects must not be minimized. Also, of great importance, it must be remembered that culture shock should be viewed a curable condition, not a terminal illness.

Major Stages of Cultural Adjustment

Stage 1. Everything is wonderful.

Stage 2. Everything is terrible.

Stage 3. Some things are wonderful, some things are not, but that's the way the world is.

Stage 4. I am now accepted as an insider in this culture, and I feel good about that.

Stage 5. I have left my first culture and totally accepted the new, and I do not intend to turn back.

Description of the Stages

STAGE ONE: For many, **Stage One** begins with an earnest reading of missionary biographies. It is a time filled with adventure into the wonderful unknown world of other cultures. The feeling is enhanced by missionary messages in one's local church in which an older, happy, well-adjusted missionary tells of his or her rewarding ministry. The highest elevation into **Stage One** occurs with one's call to service and the rewarding feeling of being obedient to God's leading.

This stage is further enhanced by pre-field courses—often not very long—that extol the merits of language learning and catalogue the pitfalls that have entrapped others. It is accompanied by a determination that "I will not make the same mistakes as others." (Allow me to continue in first person.) "More reward comes as people notice my dedication. They slip paper money into my hand after a church meeting in which I tell about my calling. I really feel good sitting on the platform with other candidates while mission executives tell how important each of us is in carrying on the program of the mission. Commissioning follows, and I am ready to leave for field service in Mamba Bamba or some other exotic place."

Later in Mamba Bamba—Still in Stage One:

"These people are wonderful! They seem so happy. I love them. I will learn their language. I enjoy the church services. Even the hymn tunes are the same as back home, and I can read the syllables in their hymnbook and follow along. Imagine helping to sing in another language from the very first week! I learned to greet in the local language within the first few days, and it is wonderful. People smile when I say only a few words in their language. I will learn this language, I surely will.

"I have already eaten in a few local homes. They served the local staple plus tasty chicken with a unique spicy flavor. I am still excited at the shape of their homes and I enjoy sitting on their homemade stools and chairs. In short, missionary work is everything I had ever hoped it would be. Sure, there is a little less hygiene than I like; but if I am careful, I'll have no problem. I'll just wash my hands when I sense the need to do so."

Stage Two: "During the past few months in Mamba Bamba, the feeling that 'these people are all wonderful' isn't lasting the way I thought it would. I learned that some of those that I really like are actually not converted. They are nice enough on the outside, but would you believe that one of them is a polygamist? Another, though married, has a child to an unmarried schoolteacher in another village.

"Something else bothers me. This language isn't as easy as I thought. There seem to be more exceptions to the rules of grammar than there are rules. How can I master all the exceptions? I particularly don't like it when people laugh at the way I say things. After all, I am trying my best.

"There is more. This place has problems I was never told about. The hospital has more in-patients than the number of beds. The school has financial problems, and at church, people hardly put anything into the offerings on Sunday.

"There is so much dust that I wonder if I will ever be able to keep my house clean. The local water isn't totally safe and I am tired of boiling it for drinking and cooking.

"At least there are a few friends I can talk to. Though they have their problems, one in particular is a real believer. When everything else looks bleak, I can at least hold on to him (or her). I don't know what I would do if I ever heard that one committed a sin.

"So even though things around me aren't perfect, at least I have my work. I enjoy it and when things get rough I'll just concentrate on what I do best. Unfortunately, right now I am beginning to feel a little unnerved about that, too. I thought I was a pretty good teacher but this past year my students didn't do very well in the annual government exams. As long as no school inspector or administrator brings up that subject I'll be fine. In fact, if they do I am ready to tell them the truth. Actually sometimes I question the intellectual capability of people like this. Anyway, what more can they expect? I am doing my best.

A Few Months Later — Still in Stage Two:

"All right, I'll admit it. This place is the pits. When I visit in their homes, instead of serving spicy chicken with the staple, they give me only vegetables. In fact, the last time they gave me pumpkin leaves which nobody eats where I come from. And I don't enjoy the Sunday services anymore. I can't follow the sermon and they won't interpret the announcements into English so at least I know what's going on. I dread the year-end examination results due to come out again. And to top it all off, I just heard the most awful rumor. I heard—if you can believe this—that this man I thought was a true believer (you know, the one I thought I could really trust?) I heard that when his nephew was sick and was taken to the local herbalist, my alleged friend did nothing to stop them. Can't I trust anyone around here?

"You know what I am going to do? I am going to my house. I am going to close the curtains, put on a cassette tape of Handel's Messiah, and I am going to read a good book. I still have some homemade ice cream in the freezer which I made the last time I felt like this. If I had a do-not-disturb sign, I'd put it on the outside of my door. I don't need one more request from anyone. These people have more needs than anyone can meet anyway.

"Another thing—if this feeling doesn't change, I am going to call it quits at the end of this term. By the way, did you know that this car I was given to use is actually registered in the name of the church? You might as well say that some ordinary church member around here is as much an owner of it as I am. Imagine an illiterate person being part owner of a car driven by someone with a Master's degree in English. I'll tell you right now that's only a symptom of the problems this place has. You never heard of such a thing back home where I come from!"

Following Three Years in Mamba Bamba—Stage Three Begins: "I am now on furlough, and it is doing wonders for me. Our pastor in the home church really preaches well, and I just love this pipe organ music. In fact, last Sunday the chancery choir sang part of Handel's Messiah, and I got to hear the Hallelujah Chorus. It made the tears come!

"It is amazing what a little rest in the homeland has done for me. I'm feeling a lot better than I did those last six months in Mamba Bamba. I heard they had a good annual conference since I left and that a spirit of revival was evident on the last day. If those two local people confessed their sin as it was reported, that's reason for hope. That's what that whole church needs!

"Something else strikes me just now. I found out that several couples in the home church here are having marriage difficulties. I still can't believe that one of the couples is actually considering divorce. Why doesn't someone do something? We'd have done something in Mamba Bamba!

"Another thing, the news here at home is kind of depressing. There are robberies and murders reported in almost every newscast. And now several government officials are under indictment for who knows what. They won't even talk. At least in Mamba Bamba they make people talk.

"The job I left when I went to the mission field has been eliminated, and that means I can't get it back if I decide not to return to Mamba Bamba. If I do stay here, I'll have to start all over. I am too young to retire. If I can just come to some agreement with our mission board, maybe I can return to the field. I heard that one can now get a full six months of language study upon request. In fact, that's a must if I am to return to Mamba Bamba.

"I am pleased about the reports of continuing revival among the church people. In fact, if they let me study the language and give me a ministry of evangelism and leading Bible studies, I really think I could be happy in Mamba Bamba.

A Year Later — Back on Assignment:

"They got electricity here in Lower Zax province since I left. That has improved things a lot. I finished the language course and preached my first sermon. I admit it took a lot of preparation, and it wasn't very profound. But I really enjoyed it. In fact, I always felt a little guilty using an interpreter when I spoke in public. Speaking on my own is so much better.

"Another thing — I am glad I no longer have to be involved in every meeting that goes on around here. I found out that they really can get along without my kind of influence in every business meeting. Furthermore, it gives me more time to do what I am here to do — encourage other people. I genuinely enjoy seeing the spiritual growth that is taking place.

"I finally feel that I can objectively see both the strengths and weaknesses in this culture as well as my own back home. Now I am able to make a contribution in both places. I am really glad I returned to Mamba Bamba."

Stage Four: A Description (not in first person)

Stage Four indicates that one has changed his or her psychological residence. One now believes he belongs to the society in which he lives. He or she has succeeded in building deep and lasting friendships. In this stage, one does not tolerate criticism of the local system lightly. In fact, one has chosen to become part of the local system: "These are now my friends. We have been through a lot together." In **Stage Four** one more than tolerates local food. By now he or she enjoys it. This stage also means joining the battle of life with local people and making their problems my problems. "When they hurt, I'll hurt."

Those in **Stage Four** become impatient with a system that allows **Stage Two** perspectives to exist indefinitely. They covet for all their co-workers the healthy relationships that have been developed in their **Stage Four** relationship with local people.

Language is now second nature. Deep meanings of terms and concepts are attractive. Proverbs in the local language are a fascination, not an insurmountable challenge. The way people do things in Mamba Bamba is worthy of investigation. One comes to the realization that local people do not need to change so much as outsiders need to learn from them.

In **Stage Four**, practices which reflect cultural insensitivity are difficult to tolerate. There is real danger here for the person in **Stage Four**. Unless he or she learns to handle it, an unhealthy reaction to cultural insensitivity can develop. It takes special grace when this stage is reached.

Stage Four is the genuine-satisfaction stage, not the "off-the-deep-end" stage. In **Stage Four**, one has adopted the new culture but has not rejected the old.

Unfortunately, **Stage Four** people (as with some in **Stage Three**) can have an unsettling influence on those struggling to survive **Stage Two**. If a **Stage Two** person encounters a well-adjusted person in

Stage Four, it may cause a negative reaction ranging from envy to denial: "That person doesn't really enjoy eating food with his fingers." Or one may experience resentment that the **Stage Four** person is fraternizing with "the enemy" -- "How can he or she enjoy being with people who do what these people do?"

The **Stage Four** person must exercise care so that the nerves of others aren't frayed unnecessarily. Sometimes that is very hard to avoid. In fact, sometimes no matter what a **Stage Four** person does, it can be a source of irritation for a discouraged person in **Stage Two**. In this case, the **Stage Four** person must cultivate spiritual graces and let understanding abound. That's not always easy.

Stage Five

In times past, **Stage Five** was referred to as "going native." In actual fact, it is the stage we expect all immigrants to reach when coming to North America or Europe, for example. But among missionaries, this stage is often perceived as a negative experience. It may involve a strong reaction to one's former culture. **Stage Five** may mean marrying into the new society, learning to live with all the ramifications of rearing children, adjusting to retirement and eventually preparing to die in that society. It is normally the no-turning-back stage. It may or may not include a conscious rejection of the former culture. For some it can be the wholesome experience to which millions of well-adjusted immigrants can testify. On the other hand, it may end in disillusionment as one realizes that even in **Stage Five** he or she cannot get away from one of the biggest problems this life poses: that of living with one's self. If that is one's problem, **Stage Five** is not the solution.

Sometimes in its extreme form, **Stage Five** can result in one becoming a hermit. It may mean rarely taking a bath or not washing one's hair for months at a time. And when one reaches this stage, he or she is likely to become an embarrassment to local people who themselves hold to higher standards.

Sometimes a person in **Stage Five** lives through the negative part of the experience and then pulls back to a more normal adjustment. In that case, a **Stage Five** person finds that the rejection of the former culture is not necessary in order to find one's own wholesome identity. In this respect, it can be a maturing experience as one reckons with the loss of his or her previous cultural identity and takes on a new one.

There can be a very positive side to **Stage Five**. Some single missionaries have married a citizen of the country in which they serve. That can speed along the process of cultural adjustment because one is forced to relate to new family members in socially appropriate ways. It is like getting "inside" help to make the adjustment. This can help to open doors in the society normally closed to outsiders. A North American mission executive recently observed that among American missionaries working in Western Europe some of the most successful are those involved in cross-cultural marriages. It should be mentioned here that cross-cultural marriages are often characterized by stress for many other reasons.

There is sometimes a very high price to pay for total acceptance of **Stage Five**. Take, for example, the person who chooses to marry someone from the new society. While that person, perhaps a missionary, may have the ability to cross the cultural gap, other family members may not. Much depends on how wide the gap really is. As the result of a cross-cultural marriage, difficulty may only surface in later years when the question of retirement arises or when there is the death of a family member. Family and individual expectations can differ considerably. Obviously not all future problems can be anticipated, and sometimes the stakes get very high.

General Observations on the First Three Stages

1. The transition from one stage to another often happens over a period of time. It is hardly ever instantaneous or single-event oriented. Sometimes one feels like he or she is completely out of one stage, and then something happens which shows that all is not over yet.

2. Some, by their nature, pass through the stages without great extremes. Their experience does not include high peaks and deep valleys. For others, the extremes are very pronounced. Many factors, including one's personality type and the support of colleagues, for example, affect the intensity of the experiences.

3. Missionary training is helpful in avoiding the extremes, but even those who are well trained may encounter events which they did not anticipate. The kind of training is critically important. Holding out unrealistic expectations can accentuate future problems considerably.

4. Some people move swiftly through the stages because of the positive nature of their assignment or working conditions. They feel fortunate to have an environment with which they are compatible.

5   Personality type has a lot to do with how one adjusts to new and unfamiliar surroundings. A rigid person who is neither intuitive nor perceptive may find it difficult to adjust to the thousands of variables in a new culture. Retreating from the unfamiliar may be one's only recourse in the attempt to maintain psychological equilibrium. On the other hand, a flexible, extroverted person who focuses on the central issues of one's Christian faith may not be disturbed by the myriad of cultural variables which he or she encounters.

Observations on the First Three Stages:

Stage One

1. **Stage One** is often unrealistic because of the nature of missionary biographies and story-telling. In other words, well-adjusted people in **Stage Three** or **Four** make things sound too easy for impressionable **Stage One** personalities.

2. Sometimes **Stage One** people are only given enough training to immunize them against real understanding. Those who have taken a three-week or three-month course sometimes feel that they are adequately prepared. For them, a little learning may truly be a dangerous thing. People differ greatly; but for many, one full year of solid cross-cultural training is essential—two years may be required.

3. **Stage One** is sometimes characterized by substantial formal western education. (Extensive training may heighten expectations.) But what is often totally missing is personal discipleship by a **Stage Three** or **Stage Four** person. Often the need to replace field personnel means that there is no time

for adequate cross-cultural preparation, and so candidates are rushed to their assignments prematurely. It is most tragic when, on top of everything else, a new person ends up getting his introduction to a new culture from a discouraged **Stage Two** person.

4. **Stage One** is characterized by a "pedestal syndrome" which elevates cross-cultural workers unfairly. Some sip too deeply from the heady wine of overseas service. One good antidote is a period of discipleship in a cross-cultural setting in the homeland. Those who have little ability to adjust to another culture can be identified before the great expense of overseas field service.

5. **Stage One** is exaggerated by mission executives who have little or no concept of servant leadership. Many candidates are given the impression that they will be given important responsibilities centered around what they "do." And so candidates anticipate being "in charge" of something. They have not been told that in many cultures "being" is a more important testimony than "doing."

Stage Two

1. **Stage Two** is the disillusionment stage. The dream of **Stage One** has clearly faded. It is the "no one ever told me it would be like this" stage.

2. In this stage, it often seems as though no one can do anything right—particularly local people. Unfortunately, the most attractive people become others who are struggling through their own **Stage Two** experiences. It is common for several people in **Stage Two** to regularly play parlor games and to talk about how bad things are. On such occasions, unkind joking about local people is often used to break the tension.

3. Stress is managed differently by different people in **Stage Two**. Some become vocal about their problems and thereby avoid an ulcer or high blood pressure. Others quietly retreat and talk things out with no one. The first is difficult for the community; the second puts the individual under stress.

4. Most unfortunate, the **Stage Two** person often avoids local people who could help in the adjustment process. In this stage, it is almost impossible to recognize local people as a resource. After all, they appear to be the cause of one's problems!

5. Anger is often at the bottom of the **Stage Two** dilemma — anger at one's inability to control the circumstances in one's life. If the road were just paved . . . If this drinking water were just safe . . . If these people would not steal . . . If . . . If . . . If . . .

6. In **Stage Two** it is often impossible to rationally distinguish between what can be controlled and what cannot. Some things can be changed simply by an attitude change. For example, "these people are unfriendly" may be changed simply by my becoming friendly to them. But paving the bumpy road may not be done during one's lifetime. For the person in **Stage Two**, it is helpful to distinguish between those things that can be changed and those that can't.

7. Some factors causing stress in **Stage Two** are physical in nature. Such things exaggerate problems that would otherwise be taken in stride. For example, if one is already discouraged, dysentery caused by dirty water can be much more difficult to handle. If one is already disillusioned, an allergy related to tree blossoms can make cultural adjustment harder to endure. An extreme example would be a physically handicapped person who must endure a long vehicle ride just to get to town for a break. Physical limitations can exaggerate problems of cultural adjustment.

8. It is difficult for a **Stage Two** person to tolerate the buoyancy of a **Stage Three** or **Four** co-worker. One reaction is to resent their ability to adjust to the local conditions. Another is to envy their ability to learn the language. Yet another reaction is to simply deny that a person in **Stage Three** or **Four** really is as happy as he or she seems. "They just aren't being realistic." In such a situation, it is difficult to think of people in **Stage Three** or **Four** as a resource; they are more likely to be resented. Here again, a simple attitude change can make a positive difference.

Stage Three

1. This is the leveling out stage. It is the beginning of the restoration of one's psychic unity. Balance is now becoming a possibility.

2. It is characterized by a feeling that the battle can be won. It is recognition that the whole world is not diseased; and in fact, there is a vaccine available for my particular ailment. It doesn't mean problems no longer exist; but they exist everywhere, not just where I am. That's why seeing a few problems in one's homeland can help to put things into perspective.

3. In **Stage Three**, one discovers that local people can be a tremendous resource, and need not be considered adversaries. If one has a challenge or problem to be overcome, local people are likely to be the best resource — sometimes the only resource — in reaching the goal.

4. **Stage Three** is the recognition that I can be happy if I change my attitude toward the situation. It doesn't mean, for example, that one loses all consciousness of hygiene. It means that one purposes to live carefully and joyfully.

Conclusion

As I mentioned in the beginning, culture shock need not be viewed as a terminal illness. With the determination of the individual involved and the concern of those who surround him or her, a successful adjustment can usually be made.

What's more, the adjustment is worth making. Those happy **Stage Three** and **Stage Four** people aren't all pretending. They do enjoy what they are called to do. God has given them a love for the people with whom they live and serve, and He rewards them with personal satisfaction for showing that love.

The message of hope for the person in the **Stage Two** valley of despair is that it is not necessary to live one's whole life there. Jesus doesn't call cross-cultural missionaries to be discouraged servants all their lives. He calls them to be living examples of how He would live if He could be everywhere, in person, all the time. What a challenge, and what a privilege!

When one is in the valley of discouragement, it may be difficult, but it is critically important to reach out to others. There is usually a good listener somewhere, either among one's colleagues or among local people. One must not only talk with those who, like themselves, are unable to cope with cultural adjustment. That can be counterproductive in overcoming the syndrome.

An engineer was once asked how it was possible to build tall skyscrapers in a place like Los Angeles, California where severe earthquakes sometimes occur. He said there are two secrets. One is to dig down deep enough to pin the building to solid rock. The second is to put flexibility in the joints of the building. Someone then suggested the same advice for believers and, I would add, cross-cultural workers. Pin your foundation on solid rock and put flexibility in your joints. We all know who The Foundation is. The challenge is to build in the flexibility.

Becoming culturally well adjusted is a goal worth striving for. My encouragement is to seek to unravel the mystery of cross-cultural adjustment to the best of one's ability. Having done that there is no alternative but to commit to the Lord everything else which seems beyond human control.

PARTIAL LIST OF SUGGESTED READING

Brewster, E. Thomas and Elizabeth S. *Bonding and the Missionary Task*. Pasadena: Lingua House, 1982.

Foyle, Marjory F. *Overcoming Missionary Stress*. Wheaton: EMIS, 1986.

Heibert, Paul G. *Anthropological Insights for Missionaries*. Grand Rapids: Baker Book House, 1985.

Heibert, Paul G. *Perspectives on the World Christian Movement, Culture and Cross-Cultural Differences*. (Pages 367-375), Pasadena: William Carey Library, 1981.

Lingenfelter, Sherwood G. and Marvin K. Mayers, *Ministering Cross-Culturally*, Grand Rapids: Baker Book House, 1986.

Loss, Myron. *Culture Shock*. Middleburg: Encouragement Ministries, 1983.

Nida, Eugene A. *Customs and Cultures: Anthropology for Christian Missions*. Pasadena: William Carey Library, 1975.

Oberg, Kalervo. *"Culture Shock: Adjustment to New Cultural Environments." Practical Anthropology*, Vol. 7, 1960.

General Bibliography

"A Champion for Self-Reliance." An interview with Glenn Schwartz. *Mission Frontiers*, Jan-Feb 1997.

Adeyemo, Tokunboh. *Salvation in African Tradition.* Nairobi: Evangel Publishing House, 1979.

Allen, Roland. *Missionary Methods: St Paul's or Ours?* London: World Dominion Press, 1960.

Allen, Roland. *Missionary Principles.* Grand Rapids: Wm. B. Eerdmans, 1964.

Allen, Roland. *Spontaneous Expansion of the Church and the Causes Which Hinder It.* Grand Rapids: Wm. B. Eerdmans, 1962.

"An Open Letter on Giving in Kenya." Gideon Kiongo, *Mission Frontiers*, June 2001.

"Avoiding Dependency – Mobilizing Local Resources." Glenn Schwartz. *Mission Frontiers*, Sept-Dec 1998.

Barrett, David. *Schism and Renewal in Africa.* Nairobi: Oxford University Press, 1968.

Befus, David R. *Where there are no Jobs: Enterprise Solutions for Employment and 'Public Goods' for the Poor.* Miami: LAM, 2005.

Bolling, Landrum. *Private Foreign Aid.* Boulder: Westview Press, Colorado, 1982.

Bonk, Jonathan J. *Missions and Money: Affluence as a Western Missionary Problem.* Maryknoll, NY: Orbis Books, 1991.

Brewster, Thomas and Elizabeth. *Bonding and the Missionary Task.* Lingua House: Dallas, 1982.

Christian, Jayakumar. *God of the Empty-Handed: Poverty, Power and the Kingdom.* Monrovia: MARC Publishing, 1999.

"Church and Mission in Central Africa: A Missiological Study in Indigenization." Glenn Schwartz (available on the WMA website www.wmausa.org).

Cotterell, Peter. *Born at Midnight.* Chicago: Moody Bible Institute, 1973.

"Cutting the Apron Strings." Glenn Schwartz, *Evangelical Missions Quarterly* (January 1994). Reprinted in *Mission Frontiers,* Jan-Feb 1997.

Dekker, John. *Torches of Joy.* Westchester (Illinois): Crossway Books, 1985.

Douglas, J. D., ed. *Let the Earth Hear His Voice.* Minneapolis: World Wide Publications, 1975.

"Fighting Dependency Among the 'Aucas': An interview with Steve Saint ." *Mission Frontiers,* May-June 1998.

Foyle, Marjory F. *Overcoming Missionary Stress.* Wheaton: EMIS, 1986.

"From Dependency to Fulfillment." Glenn Schwartz, *Evangelical Missions Quarterly,* July 1991.

George, Susan. *How the Other Half Dies: The Real Reasons for World Hunger.* Harmondsworth: Penguin Books, 1976.

George, Timothy. *Faithful Witness: The Life and Mission of William Carey.* Worcester: Christian History Institute, 1991.

"Going South of the Border for a Short-Term?" Rick Johnson. *Mission Frontiers,* June 2000.

Greenleaf, Robert K. *Servant Leadership: A Journey into the Nature of Legitimate Power and Greatness.* New York: Paulist Press, 1977.

Hancock, Graham. *The Lords of Poverty: The Power, Prestige and Corruption of the International Aid Business.* New York: Atlantic Monthly Press, 1989.

Hastings, Adrian. *Church and Mission in Modern Africa*. Condon: Burns & Oats, 1967.

Hattaway, Paul. *Back to Jerusalem: Three Chinese House Church Leaders Share their Vision to Complete the Great Commission*. Waynesboro: Gabriel Publishing, 2003.

Heibert, Paul G. *Anthropological Insights for Missionaries*. Grand Rapids: Baker Book House, 1985.

Heibert, Paul G. *Perspectives on the World Christian Movement, Culture and Cross-Cultural Differences*. (Pages 367-375), Pasadena: William Carey Library, 1981.

Hodges, Melvin L. *On the Mission Field — The Indigenous Church*. Chicago: Moody Press, 1953.

Hughes, Dewi and Matthew Bennett. *God of the Poor: A Biblical Vision for God's Present Rule*.

Lingenfelter, Sherwood G. and Marvin K. Mayers, *Ministering Cross-Culturally*, Grand Rapids: Baker Book House, 1986.

"It's Time to Get Serious About the Cycle of Dependency in Africa." Glenn Schwartz. *Evangelical Missions Quarterly*, April 1993. Reprinted in *Mission Frontiers*, Jan-Feb 1997.

Jacobs, Donald R. *From Rubble to Rejoicing: A Study of Effective Christian Leadership Based on Nehemiah*. Pasadena: Wm. Carey Library, 1991.

Kaluzi, Jackson. *A Mission Strategy for Tanzania*. Unpublished thesis, Nantwich (England); Flim Bible College, 1995.

Kraft, Charles H. *Christianity in Culture: A Study in Dynamic Biblical Theologizing in Cross-Cultural Perspective*. Maryknoll: Orbis Books, 1979.

Christianity with Power. Ann Arbor: Vine Books, 1989.

Defeating Dark Angels. Ann Arbor: Vine Books, 1992.

Kraft, Charles H., ed. *Readings in Dynamic Indigeneity*. Pasadena: Wm. Carey Library, 1979.

Kriel, Jacques and Willem Sayman. *AIDS: The Leprosy of Our Time.* Johannesburg: Orion Publishers, 1992

Lingenfelter, Sherwood G. and Mayers, Marvin K. *Ministering Cross-Culturally.* Grand Rapids: Baker Book House, 1986.

Little, Christopher R. *Mission in the Way of Paul: Biblical Mission for the Church in the Twenty-First Century.* New York: Peter Lang Publishing, 2005.

Luzebetak, Louis J. *The Church and Cultures: An Applied Anthropology for the Christian Worker.* South Pasadena: William Carey Library, 1970.

"Looking at Missions from Their Side, Not Ours." Steve Saint, *Mission Frontiers*, May-June 1998.

Loss, Myron. *Culture Shock.* Middleburg: Encouragement Ministries, 1983.

Madeley, John. *Trade and the Poor: The Impact of International Trade on Developing Countries.* London: Intermediate Technology Publications, Ltd, 1992.

Mbiti, John S. *African Religions and Philosophy.* London: Heinemann, 1969.

McGavran, Donald A. *Bridges of God.* New York: Friendship Press, 1955.

McGavran, Donald A. *How Churches Grow: New Frontiers of Mission.* London: World Dominion Press, 1959.

McGavran, Donald A. *Understanding Church Growth.* Grand Rapids: Wm. B. Eerdmans, 1970.

MacMaster, Richard K. with Donald R. Jacobs. *A Gentle Wind of God: The Influence of the East Africa Revival.* Scottsdale: Herald Press, 2006.

Mfwilwakanda, Nlongi. *Mandate for a Missionary Church in Africa.* Unpublished thesis. Ann Arbor: University Microfilms, 1982.

Museveni, Yoweri K. *What is Africa's Problem?* Kampala: NRM Publications, 1992.

Nevius, John L. *The Planting and Development of Missionary Churches.* Philadelphia: Presbyterian and Reformed Publishing Co, 1958.

Nida, Eugene A. *Customs and Cultures: Anthropology for Christian Missions.* Pasadena: William Carey Library, 1975.

Nthamburi, Zablon. *From Mission to Church: A Handbook of Christianity in East Africa.* Nairobi: Uzima Press, 1991.

Oberg, Kalervo. *"Culture Shock: Adjustment to New Cultural Environments." Practical Anthropology,* Vol. 7, 1960. Carlisle: OM Publishing, 1998.

Olasky, Marvin. *The Tragedy of American Compassion.* Washington: Regnery Publishing, 1992.

Pearse, Meic. *Why the Rest Hates the West: Understanding the Roots of Global Rage.* Downers Grove: InterVarsity Press, 2004.

Read, William R., Victor M. Monterroso, Harmon A. Johnson. *Latin American Church Growth.* Grand Rapids: Eerdmans, 1969.

Reese, Robert. *Dependency and Its Impact on Churches Related to the Baptist Convention of Zimbabwe and the Zimbabwe Christian Fellowship.* Unpublished manuscript. MidAmerica Baptist Seminary, Memphis, 2005.

Sachs, Jeffrey D. *The End of Poverty: Economic Possibilities for Our Time.* New York: Penguin Press, 2005.

Sanders, J. Oswald. *Spiritual Leadership.* Chicago: Moody Press, 1967.

Shorter, Aylward. *African Christian Theology: Adaptation or Incarnation?* Maryknoll: Orbis Books, 1977.

Speer, Robert E. *Christianity and the Nations.* New York: Fleming H. Revell, 1910.

Stearns, Bill and Amy. *Catch the Vision 2000.* Minneapolis: Bethany House Publishers, 1991.

Steffen, Tom A. *Passing the Baton: Church Planting that Empowers.* La Habra (California): Center for Organizational and Ministry Development, 1993.

"Stop Sending Money!" Robertson McQuilkin. *Christianity Today* (March 1, 1999).

Swenson, Richard A. *Margin: Restoring Emotional, Physical, Financial and Time Reserves to Overloaded Lives.* Colorado Springs: Navpress, 1992

Tangri, Roger. *The Politics of Patronage in Africa.* Oxford: James Currey Ltd., 1999.

Taylor, Mrs. Howard. *Behind the Ranges. Fraser of Lisuland, South West China.* London: China Inland Mission, 1944.

Taylor, John V. *Primal Vision: Christian Presence amid African Religion.* Alva: SCM Press Limited, 1963.

"The Church in Africa: Making Its Way from Dependency to Self-Reliance." Zablon Nthamburi. *Mission Frontiers,* Jan-Feb 1997.

"The Papua New Guinea Bible Church." Gerald Bustin. *Mission Frontiers,* April 2000.

Tippett, Alan R. *Church Growth and the Word of God.* Grand Rapids: Wm B. Eerdmans, 1970.

Tippett, Alan R. *Introduction to Missiology.* Pasadena: Wm. Carey Library, 1987.

Tippett, Alan R. *Verdict Theology in Missionary Theory.* Pasadena: Wm. Carey Library, 1973.

Tippett, Alan. *People Movements in Southern Polynesia.* Chicago: Moody Press, 1971.

"True Local Ownership Through Micro-Credit." Joseph Richter. *Mission Frontiers,* September 2000.

Tucker, Ruth A. *From Jerusalem to Irian Jaya.* Grand Rapids: Zondervan Publishing House, 1983.

Wagner, C. Peter, et al, eds. *Praying Through the 100 Gateway Cities of the 10/40 Window.* Seattle: YWAM Publishing, 1995.

Wakatama, Pius. *Independence for the Third World Church: An African Perspective on Missionary Work.* Downers Grove: InterVarsity Press, 1976.

"When the Mission Pays the Pastor." David Allen, *Evangelical Missions Quarterly* (April 1998).

"When Two Bikes Split the Church." Christopher Little, *Mission Frontiers,* December 2000.

"What Hath our Western Money and our Western Gospel Wrought?" William J. Kornfield. *Mission Frontiers,* Jan-Feb 1997.

Yamamori, Tetsunao, Bryant L. Myers, Kwame Bediako, and Larry Reed, editors. *Serving with the Poor in Africa.* Monrovia: MARC Publications, 1996.

Index